FIRST REACTIONS

FIRST REACTIONS

Critical Essays 1968-1979

CLIVE JAMES

ALFRED A. KNOPF   NEW YORK   1980

THIS IS A BORZOI BOOK
PUBLISHED BY ALFRED A. KNOPF, INC.

I should like to thank the magazine editors of the following publications, in which
some of these essays first appeared: *the Review, The Times Literary Supplement,
The Listener, Encounter, The New Review, Commentary, The New York Review of
Books*. The pieces on television first appeared in *The Observer*, and those on
D. H. Lawrence and Raymond Chandler in *D. H. Lawrence: Novelist, Poet, Prophet*,
edited by Stephen Spender, and *The World of Raymond Chandler*, edited by
Miriam Gross.

Library of Congress Cataloging in Publication Data

James, Clive [date] First reactions
Essays selected from 3 collections which were previously published under titles:
The metropolitan critic, Visions before midnight, and At the pillars of Hercules.
I. Title.
PR9619.3.J27F5   820'.9   80-7633
ISBN 0-394-51233-2

Manufactured in the United States of America
First Edition

To Jenny and Star Lawrence

Literature without tradition is destiny without history.
—*Ernst Robert Curtius*

Contents

CONTENTS

Preface

This book is a selection from the critical prose I have published during my first ten years or so as a serious writer, if that is not too grand a term. It is a further sifting, done with an eye to what might interest an American audience, of a small hill of material that had already been sifted down into three books published in England. The first of these, *The Metropolitan Critic* (1974), was a book of essays about literature and related topics. The second, *Visions Before Midnight* (1977), was a book of essays exclusively about television, drawn from my weekly column in the *Observer*. The third, *At the Pillars of Hercules* (1979), was another book of essays about literature and related topics. I can almost see the American reader's eyes glazing over as I provide this information.

Supplying notes on one's own bibliography, like making cross-references to oneself, is an attention-losing activity even if the person doing it enjoys wide fame. I am very conscious of being, to the American reader who might chance to open this book, an entirely unknown quantity, and of being likely to stay that way unless I let my work speak for itself. But the urge to have one's excesses or inadequacies understood and forgiven in advance is hard to quell. Critical prose is even more likely than any other kind to be bound up with one's autobiography. Another way of arranging this book would have been to put all the essays about poetry at the front and everything else at the back. But in their author's fond regard, some of these pieces are a young man's work or else there is no excuse for them. They either go in at the start or they don't go in at all.

When I wrote the essays collected in *The Metropolitan Critic*—and several other essays which were too obstreperous to include even in that brash volume—I was still trying to say everything at once. Style, I thought, was not only the most compressed way of speaking to the point, but a way of suggesting to your audience that you had all the other points covered too. The usual term for this kind of grandstand play is showing off, but I hope that in this case there was more to it. One tries, in one's early days, to reassure the experienced reader that he is not wasting his time.

Anyway, I found it hard to stop turning cartwheels. Most of these I have left in, even though they make me cringe to read them now. The essay on E. E. Cummings, for example—my first professionally published critical essay of any length—is written throughout with a would-be bravura which would nowadays, if I found myself even thinking like that, cause me to go somewhere dark and sleep off the fever. But at the time, when beatnik poets who could hardly string ten words together were being hailed as geniuses, it seemed important to convey something of the excitement contained in the collected works of an old bohemian who, for all his protestations of spiritual liberty, belonged firmly in the eternal tradition of schooled art. Though I was never quite foolish enough to believe that I had discovered this tradition all by myself, I was certainly foolish enough to behave as if I had. Yet if I were to calm myself down retroactively it would be to play false not just with an early self but with the temper of those times.

During the late sixties and early seventies, both in the little magazines such as *the Review* and in the established literary papers such as the *Times Literary Supplement,* the younger critics did their best not merely to say abrasive things, but to sound like abrasiveness incarnate. It wasn't enough to make astute remarks. You had to defend the faith. Trendiness had taken over in London to a degree that seems incredible even at this short distance. The enemy was at the gates; he was within the gates; he had appointed himself gate-keeper. He talked like a self-satisfied fool. It was necessary to sound nothing like him, especially when your opinions happened to coincide with his. Writing in praise of Baudelaire you could perhaps relax, but writing in praise of the Beatles you had to sound like an oracle.

Viewed in the long term, most of this doggedly cultivated razzle-dazzle was a waste of effort. In Great Britain there was no direct involvement with the Vietnam war and hence no political reinforcement for the social pretensions of the counterculture, which soon bored itself out of existence. Unshaken throughout the event, the educated reading public had retained its traditional homogeneity. You could speak quietly and your drift would still be caught. Realizing this, and relieved at the realization, I tried hard to write straightforward critical prose. But the impulse towards pyrotechnics had to go somewhere.

It went into television criticism. I became the *Observer*'s television critic in 1972 and instantly found myself faced with the task of interpreting the entire range of human experience in one thousand words per week. Here was not just an excuse, but a demand, for every elliptical trick in the bag. A television column *had* to be allusively conversational: quiddities, quibbles and riddles were the only means of keeping up with the requirements for comment that came gushing out of the screen. Every Sunday morning a million sharp-witted readers were waiting to test my responses against theirs. I won't presume to say that I rose to the challenge. All I can be sure of is that the urge to shine was well taken care of.

I am still writing the column eight years later, and still find, every Friday morning when I sit down to compose it, that the condition of elementary adequacy is to leave no phrase unturned. *Visions Before Midnight* was selected from my first four years at the task. American readers who wonder why there is nothing about *Upstairs, Downstairs* will not, I hope, feel insulted if they are told that some of the British television programmes which are screened on *Masterpiece Theatre* in the U.S.A. are regarded as run-of-the-mill fantasy in their land of origin. The same applies, perhaps, in the reverse direction. In Britain *The Rockford Files* is admired not just for its qualities of story and character but for James Garner's miraculous social ease and the way the California air looks so warm.

With the impulse to startle being satisfied elsewhere, the essays in *At the Pillars of Hercules* show, I hope, a more tranquil ego. That they hint at less, while feeling obliged to get more said, is surely some advantage. There are enough deficiencies to ensure continuity with earlier work. Among these are some errors of emphasis which will be particularly apparent to an American reader, since they concern American subjects. I think I was right in tracing Edmund Wilson's early radicalism to the American past rather than to the Soviet present, but I was probably wrong to make light of it. An informed American will no doubt smile at my naïvety. At the time I wrote the essay, however, Wilson was on the verge of death and it was time to pay tribute, even at a distance and before one was ready.

The essay on Shaw, and the long essay on Solzhenitsyn, both need some measure of apology. I am well aware that Shaw's imagination failed catastrophically in later life, so that he became a promoter for the totalitarian regimes whose evil he should have been the first to see. But in the second volume of his collected letters—the book I was reviewing—his moral qualities are all on show, and I persist in believing them to be great ones. As for attributing cool reason to Solzhenitsyn, it was the right thing to do at the time. Having praised him for his avoidance of messianic rant, I had the choice, when messianic rant subsequently turned out to be exactly the thing he wanted to go in for, between suppressing my original remarks or else letting them stand as an example of what seemed reasonable to say about Solzhenitsyn in 1974. Nor indeed, on that subject, is there much that I would want to say differently in the light of later developments. Solzhenitsyn, like Shaw, is a master spirit who has the limitations of a master spirit. He wants the free world to have an integrated sense of ethical purpose, such as he has himself. The free world can't have that, but if he were not the man who thought it could, then he would never have given us his analysis and evocation of what an unfree world is actually like.

Most of my essays about literature, and a good proportion of the ones about television, are written in praise of something. It would be pharisaical thus to concoct an unwarranted reputation for easy charm. In fact there is a good deal of bitchery in the essays I have left out. The London literary world is a cockpit clouded with flying feathers. On the other hand it has a remarkable unity. The feuds are more personal than political. Sworn ideological enemies quite commonly join each other for lunch each week. The bitter divisions of New York intellectual life are difficult for the London literati to comprehend. Similarly the American onlooker would perhaps regard the typical London literary quarrel as a teacup-sized storm strangely without aftermath.

But these differences, though they are the most subtle and pervasive cultural differences of all, are essentially differences of tone. On the whole, with due allowance for disparate concerns, London and New York share the same literary culture. Perhaps I am bound to believe that, since lately I have been publishing essays with equal frequency on either side of the Atlantic. But I think I would believe it anyway. The language of considered judgement is spoken in both cities. Eugenio Montale, somewhere amongst his marvellously sane critical prose, defines poetry as a dream in the presence of reason. Once again I don't claim that these essays embody reason; but they all aspire to it, and could never have been written without the belief that it exists.

London, 1980

THE
METROPOLITAN CRITIC

The Metropolitan Critic

Edmund Wilson writes in the 1957 chapter of *Upstate*:

Looking out from my window on the third floor, I saw the change made here by autumn in the landscape and the atmosphere: they become distinctly more serious. Nature begins to warn us, reassuming her august authority; the luxury of summer is being withdrawn.

In context, this passage carries many times the weight of any ordinary nature notes: the book is already half over, a splitting head of steam has been built up and the reader is by now in no doubt that the luxury of summer is being withdrawn from the writer himself, from the historical district in which he writes, from all the artists he has ever personally known and from the America which he has for so long chronicled and which he is now ceasing even to distrust—*Upstate* shivers with the portent of an advancing ice-cap. Wilson's monumental curiosity and zest of mind have not grown less, but by now they are like Montaigne's, exiled within their own country and awaiting, without real hope, a better age which will know how to value them. Self-confidence remains, but confidence in one's function ebbs; one's books do not seem to have been much use; the public weal has proved itself an illusion and private life is running out of time. *"C'est icy un livre de bonne foy, lecteur,"* wrote Montaigne, dampening the reader's ardour.

Il t'advertit dez l'entree, que ie ne m'y suis proposé aulcune fin, que domestique et privee: ie n'y ay eu nulle consideration de ton service, ny de ma gloire; mes forces ne sont pas capables d'un tel dessein.

Just so long as we understand each other.

Wilson's tone is similarly self-sufficient. "The knowledge that death is not so far away," he writes in 1963,

> that my mind and emotions and vitality will soon disappear like a puff of smoke, has the effect of making earthly affairs seem unimportant and human beings more and more ignoble. It is harder to take human life seriously, including one's own efforts and achievements and passions.

That was the year in which he was writing *The Cold War and the Income Tax*—a profound growl of dissatisfaction about owing the United States Government a swathe of back-taxes which it would only have wasted on building and dropping bombs if he had handed it over. Dealings with the revenue men were prolonged and wearying, making a general disappointment with life understandable. In 1966 things were going better, but his view of existence didn't much lighten. To go with his Kennedy Freedom Medal he was given a $1,000 award by the American Academy of Arts and Sciences and a $5,000 National Book Award, but he found himself feeling let down rather than puffed up. "They make me feel that I am now perhaps finished, stamped with some sort of approval and filed away. . . ." He is hard on himself, and no softer on humanity as a whole. "Reading the newspapers, and even the world's literature, I find that I more and more feel a boredom with and even scorn for the human race." In such ways his darkening mood is overtly stated, but what gives it power—and makes *Upstate* such an elegiac and at times unmanning book—is the way in which the selectivity of his impressions presents picture after picture of decay, confusion and loss. Talcottville, N.Y., is presented as a last vestige of the old, hopeful America, and Wilson—not hiding or even sheltering, just waiting—takes up residence there each summer to find that the new and vengeful America has always moved a bit closer. Not that it matters much any more.

By the end of the book we're a long way from the mood in which Wilson first evoked Talcottville, in his "The Old Stone House" essay of 1933, later collected in *The American Earthquake*. In the first place, that essay recalled the hopes of the New Englanders who had grown sick of narrowness and were all for pushing on into the realm of unlimited opportunity:

I can feel the relief myself of coming away from Boston to these first uplands of the Adirondacks, where, discarding the New England religion but still speaking the language of New England, the settlers found limitless space. They were a part of the new America, now forever for a century on the move.

The thrill of the great American experiment is still there in the writing, and even though this old essay was just as disenchanted as the new book is, the disenchantment worked in reverse: Talcottville was the opposite of a refuge, representing a past that needed to be escaped from, not returned to.

Thirty years or so later, in *Upstate,* he is cricking his neck to get back to it, but it is too late. Material progress has already made its giant strides. Juvenile delinquents and uproarious bikers maraud and destroy. The John Birch Society slaps up flagrant stickers. Treasured windows on which poet friends have inscribed verses with a diamond pen are shattered in his absence. The Sunday *New York Times* is too heavy for him to carry. There is a spider in the bathtub of a motel. An old acquaintance, Albert Grubel, keeps him abreast of the ever-escalating car-crash statistics. His daughter Helena grows up and starts having car crashes of her own. In 1963 he finds out that he has for all this time been living virtually on top of a SAC air-base, and is therefore slap in the middle of a prime target area. By the end of the book there is a distinct possibility that a four-lane highway will be constructed a few inches from his front door.

The detail is piled on relentlessly, and if there were nothing else working against it, then *Upstate* would be a dark book indeed. But several things stop it being disabling. First, there are revelations of the Wilsonian character, as when he faces the bikers and asks them why they can't ride on the highway instead of around his house, or when he argues about iambic pentameters with Nabokov (who insists that Lear's "Never, never, never, never, never" is iambic), or when he tells Mike Nichols that Thurber is not alone in lacking self-assurance and that he, Wilson, often gets up at four o'clock in the morning to read old reviews of his books. In bits and pieces like these there is enough singularity and sheer quirkiness to keep things humming.

Second, there is evidence of the Wilsonian curiosity, as when he deepens his knowledge of the county's history, or when he becomes interested in the founding and the subsequent fate of the old Oneida community. Wilson can't stop learning things, and it's worth remembering at this point that the curious information which crops up in the book is only the topmost molecule of the outermost tip of the iceberg. In the period covered by *Upstate* (1950–1970), Wilson was producing the exhaustively prepared *Patriotic Gore* and the expanded second edition of *The Shock of Recognition,* breaking into new cultures with *The Scrolls from the Dead Sea, Apologies to the Iroquois* and *O Canada,* turning out important investigatory pamphlets such as *The Cold War and the Income Tax* and *The Fruits of the MLA* (a crucially important attack on boondoggling academicism which has yet to be published in Britain) and editing *A Prelude* and the second and third in his series of literary chronicles, *The Shores of Light* and *The Bit Between My Teeth*—the first, *Classics and Commercials,* having appeared in 1950.

Only the European panoptic scholars come near matching Wilson for learning, and for sheer range of critical occupation there is no modern man to match him, not even Croce. If *Upstate* tends to give the impression that his wonted energy now only faintly flickers, the reader needs to remind himself sharply that the mental power in question is still of an order sufficient to illuminate the average city. Seemingly without effort, Wilson dropped *A Piece of My Mind* (1957) somewhere into the middle of all this hustle and bustle, and in the chapter entitled "The Author at Sixty" announced:

> I have lately been coming to feel that, as an American, I am more or less in the eighteenth century—or, at any rate, not much later than the early nineteenth. . . . I do not want any more to be bothered with the kind of contemporary conflicts that I used to go out to explore. I make no attempt to keep up with the younger American writers; and I only hope to have the time to get through some of the classics I have never read. Old fogeyism is comfortably closing in.

Taking him at his word on this last point, most critics and reviewers were relieved, which was very foolish of them.

But on the first point, about feeling himself to be an eighteenth-century or nineteenth-century figure, Wilson was making a just estimate, even if he meant only that he didn't drive a car and couldn't bear to pronounce the word "movies." As Alfred Kazin argued in his review of *The American Earthquake* (collected in his fine book *Contemporaries*), the men to compare Wilson with are the literary artists driven by historical imaginations—men like Carlyle.

The third thing which lightens the darkness of *Upstate* is the author's gradually revealed—and revealed only gradually even to himself—interest in a local young woman striving to better herself. Perhaps without really willing it, Wilson is telling a subtle story here: flashes and fragments are all we get. But by the time the book is over, we are convinced that her story is the story of the book, and that the story has gone against the mood. Kazin suggested that Wilson's secret was to gaze at America with a cold eye without being cold on America. *The American Earthquake* inexorably recorded the shattering effects of industrialism and the spiritual confusion of the New Deal, but it was not a hopeless book—it responded to the period's vitalities, even (while castigating it) the vitality of Henry Ford. *Upstate* very nearly *is* a hopeless book, and for a long while we suspect that Wilson *has* gone cold on America. But finally we see that he hasn't, quite: as the girl Mary works to establish herself in a way that her European origins would probably not have allowed, the American adventure haltingly begins all over again, at the eleventh hour and in the fifty-ninth minute.

Against the Stygian background of the book's accumulated imagery it is not much hope to offer, but it is not nothing, and Wilson was never in the consolation business anyway. Which leaves us—as we shelve *Upstate* beside *A Prelude* and prudently leave room for the books dealing with the thirty uncovered years between them—with the question of what business Wilson *has* been in.

What does Wilson's effort amount to? Is there an atom of truth in his dispirited suggestion that his books have dated? Supposing—as seems likely—that Wilson belongs with the great, copious critical minds like Saintsbury, Sainte-Beuve, Croce, Taine: is he doomed to survive like them only as an emblem of the qualities a mind can have, Saintsbury for gusto, Sainte-Beuve for diligence, Croce for rigour, Taine for drama? Wilson makes Van Wyck Brooks's output look normal, Eliot's look slim, Empson's, Trilling's and Leavis's look famished. Just how is all this avoirdupois to be moved forward? We need to decide whether critical work which has plainly done so much to influence its time vanishes with its time or continues. To continue, it must have done something beyond maintaining standards or correcting taste, important as those functions are: it must have embodied, not just recommended, a permanent literary value. And we do not have to reread much of Wilson's criticism—although it would be a year of perfect pleasure to reread all of it—to see that it does embody a value, and embodies it in a way and to a degree that no other corpus of twentieth-century work has approached. But this value, so easily sensed, is very difficult to define, since it must perforce reside in whatever is left after opposing high estimations of Wilson have cancelled each other out. Lionel Trilling (in "Edmund Wilson: A Background Glance," collected in *A Gathering of Fugitives*) says that an interest in ideas is the very essence of Wilson's criticism. Alfred Kazin, on the other hand, says that ideas are things Wilson is not at home with. If both these men admire the same thing in Wilson, what is it?

The answer is that Wilson has a mental style—a mental style which reveals itself in the way he writes. He is proof by nature against metaphysics of any kind (sometimes to the damaging extent that he cannot grasp why men should bother to hold to them), and this characteristic gives his work great clarity. He never has to strive towards perspicuity, since he is never tempted even momentarily to abandon it. And in more than fifty years of activity he has put up such a consistent show of knowing what he means—and of writing it down so that it may be readily understood —that he has invited underestimation. The most difficult escape Houdini ever made was from a wet sheet, but since he was in the business of doing difficult-looking things he had to abandon this trick, because to the public it seemed easy. What Wilson was doing was never easy, but he had the good manners to make it look that way. If he could only have managed to dream up an objective correlative, or a few types of ambiguity, or if he had found it opportune to start lamenting the loss of an organic society, he would be much more fashionable now than he is. But we can search his work from end to end without finding any such conversation piece. What we do find is a closely argued dramatic narrative in which good judgement and misjudgement both stand out plainly. The dangerous excitement of a tentatively formulated concept is absent from his work, and for most of us this is an excitement that is hard to forgo: the twentieth century has given us a palate for such pepper.

But there is another, more durable excitement which Wilson's entire body of work serves to define. There is a clue to it in *Upstate,* in the passage where Wilson discusses the different courses taken by Eliot and Van Wyck Brooks:

> They were at Harvard at the same time, Brooks of the class of 1908, Eliot of 1910, and both, as was natural then, went, after college, to England.

Eliot took root there, but Brooks said that, during the months he spent in England, he found himself preoccupied with American subjects. This difference marks the watershed in the early nineteen-hundreds in American literary life. Eliot stays in England, which is for him still the motherland of literature in English, and becomes a European; Brooks returns to the United States and devotes himself to American writing, at the expense of what has been written in Europe. Eliot represents the growth of an American internationalism; Brooks, as a spokesman of the twenties, the beginnings of the sometimes all too conscious American literary self-glorification which is part of our American imperialism.

As it happened, Wilson was to go on to cover American subjects with all Brooks's thoroughness and more; and to parallel Eliot's internationalism while yet holding to the tacit belief that the American achievement could well be crucial in the continuity of that internationalism; and to combine these two elements with a total authority of preparation and statement. For that preparation, he had the brilliant education available in pre-war Princeton to a young man ready to grasp it. For that statement, he was obliged to evolve a style which would make his comprehensive seriousness unmistakable in every line. Out of these two things came the solid achievement of judgements based on unarguable knowledge ably supplied to meet an historical demand. From the beginning, Wilson was a *necessary* writer, a chosen man. And it is this feeling of watching a man proving himself equal to an incontestably important task—explaining the world to America and explaining America to itself—which provides the constant excitement of Wilson's work.

Commanding this kind of excitement his prose needed no other. Wilson grew out of the great show-off period of American style. He could not have proceeded without the trail-blasting first performed by Mencken and Nathan, but he was fundamentally different from them in not feeling bound to overwrite.

Wilson's style adopted the Mencken-Nathan toughness but eschewed the belligerence—throwing no punches, it simply put its points and waited for intelligent men to agree. It assumed that intelligence could be a uniting factor rather than a divisive one. In the following passage (from "The Critic Who Does Not Exist," written in 1928 and later collected in *The Shores of Light*) this point is made explicitly:

What we lack, then, in the United States, is not writers or even literary parties, but simply serious literary criticism (the school of critics I have mentioned last, i.e., Brooks, Mumford and Joseph Wood Krutch, though they set forth their own ideas, do not occupy themselves much with the art or ideas of the writers with whom they deal). Each of these groups does produce, to be sure, a certain amount of criticism to justify or explain what it is doing, but it may, I believe, be said in general that they do not communicate with one another; their opinions do not really circulate. It is astonishing to observe, in America, in spite of our floods of literary journalism, to what extent literary atmosphere is a non-conductor of criticism. What actually happens, in our literary world, is that each leader or group of leaders is allowed to intimidate his disciples, either ignoring all the other leaders or taking cognizance of their existence only by distant and contemptuous sneers. H. L. Mencken and T. S. Eliot present themselves, as I have said, from the critical point of view, as the most formidable figures on the scene; yet Mencken's discussion of his principal rival has, so far as my memory goes, been confined to an inclusion of the latter's works among the items of one of those lists of idiotic current crazes in which the *Mercury* usually includes also the recall of judges and paper-bag cookery. And Eliot, established in London, does not, of course, consider himself under the necessity of dealing with Mencken at all. . . . Van Wyck Brooks, in spite of considerable baiting, has never been induced to defend his position (though Krutch has recently taken up some challenges). And the romantics have been belaboured by the spokesmen of several different camps without making any attempt to strike back. It, furthermore, seems unfortunate that some of our most important writers—Sherwood Anderson and Eugene O'Neill, for example—should work, as they apparently do, in almost complete intellectual isolation, receiving from the outside but little intelligent criticism and developing, in their solitary labours, little capacity for supplying it themselves.

Wilson's innovation was to treat the American intelligentsia as if it were a European one, speaking a common language. "For there is one language," he wrote in the same essay, "which all French writers, no matter how divergent their aims, always possess in common: the language of criticism." That was the ideal, and by behaving as if it had already come about, he did a great deal to bring it into existence. The neutral, dignified tone of his prose was crucial here: it implied that there was no need for an overdose of personality, since writer and reader were on a level and understood one another. As Lionel Trilling has convincingly argued, Wilson's years in an editorial chair for the *New Republic* were a big help in getting this tone right—he was in action continuously (more than two-thirds of the pieces in *The Shores of Light* first appeared in the *New Republic*) before a self-defining audience of intelligent men, all of whom were capable of appreciating that opinions should circulate.

The literary chronicles, especially *The Shores of Light,* are commonly valued above Wilson's more integrated books, and although it seems likely that the people doing the valuing have not correctly judged the importance of the latter, the evaluation nevertheless seems just at first glance. As has often been pointed out, there is nothing in criticism to beat the thrill of hearing Wilson produce the first descriptions and definitions of the strong new American literature that was coming up in the 1920s—the first essays on Fitzgerald and Hemingway will always stand as the perfect objects for any literary journalist's envy and respect. But here again we must remember to avoid trying to nourish ourselves with condiments alone. What needs to be appreciated, throughout the literary chronicles, is the steady work of reporting, judging, sorting out, encouraging, reproving and re-estimating. The three literary chronicles are, among other things, shattering reminders that many of the men we distinguish with the name of critic have never judged a piece of writing in their lives—just elaborated on judgements already formed by other men.

A certain demonstration of Wilson's integrity in this regard is his ability to assess minor and ancillary literature about which no general opinion has previously been built up: *The Shock of Recognition* and *Patriotic Gore* are natural culminations of Wilson's early drive towards mining and assaying in territory nobody else had even staked out. Wilson is a memory; he never at any stage believed that the historic process by which writings are forgotten should go unexamined or be declared irreversible. Remembering is one of the many duties the literary chronicles perform: not so spectacular a duty as discovering, but equally important. For Wilson's self-posed task of circulating opinions within an intelligent community (a community which depends on such a process for its whole existence), all these duties needed to be scrupulously carried out, and it is the triumph of the literary chronicles that they were carried out in so adventurous a way.

Unless all these things are held in mind, the true stature of the literary chronicles cannot be seen, even by those who value them above the rest of Wilson's work. In *The Shores of Light* it is necessary to appreciate not just "F. Scott Fitzgerald" and "Emergence of Ernest Hemingway" but also pieces like "The Literary Consequences of the Crash," "Talking

United States," and "Prize-Winning Blank Verse." In *Classics and Commercials* we need to cherish not only the stand-out hatchet jobs like "Who Cares Who Killed Roger Ackroyd?" and "Tales of the Marvellous and the Ridiculous" but also the assiduous labour of weighing up—never impatient, even when repelled—which went into essays like "Glenway Wescott's War Work" and "Van Wyck Brooks on the Civil War Period." And unless we can get rid of the notion that picking winners was Wilson's only true calling in life, we will have no hope at all of reaching a true estimation of *The Bit Between My Teeth*—a book disparaged as tired and thin by reviewers who in the full vigour of youth could not have matched the solidity of the least piece in it. "The Pre-Presidential T.R." and "The Holmes-Laski Correspondence" are masterly examples of what Wilson can accomplish by bringing a literary viewpoint to historical documents; and "The Vogue of the Marquis de Sade" got the whole Sade revival into focus and incisively set the limits for its expansion.

The literary chronicles would have been more than enough by themselves to establish Wilson's pre-eminence: to a high degree they have that sense of the drama of creativity which Taine had been able to capture and exploit. If people are going to read only some of Wilson instead of all of him, then the chronicles are what they should read. But it is one thing to say this, and another to accept the assumption—distressingly widespread in recent years—that *Axel's Castle* and *The Wound and the Bow* and *The Triple Thinkers* have in some way done the work they had to do and may be discarded, like used-up boosters. There is not much doubt about how such an idea gained currency, books of long essays being so much harder to read than books of short ones. But there is no reason for anyone who has actually read and understood a book like *Axel's Castle* to go along with such a slovenly notion. When, in the Yeats chapter of that book, Wilson compared the Yeats of 1931 to the Dante who was able "to sustain a grand manner through sheer intensity without rhetorical heightening," he was writing permanent criticism, criticism which can't be superseded, certainly not by pundits who are boning up their Dante from a parallel text instead of learning it the hard way from a teacher like Christian Gauss. It is barbarism of a peculiarly academic kind to suppose that truths of this order—not insights, explications or glosses, but truths —can be appropriated to a data bank or dismissed as obsolete. A Dantesque "epigrammatic bitterness" is *precisely* the quality to see in the mature Yeats, and in 1931, before the last poems were written, it was virtually prescient to be able to see it, since that quality had not yet reached its full concentration.

Wilson paid heavy penalties for being plain—or rather we paid heavy penalties for not seeing the force of his plainness. In the Eliot chapter of *Axel's Castle* he said something about Eliot that forty years of theses and learned articles have done their best to bury, something which we are only now capable of seeing as criticism rather than conversation, the intervening hubbub of academic industry having revealed itself as conversation rather than criticism:

> We are always being dismayed, in our general reading, to discover that lines among those which we had believed to represent Eliot's residuum of original invention had been taken over or adapted from other writers. . . . One would be inclined *a priori* to assume that all this load of erudition and literature would be enough to sink any writer, and that such a production as "The Waste Land" must be a work of second-hand inspiration. And it is true that, in reading Eliot and Pound, we are sometimes visited by uneasy recollections of Ausonius, in the fourth century, composing Greek-and-Latin macaronics and piecing together poetic mosaics out of verses from Virgil. Yet Eliot manages to be most effective precisely—in "The Waste Land"—where he might be expected to be least original—he succeeds in conveying his meaning, in communicating his emotion, in spite of all his learned or mysterious allusions, and whether we understand them or not.
>
> In this respect, there is a curious contrast between Eliot and Ezra Pound.

With Pound, Wilson was like Tallulah Bankhead faced with a tricksy production of Maeterlinck: he wasn't afraid to announce, "There's less in this than meets the eye." With Eliot, he was bold enough to say that things were simpler than they appeared at first blush. Both these judgements were backed up by a deep learning which had nothing to fear from either man, by a sense of quality which knew how to rely on itself and by a seriousness which was not concerned with putting up a front.

There is no need to go on with this part of the argument. It's more merciful simply to state that Wilson's entire critical corpus will go on being read so long as men are prepared to read widely and well. His strategy of using magazines—first the *New Republic*, later *The New Yorker*—as shipyards in which to assemble books was triumphantly successful. He is the ideal of the metropolitan critic, who understood from the beginning that the intelligence of the metropolis is in a certain relation to the intelligence of the academy, and went on understanding this even when the intelligence of the academy ceased to understand its relation to the intelligence of the metropolis. When Wilson called the Modern Language Association to order, he performed the most important academic act of the post-war years: he reminded the scholars that their duty was to literature.

For Wilson literature has always been an international community, with a comprehensible politics of its own. He learnt languages not just out of passionate curiosity but out of quasi-political purpose, becoming acquainted with whole literatures in the same way that a man who carries an international passport proves himself a part of the main. As late as the mid-1950s, Wilson was apologizing for not having done enough in this line: he has always been a trifle guilty about failing to get interested in Portuguese and Spanish. But to a chastening extent he had already made himself the universal literatus, and in the later decades of his life we find him becoming increasingly conscious that this is his major role—if he has any significance in the realm of action, then this is it. Modesty has never been among Wilson's characteristics, but a certain diffidence does creep in, of which the quietism and resignation of *Upstate* are the logical culmination. The central paradox of Wilson remains unresolved: he has put himself above the battle, inhabiting an Empyrean of knowledge by now fundamentally divorced from an unworkable world. The paradox was vicious from the beginning, becoming more and more so as modern history unfolded in front of him. Wilson was a born internationalist in literature and a born isolationist in politics, and there is a constant tension between the achieved serenity of his literary judgement and the threatening complexity of his self-consciousness as an American.

A patrician individualist by nature, Wilson was automatically debarred from running with the pack. His radicalism in the 1920s and 1930s had a decisive qualitative difference from any Marxist analyses currently available: it was élitist, harking back to the informed democracy of the American past, and therefore on a richer historical base than the hastily imported European doctrines which bemused his contemporaries. Wilson's reports on Detroit are as devastating as Marx on the working day, but the intensity is the only connection. Wilson was revolted by industrialism's depredations—if the ecological lobby ever wants to put a bible together, there are sections of *The American Earthquake* which could go straight into Revelations—but the revulsion was just as much on behalf of what America had previously been as on behalf of what it might become. Marxism is future-directed metaphysics: Wilson's thought was bent towards the literary recovery of the estimable past.

Making no commitment to Communism, Wilson was never compelled to scramble away from it, and he maintained his dignity throughout the 1930s. By 1940 he had completed his analysis of the revolutionary tradition in Europe and published it as *To the Finland Station.* In the final paragraph of that book, he declared it unlikely that the Marxist creeds would be able to bring about

> a society in which the superior development of some is not paid for by the exploitation, that is, by the deliberate degradation of others—a society which will be homogeneous and cooperative as our commercial society is not, and directed, to the best of their ability, by the conscious creative minds of its members.

America went to war again, and again Wilson was isolationist: as with the First World War, so with the Second, he saw no point in America becoming involved. He was still explaining such phenomena by market pressures and the devious conniving of Big Business—it was a Fabian position, never much altered since he first picked it up from Leonard Woolf.

Wilson has difficulty in understanding how irrational forces can be so potent. In *Europe Without Baedeker* and *A Piece of My Mind,* he came close to holding the Europeans collectively responsible for pulling their own houses down in ruins about their heads. It was the high point of his isolationism, further reinforced by a commitment to the American past amounting to visionary fervour. In his admiration for Lincoln we find Wilson getting very near the mysticism he spent a lifetime scrupulously avoiding. Finally he found an historical base solid-seeming enough to justify the relieved rediscovery of a Platonic Guardian class. "To simplify," he wrote in *A Piece of My Mind* (1957),

> one can say that, on the one hand, you find in the United States the people who are constantly aware . . . that, beyond their opportunities for money-making, they have a stake in the success of our system, that they share the responsibility to carry on its institutions, to find expression for its new point

of view, to give it dignity, to make it work; and, on the other hand, the people who are merely concerned with making a living or a fortune, with practising some profession or mastering some technical skill, as they would in any other country, and who lack, or do not possess to quite the same degree the sense of America's role.

That was as far as he got: the Republic he loved began to be overwhelmed by the Democracy he had never been sure about, and in the new reality of the 1960s he found himself taxed but unrepresented.

In *Upstate* Wilson is faced with the ruins of the American Dream, and appears to be forgetting what we are bound to remember: that the fragments can be built with and that this fact is in some measure due to him. The intellectual community which is now fighting for the Republic against its own debilitating tumours was to a considerable extent his personal creation. That Americans of goodwill, in the midst of wearying political confusion, can yet be so confident of their nation's creativity is again in a large part due to him. As Christian Gauss was to Wilson— master to pupil—Wilson is to nobody: nobody he can see. He now doubts the continuity he helped to define. But, beyond the range of vision now limiting itself to Cape Cod and Talcottville, there will always be young men coming up who will find his achievement a clear light. He is one of the great men of letters in our century.

(*Times Literary Supplement*, 1972)

Big Medicine

As a media event, A. Alvarez's *The Savage God* has turned out to have a lot in common with the all-star expedition to Everest, which to a great extent was insured against failure through being heavily pre-sold. Bits of the book have been trailed in *Partisan Review, New American Review,* the *Atlantic Monthly,* the *Listener* and finally the *Observer,* where heavy static was kicked up by the intervention of an interested party and by the editor's inexplicable desire to print the author's photograph at an even greater angle of tilt than puzzled the world on the front cover of *Beyond All This Fiddle:* at this rate, the lay reader might soon get the idea that Alvarez has adopted the supine position as a matter of course. And just as it is doubtful whether the majority of mankind really knows whether the polyglot assemblage of climbers got all the way up there or not, it is doubtful whether the intelligentsia really knows about *The Savage God* or not—the publicity and free samples probably used up most of the available response, and the task of reading a dozen polite reviews perhaps exhausted what was left. To rub the point home, Weidenfeld & Nicolson have made the book only slightly less expensive than a Ferrari Dino, thereby ensuring that the smooth curve of its commercial success shan't be dented by too many poor clucks actually trying to get hold of it and read it.

I hate to break up the party, but feel bound to announce that quite apart from its hit-parade status *The Savage God* is an important contribution to recent criticism. Alvarez has been one of the key literary intellectuals of the last decade and in this new book certain components of his thought have been pushed to their limits. In my view this mainly serves to demonstrate the contradictions which have at all previous stages obtained between them, but that doesn't mean that the book lacks the excitement (the real excitement, not the media excitement) and the *gravitas* which we associate with an intellectual venture. And the best way to pay tribute to these qualities is to trace within Alvarez's total argument those subsidiary lines of argument which have hit an impasse: to locate and examine the points at which discourse has ceased and forceful assertion (and there isn't much assertion more forceful than his) has taken over. There will then be a chance for discourse to begin again—and it needs to do that. In *The Savage God* Alvarez's critical effort has finally revealed its false emphasis in full clarity, but this only means that his critical effort has now reached the point where it can be valued exactly and so retained. There is no question of sweeping over the path he has taken and forgetting about it. To put it briefly, Alvarez since the late 1950s has been occupied with the central question about the relationship of poetry to contemporary reality. I think it can now clearly be seen that he has got the wrong answer: but he has also helped clarify the question.

As many will by now have heard, the book takes the form of an anti-sandwich: a hunk of bread between two slices of meat, the bread being a long study of suicide through the ages and the two slices of meat being accounts of suicide attempts by Sylvia Plath and the author, the first unhappily successful, the second fortunately a misfire. These two sections on Plath and himself are the stretches of Alvarez's writing most likely to be widely remembered: they have the muscular narrative drive of the "Shiprock" essay in *Beyond All This Fiddle*— which is to say, they draw you forward into regions where it seems at least plausible, if not natural, for a man to pit himself against extreme conditions as a necessary part of some kind of mental exploration. I for one am never going to understand why Alvarez should want to cling by his finger-nails to a vast slab of naked geology while vultures stagger past with one wing folded over their eyes, but I can't deny that such experience gives his narrative writing a certain edge: he seems to go about with his nervous system worn externally, and I suppose it is true that if you conduct your life in this way you will face and resolve problems that most people shirk, and restrict the range of their sensibilities by so shirking. But I can suppose this without supposing that it is *better* to push things to the limit: in fact it seems clear to me by now, having lasted this long, that limits are dangerous things which a wise man best avoids, since he is more likely to lose than find himself when he gets near them—and very likely to lose his wisdom.

But obviously for Alvarez it is not like this. Basic to both the Plath chapter and the chapter on himself is the assumption that something was being found out, and such is the seductiveness of the writing that the assumption gains great weight. Without, however, being clarified. If Alvarez is right about Plath's suicide not being meant as a real attempt, then plainly it is nonsensical to suppose that her last writings are tangible products of the supposedly special mental territory opened up by deciding not to live. And from his own attempt, Alvarez apparently gained no special insight beyond a definitive experience of whatever it is that pulses and throws off rays in the fiery centre of a king-sized hangover. That, and this:

> . . . when death let me down, I gradually saw that I had been using the wrong language; I had translated things into Americanese. Too many movies, too many novels, too many trips to the States had switched my understanding into a hopeful, alien tongue. I no longer thought of myself as unhappy; instead, I had "problems." Which is an optimistic way of putting it, since problems imply solutions, whereas unhappiness is merely a condition of life which you must live with, like the weather. Once I had accepted that there weren't ever going to be any answers, even in death, I found to my surprise that I didn't much care whether I was happy or unhappy; "problems" and "the problem of problems" no longer existed. And that in itself is already the beginning of happiness.

I don't think it is, but it's certainly the end of adolescence. Here at the finale of his book, as with Plath at the beginning and with all the historical data in the middle, Alvarez is commendably scrupulous about attaching the suicidal impulse to events in the exterior world of the suicide: eventually, he seems to suggest, suicide is a question of what formative conditions obtain in the irreducible self, and must always retreat beyond simply sociological understanding. Whole races have suicided under the threat of oppression, but others have not; people who had "everything to live for" have chosen to die; people who had every reason to die have striven to live. If there is already an inclination to suicide, circumstances might bring it out: if there is not already an inclination to suicide, circumstances tend not to put it in.

Alvarez has been more scientifically minded—more objective, more resistant to easy mental patterning—than suits him as a critic. For his own major critical assumption is still there, but now looks shakier than ever in the face of his own arguments. He is saying that the casualty rate among modern artists has been, and has had to be, unusually high, but one of the salient conclusions of his historical investigation is that the "rate" must be dependent on statistics and the statistics dependent on the deed being declared for what it is—on his own terms, he has not satisfactorily established the previous casualty rate among artists as being low. He is saying (as he has always said) that contemporary evils take unique forms and that the pertinent artistic reaction to them, since it must be extreme, will look suicidal and in a disturbing number of cases may end suicidally: but he is also saying that a correspondence of the suicidal impulse to a perceived deterioration in the external world is problematical and tends to retreat beyond investigation.

As an "extremist" Alvarez has made the disarming tactical mistake of being too reasonable. It would have been too much to ask that he should go on to demolish his own critical base—but that is the way his arguments tend, and a reviewer with any sense of the high comedy of intellectual affairs ought to evince, momentarily at any rate, a proper delight at being presented with a treatise so honestly done that it contains within itself all the material necessary for its own correction.

If Alvarez had not pinned his "casualty rate" to suicide, his famous death-roll in the title chapter could have been a lot longer. As it is, the death-roll has already been subject to fluctuations within the chapter's own short lifetime, and might well be altered again before the book comes out in paperback—Berryman is now fully eligible and Mishima needs at least a mention. On its first appearance (as "The Art of Suicide" in *Partisan Review*), Albert Camus was numbered among the missing: "Camus died absurdly in a car crash." It must have crossed the author's mind that either everybody who dies in a car crash dies absurdly or else nobody does. Anyway, Camus is now out and Joe Orton is in, and the point this time is that although Orton was murdered, his *murderer* suicided, so it qualifies as a pretty suicidal scene. Alvarez still clings to his list of painters: Modigliani, Arshile Gorki, Mark Gertler, Jackson Pollock and Mark Rothko. It's hard to see how Gertler qualifies at that level of achievement (if he does, then Dora Carrington ought to as well), but it's all too easy to see that at some point Alvarez was unimpressed with his own casualty list and felt compelled to pad it out a bit. He has widened his preoccupation from suicide to extreme self-neglect, and beyond that to ordinary carelessness, shading finally into the area where people just happen to be standing around when a hunk of twentieth-century technology goes haywire. If he had widened his definition of "artist" to include the jazzmen, he could legitimately have pushed his casualty rate up to something staggering: the fatal car crashes began with Bessie Smith and included Clifford Brown, who conceivably might have been a more important trumpeter than Dizzy Gillespie and Fats Navarro combined. The drug casualties have included Navarro, Bud Powell and pre-eminently Charlie Parker, whom I would put without hesitation among the two dozen most important twentieth-century artists in any medium. It's been a massacre, and of necessity a peculiarly modern one. But for the jazz casualty list you would be compelled *ab initio* to take account of the informing sociological conditions—Jim Crow, insecurity and the constant, tired travelling from job to job by road.

Having left jazz out of account, it's not surprising that Alvarez ignores rock music too, although it has already supplied several exemplary figures who would fit well into his sad gallery. If ever three young artists had "everything to live for," they were Janis Joplin, Jimi Hendrix and Jim Morrison—quite apart from the fact that on the material plane they were among the richest artists the world has ever known. If Alvarez doesn't want to cover this shady part of the waterfront, he's well within his rights, but the point is that in jazz and rock, precisely because their connection with the grand flow of modern events has no wide intellectual acceptance, it can more easily be seen that the casualty rate has something intimately to do with the way the life is lived. Taking the received "high" art as his field, Alvarez finds it all too easy to connect the casualty rate with the "collapse of values" which in his more thoughtful moments he is careful to present as a stimulus to creation rather than as an invitation to end it. Prematurely and fatally, he subsumes and denatures a multiplicity of sociological changes within a notion of total historical change—the one thing historical change can never be.

But a simple point emerges: before the twentieth century it is possible to discuss cases individually, since the artists who killed themselves or were even seriously suicidal were rare exceptions. In the twentieth century the balance suddenly shifts: the better the artist the more vulnerable he seems to be.

Obviously, this is in no way a firm rule. The Grand Old Men of literature have been both numerous and very grand: Eliot, Joyce, Valéry, Pound, Mann, Forster, Frost, Stevens, Ungaretti, Montale, Marianne Moore. Even so, the casualty rate among the gifted seems out of all proportion, as though the nature of the artistic undertaking itself and the demands it makes had altered radically.

There are several objections that can be made to this crucial passage. First, Alvarez hasn't been able to assemble an overwhelmingly impressive list of twentieth-century artists who "killed themselves or were even seriously suicidal"—certainly there aren't enough of them mentioned to convince us that they are any less the rare exception now than they were then. Second, a galaxy might produce smooth and homogeneous light as you look back through it from its perimeter, but it is still made of individual stars, and properly examined is seen to be very violent. If Dylan Thomas is on the modern list because he drank too much, Mozart ought to be on the older list because he ate too little. Nobody knows what happened to Masaccio, and we only know a little more than nothing about Giorgione: what we can be sure of is that their loss was cataclysmic at the time. Masaccio may very well have been the most talented painter ever born—but the point is that history absorbed the shock and continued. The shocks in all these cases were tremendous, but history absorbed them and continued. That is one of the things that makes history look different from now—it contains these explosions and continues. Nor does history very well remember lost promise.

As Alfred Einstein suggested, *frühvollendet*—"too early completed"— is a misleading term for the musicians who died young. In retrospect we see them whole and tend to forget that their premature deaths were crushing deprivations. Mozart, Weber, Purcell, Pergolesi, Mendelssohn, Chopin, Vincenzo Bellini, Schubert—they all died young, all but three within a single half-century. Or consider the Elizabethan age in poetry: Marlowe never saw thirty, Greene, Peele, Nash and Kyd all died before they were forty and Shakespeare only just made it past fifty. They drank to die in those days—Dylan Thomas would have looked like a piker. (Exercise: think of an artistic era free of visitations from the Savage God.)

Third, Alvarez's qualifying list of Grand Old Men might well have been extended—the one thing the modern era *has* got that previous centuries were short of is creative longevity. Masaccio never reached thirty, Raphael never reached forty, and in their day they were not exceptional: it was Leonardo, Michelangelo, Giovanni Bellini and Titian who were exceptional. In literature alone (Alvarez's chosen field in this passage, although elsewhere he sweeps outward without warning to take in such other arts as suit his book), the last two centuries are stiff with senescent masters, a Tolstoy and a Wordsworth paired off against every Keats, just as there is a Monet and a Renoir paired off against every Seurat. But none of this means that Alvarez has got things backwards and that history has taken the opposite turn from what he thinks. It means that history has taken no turn at all. All wars and revolutions aside, what it means is that medically speaking these are far safer times to be alive. Unless you happen to be dwelling in the vicinity when a political crisis bursts, there are incomparably fewer effective forces operating to nail you. It is one strand of history, not history itself; but it is an important strand, and Alvarez is forced into some elegant high-stepping in order to avoid it. If he had been content to stick with the genuine disaster areas of modern history, his casualty lists would have retained real weight. But by spreading his field of argument to the whole literate world he forces himself towards mysticism: he vaguely puts it about that there is something dangerous in all this safety. The liberal-humanist tradition can't cope with modern events. It takes extremism to do that. And extremism is especially required when modern events, with their ineluctable cunning, have carefully contrived to leave one sitting safely on one's duff in England or America instead of getting boiled down for soap or freezing to death above the Arctic Circle.

Eventually Alvarez's whole argument depends on the twin assumptions that modern evils are unique and that, being so, they require a unique artistic response. Not only are these assumptions separately questionable, their connection is questionable too. The first assumption is, I think, entirely without useful meaning. The second, however, has the advantage of not being so vulnerable as the first: since its connections with it were tenuous in the first place, to some extent it can break free, and in fact Alvarez's formidable critical value is dependent on the paradox that though largely wrong about what has happened he is to some extent right about what art should do about it. But to begin with the first assumption.

If anyone contends that there was nothing which happened in the concentration camps which did not happen in the Thirty Years' War, he is likely to be informed that he cannot imagine what a concentration camp was like. It's a failure of imagination, but not necessarily on the contender's side: it's far more likely that the informant has failed to imagine what the Thirty Years' War was like. History has been one long holocaust. Most arguments for the uniqueness of our own age in this department are based on the way in which technology has inflated the scale of operations while reducing the blood-heat of the people conducting them. Certainly there is a lot to this, but there is no reason to think that pre-twentieth-century life was any more readily intelligible, or tolerable, for the victim just because he was able to look his executioner in the eye—then, as now, the innocent were likely to be chosen as the very people to be slaughtered first. The true change from previous centuries to our own has been not in the way evil manifests itself, but in the way we react to it. For large-scale crimes to look so shockingly unnatural in our own century, it first had to be widely assumed that history had grown out of them—and this, broadly, was what the nineteenth century strove to assume. The nub of the matter is that the nineteenth-century enlightened mind—the mind that had studied history in a way that history had never previously studied itself—was simply not expecting these things to happen. The twentieth century began with a very widely diffused belief in progress. The heritage of Hegelianism was Great Expectations, and they were greatly disappointed. The systematic, developmental philosophies (the philosophies which governed the study of history and, by extension, of literature too) were optimistic. Either they turned to pessimism in the face of the new twentieth-century events, or else they lived on as virulent dogma.

The intellectual consequences of enforced pessimism may be seen at their most poignant in the culminating works of the European panoptic scholars—Huizinga, Curtius, Auerbach. Eventually the notion of cultural breakup was everywhere, and in one form or another its concomitant was too: if unity had been shattered, unity must once have existed, somewhere back when Christendom was still integrated, sensibility had not dissociated, society was still organic. Pessimism is the driving force of most of the finest scholarly work in our century, which means the finest there has ever been. But pessimism is no better than optimism at being realistic about history. A view of history is either pluralist or it is unreal, and on a pluralist view of history civilization and evil were never so mutually exclusive that the first could give way to the second in so complete a way. Prisoners were worked to death in the Spanish galleys while Titian painted for the court; his pictures didn't make their suffering less horrible, their suffering didn't make his pictures less beautiful; the unity was never there, it was always conflict. For anyone with the imagination to sense what life has always been like, and always will be like, it must seem almost miraculous that civilization can be so tenacious—that values do *not* collapse, and that even when a whole race is driven to the wall there are forces left which unite to condemn the crime.

Alvarez doubts the capacity of the liberal-humanist intellectual tradition to act in the face of modern events, but I doubt if it is obliged to act. (I should note that Alvarez in fact uses the term "liberal-humanist" mainly to describe what came about in New York after the intellectual defeat of Marxism in the thirties. This is to debase the term and I feel entitled to snatch it back again.) It is obliged merely to give an account of what takes place. To the extent that it got itself attached to the optimistic philosophies, it was taken for a ride: but then, it was the liberal-humanist tradition which eventually mounted the decisive critique against the optimistic philosophies. Evil, barbarism, illiberalism and inhumanity have done such a precise job of defining themselves in this century that the liberal-humanist tradition was never better placed to do its part (the intellectual part, which is not the only one) in preserving and furthering civilization. That it withdrew from compromising positions—positions it was tempted into by the promise of extra-intellectual action—ought to redound to its credit. But Alvarez is a man of action all the way to the roots, and for him it was a logical progression to ask of art what intellect had failed to do—act in the world as a strategically contending power.

It's from this desire that Alvarez's second basic assumption springs: a unique artistic response to the unique contemporary evils. The desire itself is part of a feeling for history that gets history wrong—art is certainly in conflict with other forces but is not compelled to allow for the way those forces move, and might well choose to ignore them. The assumption is wrong to the extent that it is governed by the desire. But it is right to the extent that while art might choose to ignore other forces it cannot presume to be unaware of them. Alvarez was incorrect about contemporary evils being unique but was correct about them being *there*, and his critical requirement that the artistic intelligence should take account of what had been going on was the key critical requirement as the fifties shaded into the sixties. The "end of ideology" had given the artists a dangerous opportunity to relax into insularity, withdrawing their work not just as a contending power but as any kind of force at all.

Unfortunately Alvarez phrased his warning as an invitation to get out there and fight—not just to take account of modern events, but to incorporate them, holding the mirror up to the A-blast and the torture cell. If his powerlessness in the face of modern events had driven the artist to desperation, that desperation was what he ought to express; was what the best artists were already expressing. It followed that anyone who kept a contemplative equilibrium was somehow suspect. And it was never questioned that extremist expression would have (when properly controlled) an ameliorative effect. Alvarez was far too experienced to place any value on possible therapeutic effects for the artist, but, like all theorists of art as a contending power, he was obliged merely to assert, without demonstrating, the probability of a beneficial effect on the recipient. Finally it all came down to the assurance that Lowell, Berryman, Plath and Hughes were good for you.

If the realization of what has happened in modern history forces a sensitive man towards breakdown, then a poet who does not transmit such turmoil has to be fibbing. That, crudely, was the big idea. It started as a footnote to a few sentences on Lowell in the "Art and Isolation" essay which closed *The Shaping Spirit* in 1958. The footnote didn't go in until the 1961 edition: Alvarez had been reviewing recent poetry regularly for the *Observer* in the interim, and during that time *Life Studies* had come out—at which point his criticism crossed the Rubicon with a mighty clashing of shields.

Not all these poems are successful. There is a certain air of poetic therapy about them which encourages looseness and makes some seem almost prattling. But apparently they produced the necessary results: by writing them Lowell seems to have set his house in order and so assured himself of a firm, known base from which his work could start afresh. So in the poems which end *Life Studies* and in those which have followed it—particularly his superlative version of Villon's *Testament*—Lowell handles themes quite as personal and exacerbated as those of his earlier work, but now he does so with a control and clarity which greatly add to their power. In the process, he has also opened up a fresh area of verse—the dispassionate artistic use of material salvaged from the edge of breakdown—which several talented young writers, such as Anne Sexton, have begun to develop. He has given poetry a new impetus.

The emphasis on "personal" poetry had been there since *The School of Donne,* most of which had been written in 1958. But to salvage material from the edge of breakdown—this was a new requirement, and gradually through the sixties it became a requirement which divided the good from the bad in modern poetry as decisively as Metaphysical poetry was divided from the Renaissance. In 1962 Berryman and Lowell were placed at the head of the pugnacious Penguin anthology *The New Poetry*, for which Alvarez wrote an introduction that committed him firmly to a rejection of the gentility principle. As well as giving an account of what was happening, it is quite possible that his editing of this anthology helped shape what happened later—at any rate here was intellect in action and no mistake. In 1965 Alvarez placed it on record, in *Under Pressure*, that he had seen at least one of the dangers a personal poetry of breakdown might conceivably run into.

> But when artists begin to internalize everything—nature and society, art and life, intimacy and response—they have to face a simple but overbearing difficulty: beyond a certain point, the self is also boring. . . . Extremism in the arts —the cultivation of breakdown and all the diverse facets of schizophrenia— ends not so much in anarchy as in a kind of internal fascism by which the artist, to relieve his own boredom, becomes both torturer and tortured.

This essay ("America and Extremist Art," the final chapter of *Under Pressure*) was his last chance to get out of his own aesthetic before it trapped him. But faint heart never won fair copy, and it must have seemed more interesting just to push on up the tunnel and see where it led. Finally it led him to those four figures—Lowell, Berryman, Hughes and Plath— and a formulation of Extremism (in the title essay of *Beyond All This Fiddle*, 1968) calculated to neutralize the objections he himself had already thought of.

> Perhaps the basic misunderstanding encouraged by Extremist art is that the artist's experience on the outer edge of whatever is tolerable is somehow a substitute for creativity. In fact, the opposite is true; in order to make art out of deprivation and despair the artist needs proportionately rich internal resources. Contrary to current belief, there is no short cut to creative ability, not even through the psychiatric ward of the most progressive mental hospital. However rigidly his experience is internalized, the genuine artist does not simply project his own nervous system as a pattern for reality. He is what he is because his inner world is more substantial, variable and self-renewing than that of ordinary people, so that even in his deepest isolation he is left with

something more sustaining than mere narcissism. In this, of course, the modern artist is like every other creative figure in history: he knows what he knows, he has his own vision steady within him, and every new work is an attempt to reveal a little more of it. What sets the contemporary artist apart from his predecessors is his lack of external standards by which to judge his reality. He not only has to launch his craft and control it, he also has to make his own compass.

So there has to be a steadiness inside the turmoil, and all the control necessary to control the uncontrollable. ("It is an art like that of a racing driver drifting a car," he said of Plath in the same essay; "the art of keeping precise control over something which, to the outsider, seems utterly beyond all control.") By this time Alvarez had got his Extremist aesthetic into shape, with all the loopholes plugged: the result was that it was critically inapplicable. As Lowell, Berryman, Hughes and Plath became elevated uniformly to exemplary status, it became increasingly difficult to criticize their work in any way beyond the simple assertion of inner resources (deduced from the outer resources, i.e., the poems) and control. It's almost a Leavisite fix. The Leavisite fix runs something like this: "This is great writing and the reason it's great writing is you can *see* it's great writing and if you can't see it's great writing you're not a fit reader." The Alvarez fix runs something like this: "This poem manifests control through not looking quite uncontrolled enough to be out of control and somehow implies inner resources sufficiently complex to justify the presence of the material being presented as salvaged from the edge of breakdown." At this rate criticism was bound to become a matter of trusting a favoured poet to go on being serious. Alvarez was up to his neck in a revised version of the intentional fallacy, continually referring the work back to the mind supposedly behind it and referring the mind supposedly behind it sideways to the supposed state of the world. His initial response to the quality of the language on the page was still operating, but it had precious little room to move. The trouble can be traced to the primal requirement of incorporating extreme experience. Despite the disclaimers he steadily built into his aesthetic over the ten years or so it took him to develop it, this requirement remained fundamental. It wasn't enough merely to mention an H-bomb or a concentration camp, they had to be *in* there somewhere: somehow the contemporary violence had to be reflected.

When a writer tries to hitch a ride from these themes, he usually ends only by exposing the triviality of his responses. What is needed is that extreme tension and concentration which creates a kind of silence of shock and calm around the images:

> I have done it again.
> One year in every ten
> I manage it—
>
> A sort of walking miracle, my skin
> Bright as a Nazi lampshade,
> My right foot
>
> A paperweight,
> My face a featureless, fine
> Jew linen.

Consider how the penultimate line-ending is cannily used to create a pause before the epithet "Jew." The effect is twofold: first shock, then an odd detachment. The image is unspeakable, yet the poet's use of it is calm, almost elegant. And this, perhaps, is the only way of handling such despair: objectively, accurately, and with a certain contempt. (*Beyond All This Fiddle,* title essay.)

I have never been able to accept unquestioned the rightness of Sylvia Plath assimilating such infinities of torture to her own problems. I admire her late work but not this aspect of it, and would argue that it was her *distance* from these events that made her so appallingly free with them, and that this propensity for absorbing history into the self (and being under the impression that it *fits*) is the biggest and best of the very good reasons for not going to the limit. The shock around those images is the shock of sentimental excess, as the poet tries to embody what boozy old Saroyan used to call the Whole Voyald. I don't mean that there is material which poetry can't by its nature encompass—only that there is material which the poet can't by the material's nature render personal. It just can't survive the scaling down. Where such stuff works at all in Plath, it works because of the pathos of the attempt.

Trapped in his intentional fallacy, Alvarez is betting everything on the artist's sincerity: even if the artist hasn't actually been scarified by the perception of some external event, he will possess, it is hoped, the internal equipment to justify the pretence that he has. But pretend or not, the material presented needs to be judged with some view towards the external world and away from its creator's supposed mental condition. It's possible to gesture too blithely, whatever the motivation. Here, for example, is Lowell, in a recent sonnet about Sylvia Plath. The immediate occasion for this poem seems to have been an article on Lowell in *the Review* 24 by John Bayley, who favoured Plath with an epithet Lowell found objectionable.

> *A miniature mad talent?* Sylvia Plath,
> who'll wipe off the spit of your integrity,
> rising in the saddle to slash at Auschwitz,
> life tearing this and that, *I am a woman?*

Hannah Arendt once said that finally these matters can be understood only by the poets, but when you scan a piece of journey-work like this you start wondering if she was right. A lot of rhetoric had to go over the dam before all the concentration camps in the Reich and the occupied territories got whittled down to that one word "Auschwitz"—hundreds of journalists and television anchormen had to do their stuff. And at last, after the whole infinitely ramified nightmare had been trimmed to that one stub and the stub itself had been crushed to powder, it was time for Lowell to come along and toss off a line suggesting that in Sylvia Plath the *Endlösung* finally met its implacable opponent. Carrying a sword. Riding a horse.

In such moments of rarefied bathos from his key poet, Alvarez is confronted with the limitations of his critical position: what apparently escapes him in Hughes's *Crow* ought to seize him by the throat here. Lowell's internal condition presumably being one of routine agony, the material has undoubtedly surfaced with all the correct credentials. Nor does the technical control seem much lower than average. What is wrong is the sheer, shrieking inadequacy of the event as cited to the event as it happened. For anyone who has an inkling of what the Third Reich was like, these lines will look pitiful. For anyone who has no inkling, the notion might take flower that some German character called Auschwitz finally got pinned to the mat by Sylvia Plath. Either way, small reward. These lines are part of a closed circuit, and I might add as a conjecture that they seem to me to adumbrate a wholly new kind of complacency which Alvarez has unintentionally done his share of bringing into the world: full-frontal solemnity.

Thinking of the work and the mind as a complete circuit, Alvarez is hindered from seeing what ought to be plain on the page—the actual interior weaknesses that his four front runners are fighting, as all men must fight their own psyches at some point. He is good on Plath's problems but light on the fact that her poems are a problem too: even at their powerful best they do violence to stretches of vanished time which have had so much violence done to them already the extra flourish is simply an irrelevance, like flying a Frisbee in the Colosseum. In Berryman the magnificent multiplicity of personality—the pluralism of the mind, all out there on the paper—is continually invaded and falsified by a consciously "creative," All-American ego making its belligerent claims. In Lowell there is the determination, growing ever more obvious, to write major poetry or nothing: there is so much significance going on you can hardly hear yourself think, and the steady clangour is split by the squeal of straining verbs. As for Hughes, it's as though the Nazis had killed everybody and only the animals were left. It's part of the business of criticism to run a constant check on the intellectual component of an artist's work and help keep it from calcifying. There are large penalties to be paid if we accept without question schematic interpretations of reality which vitiate what is best in an artist's work and say nothing of interest about reality.

One absence bulks large in *The Savage God*—Solzhenitsyn. Experience doesn't come more extreme than that, and it's a token of the retrogressive nature of Soviet history that if he hadn't been a mathematician he would never have even got onto a casualty list of the young cut down in their gifted prime—he would simply have been blotted out. As it was, he lived, and wrote novels in which life lived right to the dizzy limit is contemplated and reordered by a mind detached, cool, balanced, integrated and classical. It would be interesting to see what vocabulary Alvarez would employ in dealing with his achievement. It's a safe bet that he'd have to dismantle his own aesthetic before starting work, or at least loosen it to the point where the flexibility of response in *Under Pressure* (where it wasn't required of an artist who had actually had extreme experience imposed upon him that he should imitate the action of Ted Hughes) could quietly be regained.

By turning against Movement poetry and developing his Extremist aesthetic, Alvarez brought the relationship of art to reality into closer question than it had been subject to for a long time. It was the right move at the right moment, since the emergence of a right little, tight little, know-nothing English poetry was a clear and present danger. But for Alvarez as a critic the move had damaging consequences, not the least of which was a permanent ability to undervalue Philip Larkin, who had never been "immortalizing the securities and complacencies of life in the sub-urbs" (in *The Savage God* Alvarez is still saying that the Movement poets were doing that), but had been projecting a personal despair which fulfilled every one of Alvarez's requirements except for an adequate supply of globally apocalyptic referents. A life ending in boredom, fear and age might not seem much in comparison with the larger instances of modern frightfulness, but it's the way that most of us will get ours, when it comes. (And to that one point at least in *The Savage God* Alvarez incongruously seems to agree.) Larkin's treatment of death-in-ordinary will go on being frightening—extreme, if you like—when the slain millions have gone back into time with all the other millions, out of range of the casually significant evocation. In the teeth of all the evidence, Larkin has apparently decided that he might as well live. It's hard to see this as a drawback. The suicidal frame of mind isn't adequate to the understanding of history: it is under the delusion that its own destruction might be an appropriate response to events.

Alvarez is far too ready to assess the spirit of the age. Probably the last thing he would want is to be pigeon-holed with George Steiner, but there are times when he is not too many pigeon-holes away, particularly with his picture of civilization getting into a terminal crisis and art flailing around in search of new means to do its duty. My closing quotation takes us back a decade or so nearer to one of the main events, World War II. It is from Pieter Geyl—a paragraph from one of his replies to Toynbee collected in *Encounters in History*.

In any case I know full well, as do all who live sincerely by our tradition, that the ideal of Western civilization we try to serve has not made angels of us. It is an aspiration, hallowed by the labours of many generations, even though they, too, have frequently gone off the track. It is an aspiration which has always been and is still exposed to reactions from inside. If these at times seem menacing, this must only incite us to be prepared and to persevere. At the time of the national-socialist aberration there were too many in my own country as well—I mention only Huizinga—who treated us to gloomy admonitions as if the evil was in fact the culmination of a process of decay of which they imagined to detect the symptoms all around them. Toynbee now admits, in one of those apologetic concessions which drop from his pen so frequently in his new volume [A Study of History, vol. XII—C.J.], that since he cried alarm (not against Hitler, but against ourselves) the menace had been warded off, and yet even now it suits him to dub "the cold-bloodedness and highpowered organization" of the totalitarian movements "typically modern-Western."

A. J. P. Taylor named Geyl as the modern historian he venerated most. Certainly Geyl deserved a medal for self-effacement. While arguing this point with Toynbee it apparently didn't strike him as relevant that it was he, and not Toynbee, who had been in Buchenwald. One more the Savage God missed.

(the Review, 1972)

When the Gloves Are Off

In 1962 a brace of small but influential Penguins waddled into prominence: *Contemporary American Poetry,* selected and edited by Donald Hall, and *The New Poetry,* selected and edited by A. Alvarez. Hall picked on two immediately post-war books as marking the culmination of "past poetries" and the beginning of a new poetry: these were Lowell's *Lord Weary's Castle* and Richard Wilbur's *The Beautiful Changes.* For tremendous power under tremendous pressure, Lowell was your only man. For skilful elegance—but not for passion—Wilbur was likewise nonpareil. As Hall went on to point out, it was Wilbur who had the most plausible imitators, and the typical duff poem of the fifties was the *poème bien fait* that was not *bien fait*—the Wilbur poem not written by Wilbur. By 1962, Wilbur, in addition to *The Beautiful Changes,* had published *Ceremony* (1950) and *Things of This World* (1956) and had brought out a large selection in England, *Poems 1943–1956. Advice to a Prophet* (1961) was also out here by 1962, having been brought straight across by Faber with a haste well-nigh unseemly. Wilbur's stock was high on both sides of the pond.

Turning to *The New Poetry,* though, we see that the two American poets Alvarez put forward as exemplary were not Lowell and Wilbur but Lowell and Berryman. Hanging by one well-muscled arm from an ice-axe lodged firmly in the north face of the Future, Alvarez wasn't interested in grace under pressure so much as in the registration of pressure itself. For the New Seriousness, "gentility, decency and all the other social totems" were not in themselves sufficient for the task of responding to the unique contemporary evils: if skill got in the road of urgency, then skill was out. Not much room for Wilbur there.

Getting on for ten years later, Wilbur has in fact faded right out: it's doubtful if he is now thought of, on either side of the water, as any kind of force at all. Earlier this year a further volume came out, *Walking to Sleep.* A disproportionate amount of it consists of translations, and although the original poems retain his customary technical perfection they hold no surprises beyond the usual polite sparkle of his aerated language—it's the same old *aqua minerale* and either it or our liver has lost tone. The book was greeted with muted satisfaction by the squarer critics but otherwise it was correctly thought to be a bit tired.

As it happens, I saw Wilbur in action at the American Embassy in that very Year of the Penguins, 1962. His reading was prefaced by a short expository routine from John Wain, who, while preparing us for Wilbur's qualities, unaccountably chose to impersonate one of his own characters, Charles Froulish from *Hurry on Down.* (I think particularly of the moment when the rumpled and wildly gesticulating Froulish, getting set to read his magnum opus aloud, rips off his tie and throws it in the fire.) Into the pocket of high pressure created by this performance strode Wilbur, the epitome of cool. It was all there: the Ivy League haircut, the candy-stripe jacket, the full burnished image of the Amherst Phi Bete. Riding his audience like the Silver Surfer, he took European Culture out of his pocket and laid it right on us. We were stoned. It was the Kennedy era and somehow it seemed plausible that the traditional high culture of Europe should be represented in a super-refined form by an American who looked like a jet-jockey and that the State Department should pay the hotel bills. As the world well knows, the dream couldn't last. It got ambushed in Dallas the following year. But it's sometimes difficult to remember now just how solid-sounding a civilized front the U.S. was putting up in that period: it all clicked and it was all official. The internationalism of a mind like Wilbur's, its seemingly relaxed roaming in the European tradition, fitted the picture perfectly.

Of that picture there is now nothing left, not even fragments, and looking back on it with what benefits accrue to a blighted hindsight we see that it was always false in the main—arrogant, insidious and self-serving. Better Johnson's or Nixon's instincts than Kennedy's pretensions. Yet within the Kennedy era's delusive atmosphere of distinction, Wilbur's own distinction was real. He could not, in the ensuing years, respond to his country's altered situation in the way that Lowell did, but I would be surprised if this meagreness of reactive energy turned out to be determined by complacency; up to 1956, at any rate, there is plenty in his poetry to show that he was deeply troubled by the huge dislocations that Alvarez saw as a characteristic, even exclusive, twentieth-century evil. But the point, I think, is that Wilbur's intricately coherent art is suited to the long allaying of an old mental wound, and not to the sudden coping with a new one. The evidence of his work is that he was able to employ the decade or so after the war as a time of tranquillity in which his experience of wartime Europe could be assimilated and in a way *given back:* his images of order, his virtuosities of symmetry, are particularly orderly and symmetrical when he is dealing with Italy and France, the two countries in which he served. In a sentimentalized but still powerful form, we can see the same spirit at work in the J. D. Salinger story "For Esmé, with Love and Squalor," and with the same emphasis on fluent, formal speech as the instrument of recuperation. In the strict senses of both parts of the word, it is recollection: the healing wisdom comes after the event. Wilbur's comparative silence in the face of the new (and this time American-inspired) disintegration of the world picture is less likely to be a failure of response than a need for time. There is no doubt, incidentally, about what he thinks of it all—in 1967 he wrote a shattering occasional poem against Johnson's philistinism, comparing him with Jefferson, "Who would have wept to see small nations dread the imposition of our cattle-brand." But otherwise in this decade he has mainly written mechanically in his own manner, giving the impression that an early challenge to his equilibrium had long been met and that a new one has not yet been faced. For the time being, at any rate, his poetry has lost its relevance. What I want to do now is to indicate what that relevance was when his poetry still had it.

The Beautiful Changes set the level for Wilbur's technical bravura and he has never since dropped very far below it: if the recent products look ordinary, it's worth remembering that they are ordinary in a way that Wilbur himself established. If there were no more going on in his early poems than the dextrous flourishes of the dab hand that put them together, they would still be of permanent interest. Suggestions that Wilbur is fundamentally a punster in his diction are misleading. He is fundamentally a precisionist—he will make a word divert to a parallel, or revert to an antecedent etymological stage, not to pun with it but to refurbish it.

> Easy as cove-water rustles its pebbles and shells
> In the slosh, spread, seethe, and the backsliding
> Wallop and tuck of the wave . . .

The restoration of "backsliding" to pristine condition is characteristic of his handling of language, and the enforced transfer of the reader's eye-line back and down to the next starting-point ("backsliding"—pause—"Wallop and tuck") is an elementary example of his mastery of mimesis. These lines are actually from a poem in *Ceremony:* I choose them because they contain instances of his two main technical preoccupations handily demonstrated in the one spot. But each trick was already everywhere employed in *The Beautiful Changes* and working to perfection. This, for example, is from "Cicadas":

> You know those windless summer evenings, swollen to stasis
> by too-substantial melodies, rich as a
> running-down record, ground round
> to full quiet.

Sound thickens when a disc slows down. Wilbur has noticed the too-muchness of the noise and neatly picked the word "rich" as appropriate: the connotations, partly established by the preceding use of "swollen" and "too-substantial," are of a superabundance of nutrition rather than of pelf. As for the kinetic copy-catting, it's so neatly done he makes it look easy: the two-ton spondee "ground round" slows the line to a crawl, and the enforced pause of the enjambement kills the action stone dead. Sheer class. This point-for-point matching of form to action reached one kind of excellence (I say one kind because I think that elsewhere there is another) in "My Father Paints the Summer":

> They talk by the lobby fire but no one hears
> For the thrum of the rain. In the dim and sounding halls,
> Din at the ears,
> Dark at the eyes well in the head, and the ping-pong balls
> Scatter their hollow knocks
> Like crazy clocks.

Just how it goes: ping/pong; SKAT! (could be a backhand smash); k/k/k/k/k. Less easily noticed, but still contributory, is the preceding Din/Dark, a duller pair of consonants. What we are given is a kind of Doppler effect as the writer leaves the hotel lobby and walks towards the source of the noises. Copy-cat equivalence has here reached one kind of limit (not that Wilbur didn't go on exploiting it in later volumes), but in his superb poem "Grace" it reached another kind—immediately more fruitful and eventually more troublesome. In these two stanzas from the poem, the first shows the first kind, the second the second:

> One is tickled, again, by the dining-car waiter's absurd
> Acrobacy—tipfingered tray like a wind-besting bird
> Plumblines his swinging shoes, the sole things sure
> In the shaken train, but this is all done for food,
> Is habitude, if not pure

> Hebetude. It is a graph of a theme that flings
> The dancer kneeling on nothing into the wings,
> And Nijinsky hadn't the words to make the laws
> For learning to loiter in air; he merely said,
> "I merely leap and pause."

The first stanza is Wilbur's customary five or so under par for the course, and one surfaces from the dictionary convinced that the transition from stanza to stanza by way of those two near-homophones is neat and just. What "a graph of a theme" is I don't quite grasp, and can only deduce that it is the opposite of whatever motivates a dining-car waiter. But "The dancer kneeling on nothing into the wings" is a genuinely amazing stroke, probably the best early instance in Wilbur of the mighty, or killer-diller, line. Here the mechanical principles of the mimetic effect are not fully open to inspection as they are in the earlier examples: the feeling, the "art-emotion" that Eliot said could be created out of ordinary emotions, is not reducible to technicalities. Unprogrammed instead of programmed, perhaps even irrational instead of rational, the effect has been snatched out of the air by Wilbur during a temporary holiday from his usual punishing round of meticulous fidelity. When he showed he was capable of effects like this, he showed that the bulk of his poetry—his craftsman-ship—was slightly stiff by his own best standards. As a rule of thumb, it

can be said that the really glaring moments of falsity throughout Wilbur's poetry are brought about when, in pursuit of such an effect, he snatches and misses. An early example is the last couplet of "The Peace of Cities," which like a good many of his poems has the form of a two-part contention. Cities in peacetime are characterized first, and found to be more dreadful, because more inconsequential, than cities in wartime, which are characterized thus:

> . . .there was a louder and deeper

> Peace in those other cities, when silver fear
> Drove the people to fields, and there they heard

> The Luftwaffe waft what let the sunshine in
> And blew the bolt from everybody's door.

This clinching couplet sounds transcendentally silly, like some polished and perfumed banality dropped by Oscar Wilde on an off-night. But the reasons for its emptiness go beyond a mere lapse of taste: they follow from what Wilbur is trying to do with his subject-matter. He is trying to absorb the war's evil into a continuous, self-regulating process—a process in which a subdued Manichaean principle is balanced against an aesthetic Grace. The material resists that absorption. The war is a mental hot spot Wilbur tries to cool out, make sense of, reduce to order: trying to do that, he tends to devalue the experience, and his wealth of language becomes merely expensive-looking. All his poems on wartime subjects are flawed in their handling of language—his best gift goes against him. To take another example from *The Beautiful Changes,* "First Snow in Alsace" holds a delicate balance for most of its length as the snowfall softens the deadly starkness:

> The ration stacks are milky domes;
> Across the ammunition pile
> The snow has climbed in sparkling combs.

> You think: beyond this town a mile
> Or two, this snowfall fills the eyes
> Of soldiers dead a little while.

But he rounds the poem out with an orgy of consolation, providing the exact verbal equivalent of a Norman Rockwell cover painting:

> The night guard coming from his post,
> Ten first-snows back in thought, walks slow
> And warms him with a boyish boast:
>
> He was the first to see the snow.

With the possible exception of "Mined Country" (and even that one is rounded out with a tough-tender metaphysical bromide), the poems in *The Beautiful Changes* that treat the war theme directly are failures in total form as well as in local detail. But they cast light on the poems that treat the war indirectly or leave it out altogether—they demonstrate what kind of pressure it is that makes the successful poems such convincing examples of formal order attained with technical assurance but against great spiritual stress. "Lightness," the best poem in the book and one of the finest things Wilbur ever wrote, is a two-part contention —and equation—about a falling bird's-nest and a dying old American lady. It ends like this ("he" being her husband):

> He called her "Birdie," which was good for him.
> And he and the others, the strong, the involved, in-the-swim,
> Seeing her there in the garden, in her grey shroud
>   As vague and as self-possessed as a cloud,
>   Requiring nothing of them any more,
> And one hand lightly laid on a fatal door,
> Thought of the health of the sick, and, what mocked their sighing,
>   Of the strange intactness of the gladly dying.

Aware of the countless European people whom death had found by no means intact and the reverse of glad, Wilbur picked his words here with an authority that has nothing to do with glibness. Strange, now, to think of a time when America could mean peace.

In all the elements I have so far dealt with, Wilbur's first volume set the course for the subsequent ones—except that the overt treatment of war was for the most part dropped, and any concern for current, well-defined political crises was dropped along with it. He subsumed such things in a general concept of disorderly force, operative throughout history: they were the subjects his poem would redeem, rather than deal with. Each poem was to be a model of limpidity and no disturbance would be admitted which could not be deftly counterbalanced in the quest for equipoise. From *Ceremony* onwards, successes and failures accumulated in about equal number; but what *guaranteed* failure was when the disturbing force, the element of awkwardness, was smoothly denatured before being introduced as a component. It sometimes seemed possible that Wilbur was working in a dream-factory. Here is the second half of "A Plain Song for a Comrade," from *Things of This World:*

> It is seventeen years
> Come tomorrow
> That Bruna Sandoval has kept the church
> Of San Ysidro, sweeping
> And scrubbing the aisles, keeping
> The candlesticks and the plaster faces bright,
> And seen no visions but the thing done right
> From the clay porch
>
> To the white altar. For love and in all weathers
> That is what she has done.
> Sometimes the early sun
> Shines as she flings the scrubwater out, with a crash
> Of grimy rainbows, and the stained suds flash
> Like angel-feathers.

In poems like this the images of order came too easily: out-of-the-way hamlets were stiff with peasants who knew their place, and every bucket of slops could be depended upon to house an angel's ailerons. But the successes, when they happened, were of high quality. "A Baroque Wall-Fountain in the Villa Sciarra" is the stand-out poem in *Things of This World.* Again a two-part contention, it compares an elaborate fountain with a simple one, and without the slightest sense of strain draws a subtle conclusion that doubles back through its own argument. In describing the plain fountains in front of St. Peter's, Wilbur took his copy-catting to dizzy new heights:

> Are we not
>
> More intricately expressed
> In the plain fountains that Maderna set
> Before St. Peter's—the main jet
> Struggling aloft until it seems at rest
>
> In the act of rising, until
> The very wish of water is reversed,
> That heaviness borne up to burst
> In a clear, high, cavorting head, to fill
>
> With blaze, and then in gauze
> Delays, in a gnatlike shimmering, in a fine
> Illuminated version of itself, decline,
> And patter on the stones its own applause?

Virtuose almost beyond belief, this is *perizia* taken to the limit. The way the vocabulary deflates as the water collapses, the way "patter" and "applause," already connected in the common speech, are separated and exploited mimetically—well, it'll do till something cleverer comes along.

Of the killer-diller line there were a few instances, most notably in "Loves of the Puppets" from *Advice to a Prophet.* It's symptomatic, although not necessarily sad, that the lovers in Wilbur's finest love poem should be made of papier mâché. The desperation of the last stanza and the plangency of the tremendous final line are prepared for not only by the rest of the poem but by our knowledge of Wilbur's whole attitude: to ensure order in the real world, the disorder of unbridled passion must be transferred to Toyland.

> Then maladroitly they embraced once more,
> And hollow rang to hollow with a sound
> That tuned the brooks more sweetly than before,
> And made the birds explode for miles around.

But not many attempts at the art-thrill were as startling as that one. As Wilbur solidified his position, the general run of his poetry slipped past limpidity and got close to torpor. By the time of *Advice to a Prophet* self-parody was creeping in.

> In a dry world more huge than rhyme or dreaming
> We hear the sentences of straws and stones,
> Stand in the wind and, bowing to this time,
> Practise the candour of our bones.

Here the pendulum has stopped oscillating or even shivering: it's just a softly glowing, static blob.

Ten years have gone by since *Advice to a Prophet* and for most of that time the major American poets have been sweatily engaged in doing all the things Wilbur was intent on avoiding. Instead of ordering disorder, they have revealed the disorder in order; instead of cherishing a personal equilibrium, they have explored their own disintegration; where he clammed up or elegantly hinted, they have clamorously confessed. To be doubtful about the course American poetry (and a lot of British poetry along with it) has taken, you do not have to be in entire agreement with Hannah Arendt's warning that those men are making a mistake who identify their own personalities with the battlefield of history. You need only to be suspicious about artists playing an apocalyptic role. Nevertheless it is true that there is something sadly hermetic about Wilbur's recent work.

> Though, high above the shore
> On someone's porch, spread wings of newsprint flap
>   The tidings of some dirty war,
> It is a perfect day:

Here Wilbur seems to be trying to get at something specific, but once again he can only generalize—which is not the same as being specific in an oblique way. Apart from the powerful but localized hit at Johnson mentioned earlier, the serenity of previous volumes continues untroubled by any hint of altered circumstances. A solitary war poem, "The Agent," consists entirely of formula situations sketched in flat language: the hardware is World War II surplus and the setting is a back-lot assemblage of instant Europe. It reads like a worn-out answer to a new challenge. The opening lines of the long title poem guilelessly reveal the strain of a metaphysical essay being flogged into existence:

As a queen sits down, knowing that a chair will be there,
Or a general raises his hand and is given the field-glasses,
Step off assuredly into the blank of your mind.
Something will come to you.

Something does—nearly two hundred lines of wheezing exhortation. ("Avoid the pleasant room / Where someone, smiling to herself, has placed / A bowl of yellow freesias.") Wilbur's judicious retreat from raw experience has turned into mere insularity. It's a relief to get to the collection of translations at the back of the book, and the back goes more than a third of the way towards the front.

Yet with all this taken into account, there is still no reason to think that Wilbur will not eventually come up with something. At present he is off balance, a condition he is constitutionally unfitted to exploit. While he was on balance, though, he wrote a good number of poised, civilized and very beautiful poems. They'll be worth remembering when some of the rough, tough, gloves-off stuff we're lately supposed to admire starts looking thin. The beautiful changes—nobody denies that—but it doesn't change that much. I don't think it changes into *Crow*.

(*the Review*, 1971)

Everything's Rainbow

Reviewers of Elizabeth Bishop's work have small trouble in demonstrating its perfection: she is an easy poet to quote from, and it rarely occurs to them that this very fact might indicate limitations to that perfection. The cisatlantic notices for *The Complete Poems* almost all singled out as exemplary her eyeball-to-eyeball encounter with a big fish.

> I looked into his eyes
> which were far larger than mine
> but shallower, and yellowed,
> the irises backed and packed
> with tarnished tinfoil
> seen through the lenses
> of old scratched isinglass.

You would have to catch a big fish of your own to check up on any of this, and it would have to be old and sick like the fish in the poem ("He didn't fight. / He hadn't fought at all,") if it was going to lie still enough to allow the faculty of observation full play. But the point of such writing is that it is not only precise—I will accept that she is precise here, as she is so demonstrably precise elsewhere—but it makes a point of its precision, and creates emotion in making that point. As moments like these accumulate, the buildup in authority becomes more and more convincing, to the stage where the reader simply hands over control: even if he stops long enough to admit that he finds tarnished tinfoil hard to imagine, tacitly he will insist that it can still be imagined.

An appreciation of Bishop's work travels from point to point along a line of such observational intensities, and that is the unity of her poetry —intense moments accumulating. Since there are half a dozen such instances packing out even the smaller of her poems, the tendency is to ascribe unity to the poems as well. And after all, I suppose it could be argued that any poem, no matter what shape it is in otherwise, has established its reason for being if it contains even one observation like this:

> Below, the tracks slither between
> lines of head-to-tail parked cars.
>
> (The tin hides have the iridescence
> of dying, flaccid toy balloons.)

This idea comes from "Going to the Bakery," a poem set in Rio de Janeiro. Now it happens to be a fact that a toy balloon has to be inflated and allowed to die down before its colour will take on the pastel glow that Bishop here equates with an iridescent Detroit paint-job: I can assert this with such boldness solely because a tired balloon left over from our baby daughter's party reminded me, on the day before I first read this poem, of the opalescent finishes supplied as an option on the Oldsmobiles assembled in Australia in the late fifties. A not yet inflated balloon would scarcely have worked the trick: it's something to do with the stretching and relaxation of the rubber. So to this image I bring a certain capacity of verification; and someone else who had never made that particular mental connection might see that it was nevertheless likely to be true; and one way or another we are both involved.

All well and good, and it could be said that this is involvement enough, that there are not many poets who will make the faculty of sight a public issue. The vision is personal only in its power. Otherwise, it is as community-minded as you like. We and the writer are united in identifying truths which, like scientific truths, are finally tautologies; this does not deprive them of interest, but it does deprive them of animus, and the ultimate effect is one of consolation in a universe where everything has been stripped of unpredictability through being defined in terms of something else.

Obviously this line of argument would quickly collapse if it could be shown that the moments of observation in Bishop's work are as incidental as they are powerful, and really go to serve a further purpose, that of being combined into a poem which supplies them with a transfiguring energy as well as drawing from them a store of tangibility. "One is first struck by the magnificent surfaces of her poems," the blurb quotes Martin Dodsworth, and indeed one is; "later one sees that the point is to feel something else underlying the descriptions and lending them an air of dream, despite (and perhaps because of) their clarity."

I think that Dodsworth here has intuitively recognized, without raising the problem to the plane of intellect, that "to feel something else underlying the descriptions" is an activity that needs to be *recommended* and won't come naturally to a mind discriminating enough to be impressed by her faculty of observation in the first place. In fact there is a frequently ruinous dualism at work in Bishop's poetry. A poem is likely to be critically demolished by its own best moments. The self-contained quality of the intense observations amounts to inertia, and the argumentative lines joining them together, far from being lines of force, are factitious even at their best and at worst degenerate into whimsy. Here the opening stanza and a half of "Going to the Bakery," leading up to the lines I last quoted, are sufficiently illustrative:

> Instead of gazing at the sea
> the way she does on other nights,
> the moon looks down the Avenida
> Copacabana at the sights,
>
> new to her but ordinary.
> She leans on the slack trolley wires.

Sheer marmalade. It would take a more unsophisticated poet than Bishop to indulge in anthropomorphism with a show of technical conviction: trying it, she lapses instantly into the trained poet's equivalent of automatic writing. In another poem, "Seascape," she goes all free-verse in an attempt to give the device some muscle, but there is no cure for it.

> But a skeletal lighthouse standing there
> in black and white clerical dress,
> who lives on his nerves, thinks he knows better.
> He thinks that hell rages below his iron feet,

that that is why the shallow water is so warm,
and he knows that heaven is not like this.
Heaven is not like flying or swimming,
but has something to do with blackness and a strong glare
and when it gets dark he will remember something
strongly worded to say on the subject.

The observation about the lighthouse's clerical paint-work is not enough to offset the speculative rigmarole that follows. Additionally it can be conjectured that in trying to get *above* the equation of the lighthouse and the clerical garb, in trying to make something more out of the automatic and inertial device of establishing those two entities in terms of each other, she admitted her first limitation by running slap into the second. The observation tends to precede the poem, and by preceding it precludes it. Fancy takes over from the stymied imagination.

Bishop's faculty of observation works mainly in the sense of sight and there are strict rules governing it which are occasionally made explicit, as in these lines from "The Bight":

> Absorbing, rather than being absorbed,
> the water in the bight doesn't wet anything,
> the color of the gas flame turned as low as possible.
> One can smell it turning to gas; if one were Baudelaire
> one could probably hear it turning to marimba music.

Tempted with the boundless opportunities offered by synaesthesia, she takes refuge on the far side of a semicolon and rejects the temptation by diverting it to Baudelaire. Little dramas of scrupulousness like this one are constantly fought out. They are triumphs of minor tactics. Perhaps it is an obsession with these tiny battles that allows far larger ones to rage ungoverned. Getting back to "The Fish," for example, we have more than seventy lines of meticulous observation before the speaker makes her decisive move. The local brilliance of the writing is unquestionable:

> While his gills were breathing in
> the terrible oxygen
> —the frightening gills,
> fresh and crisp with blood,
> that can cut so badly—

> I thought of the coarse white flesh
> packed in like feathers,
> the big bones and the little bones,
> the dramatic reds and blacks
> of his shiny entrails,
> and the pink swim-bladder
> like a big peony.

Now this really does go like a dream, and precisely because of its clarity: the observation (the "feathers"), the presentation (that concrete use of the abstract "dramatic") and the technique (the folded in and snapped out p-b/b-p sequence in the last two lines) are absolutely in accord. But what the poet never realizes is that seventy lines of this painstaking stuff are taking *time:* in the reader's mind the fish is croaking while she runs the micrometer over it, making nonsense of the poem's punch line.

> I stared and stared
> and victory filled up
> the little rented boat,
> from the pool of bilge
> where oil had spread a rainbow
> around the rusted engine
> to the bailer rusted orange,
> the sun-cracked thwarts,
> the oarlocks on their strings,
> the gunnels—until everything
> was rainbow, rainbow, rainbow!
> And I let the fish go.

Whereupon, muttering "Thanks for nothing, lady" with its dying gasp, it undoubtedly sank like a plummet. It's not so much the tone failing here, as the tactics. When tactics and tone fail together, the results can stagger towards the gruesome, as in her "Invitation to Marianne Moore," where her fellow poetess is made to share the attributes of Mary Poppins.

> From Brooklyn, over the Brooklyn Bridge, on this fine morning,
>   please come flying.
> In a cloud of fiery pale chemicals,
>   please come flying,

to the rapid rolling of thousands of small blue drums
descending out of the mackerel sky
over the glittering grandstand of harbor-water,
    please come flying.

But it would be misleading to suggest that there are many Bishop poems dismissible on grounds of tweeness. The tone at its lowest is usually comfortably above that, at a level where the prosaic and intellectually platitudinous are twisted towards poeticized quiddities by professionally executed changes of direction. These closing lines from "Quai d'Orléans," which cap a series of brilliantly exploited observations on water-lights and leaves, illustrate the point.

We stand as still as stones to watch
    the leaves and ripples
while light and nervous water hold
    their interview.
"If what we see could forget us half as easily,"
    I want to tell you,
"as it does itself—but for life we'll not be rid
    of the leaves' fossils."

Thus with a gasp and a quick flurry of soul-searching does the poem haul itself onto the metaphysical plateau, making the exterior interior at the price of abandoning the judicious—and genuinely suggestive—language that places "nervous" just so as to concentrate the effects of trembling the poem has already established, and places "interview" to clinch the consistently employed vocabulary of seeing.

It's instructive that when Richard Wilbur gets a poem wrong, this is exactly the way he gets it wrong: the tag falls so perfectly pat that it reads like a bromide. But Wilbur's sense of tactics, perhaps in the light of her example, has always been more highly developed than Bishop's, showing itself as an acute sense of sustained argument. So similar in many ways, the two poets differ in their approach to form. Rather than plug a gap with prose, Wilbur will tighten the argument a notch and let the sequence of thought become a riddle. Bishop, eager to be clear and unwilling to perpetrate asymmetries, will interpose something that contributes to the total sonic unity but which fails to measure up to the standards that the fully felt sections of the poem have already set. The prosaic half of the dualism feels a duty to the poetic half: it feels bound to get in there and comment, compose a motto, ask a rhetorical question, round things out. And it seems to me that she comes closest to striking a balance when she realizes that a dualism exists and makes a link out of the gap's unbridgeability, as in her classic poem "Cirque d'Hiver," whose marvellously observed toy horse has so little to say to her.

> His mane and tail are straight from Chirico.
> He has a formal, melancholy soul.
> He feels her pink toes dangle towards his back
> along the little pole
> that pierces both her body and her soul
>
> and goes through his, and reappears below,
> under his belly, as a big tin key.
> He canters three steps, then he makes a bow,
> canters again, bows on one knee,
> canters, then clicks and stops, and looks at me.
>
> The dancer, by this time, has turned her back.
> He is the more intelligent by far.
> Facing each other rather desperately—
> his eye is like a star—
> we stare and say, "Well, we have come this far."

It is probably too neat to say, but I will risk saying it, that such a poem dramatizes her own poetic situation to perfection. The whole force of her talent is to establish the thingness of things; which being done, the things have nothing much to add. It is as if a composer were to be frustrated in his symphonic ambitions by an irrepressible gift of producing short and self-sufficient melodies: he would be disabled by an excess of talent.

I don't want to suggest that this book is a record of failure. On the contrary I believe it contains more than its fair share of excellent poems, and where the poems are not excellent, their component parts are frequently enthralling. Elizabeth Bishop is an important modern poet if anybody is. But I think that the very terms in which her work is praised serve to indicate that hers is a poetry of a particular emphasis, and that it has not yet been sufficiently questioned whether or not this emphasis might be damaging to the aims implicit in her forms and themes. She aims beyond precision. If "precision" is the cardinal word in our aesthetic vocabulary, we will be praising her for the very thing that she has striven (correctly, in my view, although not often successfully) to transcend.

(*the Review,* 1971)

On John Berryman's
Dream Songs

If the contention is accepted that an excess of clarity is the only kind of difficulty a work of art should offer, John Berryman's *Dream Songs* (it is surely permissible by now to call the complete work by that name) have been offering several kinds of unacceptable difficulty since they first began to appear. It was confusedly apparent in the first volume of the work, *77 Dream Songs,* that several different personalities within the poet's single personality (one doesn't suggest his "real" personality, or at any rate one didn't suggest it at that stage) had been set talking to and of each other. These personalities, or let them be called characters, were given tones of voice, even separate voices with peculiar idioms. The interplays of voice and attitude were not easy to puzzle out, and many reviewers, according to Mr. Berryman and their own subsequent and sometimes abject admissions, made howlers. With this new volume of 308 more dream songs comes a rather impatient corrective from the author pointing out how simple it all is.

Well, the first book was not simple. It was difficult. In fact it was garbled, and the reviewers who said so and later took it back are foolish. *His Toy, His Dream, His Rest,* this new and longer book, is simpler, with many of the severally voiced conversational devices abandoned. Its difficulties are more of texture than of structure: the plan is less schematic but the indulgences are proportionately greater, eccentricity proliferating as the original intellectualized, constructional gimmicks fold up under the pressure of released expression. There are passages that are opaque and likely to remain so. Some of the language is contorted in a way designed to disguise the platitudinous as a toughly guarded verity. The range of reference is very wide (the *Dream Songs,* like dreams in sleep, draw freely and solidly on the cultural memory), but there are some references which go well beyond the legitimately omnivorous curiosity of the poetic intelligence and achieve impenetrable privacy through not being, like most of the rest, explained by their general context.

This last, the general context, is the true structure of Berryman's complete book of 385 individual, but not isolated, lyrics. It is not wise to contend that the ambitions of Structure (with a capital "S") can go hang, the individual lyrics being all that matters. In fact, the lyrics mostly explain each other's difficulties—sometimes across long distances—by tilting themes to a different angle, revisiting a location, repeating a cadence or redefining a point. It was Yeats's way and for that matter it was Petrarch's—the long poem as an arrangement of small ones. One proof that this is the operative structure in the *Dream Songs* is that the work feels more comfortable to read as one gets further into it. But if it is not wise to say that the structure is nothing and the individual lyric everything, it is still less wise to say that the work is unintelligible without a perception of its grand design. It is unlikely that a clear account of such a grand design will ever be forthcoming, although the chances of several bright young academic things building a career on the attempt are unfortunately 100 per cent. It will probably not be possible to chart the work's structure in the way that the *Divine Comedy,* for example, can be charted out in its themes, zones and stylistic areas. The development of the *Dream Songs* is much more a development by accretion: Ezra Pound and William Carlos Williams are the two obvious models. An indication of this is the already mentioned fact that the multi-voiced interplay of *77 Dream Songs* is in these later ones not so much in evidence: as a device it has yielded to ideas more productive, especially to the unabashed elegiac strain, sonorous as lamenting bagpipes, which in many ways makes this new book a convocation of the literary ghosts. One feels at the end of this new volume that there is no reason, except for the necessary eventual loss of inspiration, why the work shouldn't go on literally for ever—just as the *Cantos,* whose material is *un*digested information (Berryman digests his), could obviously go on to fill a library. The work has no pre-set confining shape to round it out, and one doesn't see why the 385th song need absolutely be the last one—not in the way one sees that the last line of the *Divine Comedy,* for many previously established reasons, must bring the poem to an end.

In brief, with the *Dream Songs* Berryman has found a way of pouring
in everything he knows while still being able to tackle his themes one, or
a few, at a time. Attacking its own preliminary planning and reducing it
to material, the progressive structure advances to fill the space available
for it—a space whose extent the author cannot in the beginning accurately guess at but must continue with the poem in order to discern.

The *Dream Songs* are thus a modern work, a work in which it is pos-
ible for the reader to dislike poem after poem and idea after idea without
imagining that what he likes could have come into existence without what
he dislikes. It is particularly worth remembering this point when one
comes across gross moments which make one feel like kicking the book
around the room. And it is particularly worth making this general point
about the *Dream Songs* having the title to a work (rather than just a
trendily labelled grab-bag) in view of the virtual certainty that the weird-
ball academic studies will soon be upon us, bringing with them the
inevitable reaction into an extreme commonsensicality which would deny
the existence of a long poem rather than have it "studied" in brainless
terms.

It was a masterfully asserted, overwhelmingly persuasive version of
commonsensicality which enabled Croce to liberate the *Divine Comedy*
(the case is again relevant) from an inhumanly attentive *Wissenschaft* and
release the poetry within it to immediate appreciation. But of course the
Crocean case was over-asserted. The poem *does* possess an informing
structure, a structure which the reader must know in detail, though better
later than sooner and better never than in the first instance. Berryman's
Dream Songs, on their much smaller, less noble scale, likewise have a
structure, and will continue to have it even when the scholars say they do.
That is the thing to remember, that and the fact that the structure is
inside rather than overall. Especially when a long poem is such a present
to the academics as this one is, the humane student is engaged in a fight
for possession from the very outset: he needs to remember that to be
simplistic is to lose the fight. He must admit complication—certainly
here, for the *Dream Songs* are extremely complicated, having almost the
complexity of memory itself. They depend on the perception that the
mind is not a unity but a plurality, and by keeping the talk going between
these mental components, by never (or not often) lapsing into a self-
censoring monologue, they convey their special sense of form. It's even
possible to say that the poorest sections of the work are the sections where

the poet's sense of himself is projected into it as a pose—where an attitude is struck and remains unquestioned in a work of art whose unique quality is to question all attitudes through the critical recollection of their history and a sensitive awareness of all the clichés attendant on the concept of the creative personality. And the personality in play is, all along, the creative one: the central motive of the *Dream Songs* can be defined as an attempt by a poet to examine himself without lapsing into self-regard. "The poem then," Berryman writes in his prefatory note,

> whatever its wide cast of characters, is essentially about an imaginary character (not the poet, not me) named Henry, a white American in early middle age sometimes in blackface, who has suffered an irreversible loss and talks about himself sometimes in the first person, sometimes in the third, sometimes even in the second; he has a friend, never named, who addresses him as Mr. Bones and variants thereof.

Not the poet and not me. But obviously, in what is mainly the story of a poet who is currently writing a poem which sounds remarkably like the one the reader is reading, the poet *is* the hero, a fact readily ascertainable from the amount of autobiographical material being used, some of which would be embarrassing if not rendered neutral by the poem's universalizing mechanisms, and some of which is not rendered neutral and consequently *is* embarrassing. The question is always being turned up, as the reader ploughs on, of whether the author *knows* that every so often a certain insensitivity, a certain easily recognizable "creative" belligerence, is getting through unqualified to the page. Here and only here is the central character "me" in the raw sense: in the refined sense the "me" is representative of all artists and hence of all men in their authentically productive moments. The embarrassments are probably best accepted as a contributory quality, a few turns of the stomach consequent upon the many thrills. The poem's devices of voicing are not meant to distance personality but to reveal it: the doubts begin when we suspect that attitudes are reaching us which the poet has not analysed, that he does not realize he is being revealing in a crude sense. But really there are bound to be these. The important thing to say here is that the personality in the poem, manifold, multiform and self-examining in an obsessive way, keeps all one's attention. The language never settles into anything less than readability, and even when the restlessness becomes a shaken glamour in which one can see little, it is evident that something is being worried at: we are not just being dazzled with an attempt to churn meaning into existence. There is not much fake significance, though quite a lot of blurred.

Thematically, these new songs are first of all a disorderly, desperate and besotted funeral for Berryman's literary heroes, who might be called, following the author's own terminology, the "lovely men." Of these, Delmore Schwartz is easily the star. His decline is convincingly (one hopes fairly) illustrated. There are sketches towards blaming this writer's collapse on society at large, but there is also a more powerful evocation of a sheer inability to cope. "Admiration for the masters of his craft" was one of the emotions Edmund Wilson picked out as characterizing *77 Dream Songs*. In the new book the simple admiration for the masters continues, but in Schwartz's case (and to a lesser extent in Randall Jarrell's) it goes a long way beyond admiration, and a good deal deeper than craft, into a disturbed exploration of the artist's way of life in America now —and this concern again, through the internalizing way the poem has, is referred back to the condition of the poet-narrator, a condition of physical crack-up and a fearful but no longer postponable facing of the unpalatable truths. Some of the evocations of Schwartz's life seem a trifle cheap, like all those Greenwich Village memoirs conjuring up the less than compelling figure of Little Joe Gould: here, as in the sporadic scenes of Irish pubbing and loosely buried claims to a hairily abrupt way with the ladies, the underlying ideas of bohemianism sound a touch conventional, the reactions provincially American as opposed to the acutely modern, prolix Western intelligence of the work's usual tone.

Exemplified by the poet's cacophonous admiration of Shirley Jones, the supposedly "genuine" identification with the straightforward and simple reads as hick gullibility and sheer bad taste. Another thumping example of bad taste is the unsufferably patronizing farewell for Louis MacNeice. A lack of "good taste" is one of Berryman's strengths, in the sense that he can range anywhere for images without a notion of fitness barring his way. But positive *bad* taste is one of his weaknesses. His tough, anti-intellectual line on the American virtues can bore you in an instant by the insensitivity of delivery alone. There are moments when Berryman writing sounds a bit like John Wayne talking. For all his absorptive capacity for the fine details of life, Berryman's conception of America and of civilization itself seems cornily limited, and even the book's elegiac strain, its congested keening for the gifted dead, edges perilously close to an elementary romanticism whose informing assumption is the withdrawal of support by the gods. Waiting for the end, boys. But at their best the *Dream Songs* are a voice near your ear that you listen to, turn towards and find that you must turn again; a voice all around you, unpinnable to a specific body; your own voice, if you had lived as long and could write in so condensed a way; a voice not prepossessing, but vivid and somehow revivifying. A solitary quotation makes an appropriate finale:

> . . . I can't read any more of this Rich Critical Prose, / he growled, broke wind, and scratched himself & left / that fragrant area.

(Times Literary Supplement, 1969)

On Theodore Roethke's
Collected Poems

When Theodore Roethke died five years ago, his obituaries, very sympathetically written, tended to reveal by implication that the men who wrote them had doubts about the purity and weight of his achievement in poetry. Now that his collected poems have come out, the reviews, on this side of the water at least, strike the attentive reader as the same obituaries rewritten. Roethke was one of those men for whom poetic significance is claimed not only on the level of creativity but also on the level of being: if it is objected that the poems do not seem very individual, the objection can be headed off by saying that the man was a poet apart from his poems, embodying all the problems of writing poetry "in our time." It is a shaky way to argue, and praise degenerates quickly to a kind of complicity when what is being praised is really only a man's ability to hold up against the pressures of his career. Criticism is not about careers.

From the small amount of information which has been let out publicly, and the large amount which circulates privately, it seems probable that Roethke had a difficult life, the difficulties being mainly of a psychic kind that intellectuals find it easy to identify with and perhaps understand too quickly. Roethke earned his bread by teaching in colleges and was rarely without a job in one. It is true that combining the creative and the academic lives sets up pressures, but really these pressures have been exaggerated, to the point where one would think that teaching a course in freshman English were as perilous to the creative faculties as sucking up to titled nobodies, running errands for Roman governors, cutting purses, grinding lenses or getting shot at. If Roethke was in mental trouble, this should be either brought out into the open and diagnosed as well as it can be or else abandoned as a point: it is impermissible to murmur vaguely about the problems of being a poet in our time. Being a poet has always been a problem. If the point is kept up, the uninformed, unprejudiced reader will begin to wonder if perhaps Roethke lacked steel. The widening scope and increasing hospitality of academic life in this century, particularly in the United States, has lured many people into creativity who really have small business with it, since they need too much recognition and too many meals. Plainly Roethke was several cuts above this, but the words now being written in his praise are doing much to reduce him to it.

This collection is an important document in showing that original-ity is not a requirement in good poetry—merely a description of it. All the longer poems in the volume and most of the short ones are ruined by Roethke's inability to disguise his influences. In the few short poems where he succeeded in shutting them out, he achieved a firm, though blurred, originality of utterance: the real Roethke collec-tion, when it appears, will be a ruthlessly chosen and quite slim vol-ume some two hundred pages shorter than the one we now have, but it will stand a good chance of lasting, since its voice will be unique. In this respect, history is very kind: the poet may write only a few good poems in a thousand negligible ones, but those few poems, if they are picked out and properly stored, will be remembered as char-acteristic. The essential scholarly task with Roethke is to make this se-lection and defend it. It will need to be done by a first-rate man capa-ble of seeing that the real Roethke wrote very seldom.

Of his first book, *Open House* (1941), a few poems which are not too much reminiscent of Frost will perhaps last. Poems like "Lull" (marked "November, 1939") have little chance.

> Intricate phobias grow
> From each malignant wish
> To spoil collective life.

It is not assimilating tradition to so take over the rhythms of poetry recently written by another man—in this case Auden. It is not even constructive plagiarism, just helpless mimicry. To a greater or lesser degree, from one model to the next, Auden, Dylan Thomas, Yeats and Eliot, Roethke displayed throughout his creative life a desperate unsureness of his own gift. In his second book, *The Lost Son,* published in 1948, the influence of Eliot, an influence which dogged him to the end, shows its first signs with savage clarity.

> Where's the eye?
> The eye's in the sty.
> The ear's not here
> Beneath the hair.

There are no eyes here, in this valley of dying stars. In his five-part poem *The Shape of the Fire* he shows that he has been reading *Four Quartets*, giving the game away by his trick—again characteristic—of reproducing his subject poet's most marked syntactical effects.

> To see cyclamen veins become clearer in early sunlight,
> And mist lifting out of the brown cat-tails;
> To stare into the after-light, the glitter left on the lake's surface,
> When the sun has fallen behind a wooded island;
> To follow the drops sliding from a lifted oar,
> Held up, while the rower breathes, and the small boat drifts quietly
>   shoreward;

The content of this passage shows the pin-point specificity of the references to nature which are everywhere in Roethke's poetry. But in nearly all cases it amounts to nature for the sake of nature: the general context meant to give all this detail spiritual force usually has an air of being thought up, and is too often just borrowed. In the volume *Praise to the End!*, which came out in 1951, a certain curly-haired Welsh voice rings loud and clear. It is easy to smile at this, but it should be remembered that a poet who can lapse into such mimicry is in the very worst kind of trouble.

> Once I fished from the banks, leaf-light and happy:
> On the rocks south of quiet, in the close regions of kissing,
> I romped, lithe as a child, down the summery streets of my veins.

In the next volume, *The Waking* (1953), his drive towards introspective significance—and a drive towards is not necessarily the same thing as possessing—tempts him into borrowing those effects of Eliot's which would be close to self-parody if it were not for the solidly intricate structuring of their context.

> I have listened close
> For the thin sound in the windy chimney,
> The fall of the last ash
> From the dying ember.

There it stands, like a stolen car hastily resprayed and dangerously retaining its original number-plates. His fascination with Yeats begins in this volume—

> Though everything's astonishment at last,

—and it, too, continues to the end. But whereas with Yeats his borrowings were mainly confined to syntactical sequences, with Eliot he took the disastrous step of appropriating major symbolism, symbolism which Eliot had himself appropriated from other centuries, other languages and other cultures. The results are distressingly weak, assertively unconvincing, and would serve by themselves to demonstrate that a talent which has not learnt how to forget is bound to fragment.

> I remember a stone breaking the edifying current,
> Neither white nor red, in the dead middle way,
> Where impulse no longer dictates, nor the darkening shadow,
> A vulnerable place,
> Surrounded by sand, broken shells, the wreckage of water.

Roethke's good poems are mostly love poems, and of those, most are to be found in the two volumes of 1958 and 1964, *Words for the Wind* and *The Far Field*. Some of his children's poems from *I Am! Says the Lamb* are also included, and there is a section of previously uncollected poems at the very end of the book including a healthy thunderbolt of loathing aimed at critics. Roethke achieved recognition late but when it came the critics treated him pretty well. Now that his troubled life is over, it is essential that critics who care for what is good in his work should condemn the rest before the whole lot disappears under an avalanche of kindly meant, but effectively cruel, interpretative scholarship.

(*Times Literary Supplement*, 1968)

An Instrument
to Measure Spring With

The plush Harcourt Brace volume of Cummings's verse *(Poems 1923–1954)* carries a line of caps on its dustcover immediately above the Marion Morehouse close-up of her husband's head: FIRST COMPLETE EDITION. The two volumes MacGibbon & Kee are now putting out in this country constitute the second complete edition, which so far as the poetry is concerned will probably remain the essential compilation of the master's work. It adds *95 Poems* (1958) and *73 Poems* (1963) to what appeared in *Poems 1923–1954*, which ended with the last poem of *XAIPE*. The layout is an improvement: much more open, so that any poem, no matter how small, gets its own page. The typesetting is modelled directly on the old standard forms worked out by Cummings with his personal typesetter at Harcourt Brace, and in fact the new face is so close to the original that it looks for a while like a laterally squeezed and longitudinally stretched photograph of it until you compare the fine detail of the serifs. Poem 44 of *No Thanks* is still blank after more than thirty years: it is still asterisked as being available "in holograph edition only." I have never seen this poem. I imagine it was originally knocked out of *No Thanks* as being too sexy (the original edition of *No Thanks* was dedicated to the fourteen different publishing houses who turned it down, Harcourt Brace being among them), but how it could still be considered so is beyond me. The copyright of the whole body of poetry remains in the possession of Marion Morehouse, which, on the assumption that only the beautiful deserve the brave, is just as it should be. Doubtless more poems will be unearthed in time, and strictly there are whole stretches of

Cummings's prose (especially in *Eimi*) which are poetry in all but name, but for the nonce this is it: the poetry collection of the year and for that matter the decade.

There is no reliable public picture of Cummings and it is doubtful if there will ever be one now. The only full-length study which existed up until the time I stopped following the secondary literature was desperately naïve, wide-eyed in worship, and as a Ph.D. subject he is too "easy": ideas-wise, he can be wrapped up in a couple of thousand words. He exists "only" as a poetic personality, in the sense that the small amount of information available concerning his life fails to enrich (i.e., contradict) the picture you get from the attitudes he strikes in his work. As a figure eating ordinary food and breathing the air of this green earth, he can be reliably caught only in age-old sketches by Edmund Wilson and a few lesser figures, sketches in which he makes momentary appearances to talk faster and more brilliantly than anyone else before abruptly departing. No argument for the essential unity of art and intellect, the compatibility of the intuitive and the considered statement and the schematic goal-achievement of an extended creative act is complete without a considera-tion of Cummings's ability to resist any such notions. His relevance to formal intellect was the relevance of a high-speed tap-dancer or a totally committed whore, both of whom he could admire and celebrate, with each of whom he was temperamentally at one.

As ideas, Cummings's themes lead to immobility when they don't lead to Broadway. He pushes a concept of individuality which would render civilization impossible to carry on, and his formulae for sexual spontaneity attained their apotheosis with Carol Lynley reading aloud from "Puella Mea" to her straight-arrow boy-friend in the movie version of *Under the Yum-Yum Tree.* But of course the ideas were never meant to be ideas. Like Lawrence, Cummings was extremely insistent, and often tedious, on the opposition of sexual expression and abstract thought but, unlike Law-rence's, Cummings's statements on the subject can't be picked off the page without going off in your hand. They are present in this life only as art, and rarely try to stop being art: where they do, as in his blurbs for his own books and the burlesques he once contributed to *Vanity Fair,* the hyperbole is monotonous and the conflated language tiresome.

As a poet, Cummings is not open to the accusation that he neglected to bar the way to people who might get him wrong, but it is certainly a pity that the emphasis of his work makes it easy for the superficial critical mind to line him up with the genuinely irrational writers in our time.

Cummings never proposed that intellect should be swept from the world. His retort to such a statement would have been "What world?" and his response to a further elaboration: "You call *this* a world?" As far as Cummings was concerned, the artist's responsibility to the world cannot be discussed, since it cannot even be proposed. Cummings presumed to test and report the quality of life directly, without reference to ideology of any kind. The results were not necessarily naïve. His purely artistic, wholesale rejection of the Soviet Union in the early thirties proved in the end to be personally less damaging than the piecemeal intellectual withdrawal of his contemporaries. *Eimi* is at least the equal of Gide's *Retour de l'U.R.S.S.* for prescience based on the creative instinct, and contains by implication everything that Cummings valued in the America he was to needle for the rest of his life. Anyone still rocking with disgusted amusement after Mr. Muggeridge's extraordinary *Observer* review of the reissue of *The Enormous Room* might like to compare *Eimi* with Mr. Muggeridge's own achievements of that period and decide whether dandies are ever right, even when they are not wrong. The two men reached the same conclusions, but look at the generosity of Cummings's book, the sweep of its pity, the prophetic urgency of its demand for the poetic in the affairs of everyday—you need to have kept your innocence to write like that.

What little we do know about Cummings's life ties in tightly with his work, and he is like Camus or Pavese in that you think of work and life together. Where they expressed doubts, he expressed certainties, but he is like them in suggesting that the writer's life must shape itself to his art or else crack open. The important thing, when your art makes claims of this kind, is that in your private life you do nothing to contradict them. And in fact Cummings never did sell himself or align himself with any dogma, was kind, was proud, was individual. That anyone should find this unity of life and work difficult to accept reveals two things, one intellectual, one temperamental, about the age in which we live. Intellectually, the fundamental modern aesthetic concept divorcing the artist's "actual" and creative personalities has been successful to the point where the academic mind has difficulty in speaking at all when faced with an individual case in which the two personalities in fact match: a two-faced, vicious phoney like Verlaine not only seems more fruitfully complicated than a man like Cummings, but also more *artistic.* Temperamentally, the age is scared stiff of being taken for a sucker: deafened by the crash of fallen idols, it scans unblinkingly for the tell-tale signs of a splitting image. Believing that faults make men human, it eventually finds corruption admirable.

Cummings wrote little confessional poetry and it's permissible to assume that this was because he had little to confess. He had seen in advance the temptations his era would offer the artist and had armoured himself against them. One tends to ascribe this invulnerability to an innate primitivism—the lucky fool—but it is probably more correct to say that it was the result of a conscious act of dedication and courage, of highly developed mentality. It isn't easy nowadays to accept the suggestion that the man of honour is not the man who exquisitely analyses his capitulation but the man who never surrenders at all. Far easier to write Cummings into a secondary category of inspiration in which his heated simplicities can be appreciated as a kind of inspired foolishness. (Some of Cummings's love poetry looks pretty naïve, of course, beside Lowell's: Cummings has few doubts, few fears, spills few beans and doesn't seem to suffer much. What century did he think he was living in, for Christ's sake?) These elementary themes of Cummings might have begun as a pose, but with some men the attitudes begun as a pose are confirmed by practice into a constitution of the mentality. Not necessarily a meretricious process: the brave men whose braveness counts usually have to talk themselves into being brave. From eccentricity to individuality, from self-assertion to a massive vocational presence, Cummings simplified and hardened his attitude to life until it supported him all by itself: he could stand up in it like a steel suit.

Cummings's poetry splits up into two main lots: poetry celebrating love, and poetry defining, satirizing and discrediting the forces trying to attack it. In the first lot, the love itself ranges from the crystal-clear concentration of a child roller-skating on a sidewalk all the way across to the titanic image of his father—

> so naked for immortal work
> his shoulders marched against the dark

—a picture of honour directly comparable with the figure of Farinata. But the bulk of this side of his work is taken up with poetry about the love between men and women, and this is the poetry most intelligent people think of when they think of Cummings. It, too, splits up: into the frankly randy and the close to holy. Almost everybody is acquainted with at least one Cummings poem of each kind. But Cummings is no nearer being two-faced here than he is anywhere else. He has no Victorian component to his mind and doesn't suffer from a pulsating pornographic vision continually bursting through to sully the serene adoration of the beloved. Nor is there any post-Victorian component: no compulsory freedom, no screwing to prove a point. It is all as unstudied, yet fully as entranced with itself, as the little girl roller-skating over the expansion strips between the slabs of cement. He simply thinks (or simply writes, if you prefer to believe he is fibbing) of a continuum between the lady lusted after as pure gash and the lady contemplated as a divine revelation: the same lady, and, in some of his really remarkable poems, at the same moment. And it seems to me that he is very successful at this, that his raunchy poems are as cleanly good as Herrick's, that his sacred ones have an affinity with the *dolce stil novo* in its most highly refined form and that he succeeded during his long creative life in joining something up which before his advent had seemed irreparably broken. In the best of the latter-day love sequences in English —Meredith's and Hardy's, to take two outstanding examples—you are given the lady on the human scale, and on the whole human scale, and are glad for the boldness. But Cummings managed something different and more difficult. Whether deeply versed in, or merely acquainted with, the sacred tradition in the love-song (I suspect deeply versed: he was well-read in several of the modern languages as well as both the classical), he succeeded in duplicating its singing voice of dedication, and produced love poems of which the greatest are comparable, even in divinity, with Dante and Petrarch. It is well known by now that Cummings's randier poems are in constant use on campuses across the English-speaking world for seducing girls. But there is a possibility, too, that his sacred poems might first seduce the seducer, making him realize that what breathes beneath him has a soul. Cummings was powerfully influenced by the figure of Beatrice and disguised as a child, a dancer or a disintegrating old slag she is in his poems often: camouflaged but not secularized. When, in "She Being Brand," he describes a deflowering in the terminology of a test-drive in a Rolls, you are immediately in roaring company with the Herrick who dreamed of his own metamorphosis into a laurel and woke to find himself the proud owner of an erection and the copious results of a wet dream. But when he writes, in "it may not always be so; and i say,"

> Then shall i turn my face, and hear one bird
> sing terribly afar in the lost lands.

you are not far from the Dante who had pushed the thematic frontier of the *stil novo* all the way to the staggering moment when Beatrice turns her silent smile from the poet to the Godhead. Whether Cummings in real life did or did not experience this continuity of feminine matter and universal spirit I have no means of knowing (Mr. Muggeridge uniquely suggests that Cummings might have been a queer), but in the best of his love poetry his implacable creative drive towards establishing exactly that continuity ignites a cluster of stellar points numerous and radiant enough to form a Milky Way of divine goodwill. Like Yeats, he learned a good deal from Dowson about how to write majestically: majesty means pomp and pomp needs drill. Sonnet III of "Sonnets—Unrealities" in *Tulips and Chimneys* is a concentration of every effect in Dowson's technical book and it can be recommended as an example of how one great poet masters another's mechanics in order to be with him in spirit. Cummings turned Dowson's tone of voice away from doom towards exaltation and from frustration to fulfilment. Also he liked *big* girls. But the sense of dedication is the same.

As an example of toughly articulated benevolence, the pagan love-song elevated to sublimity through tenderness, there is hardly anything in this century which will bear comparison with Cummings's love poetry except the very best products of Tin Pan Alley. And as his successes are Tin Pan Alley's successes—simplicity, self-definition, formal drive, the phrase pointed to revivify the words within it—so his failures are Tin Pan Alley's failures—sentimentality, self-parody, the limpidity that gels too soon. Reading Cummings through now, I skip about 60 per cent of his love poems, since they are adequately covered by the other 40. It's a failure-rate considerably smaller than that with which any song writer is content to live: eventual repetitiveness is the inevitable penalty for being plain from the beginning. In his love poetry alone he wrote himself at least seven tickets to immortality: "when thou hast taken thy last applause, and when"; "it may not always be so; and i say"; "this is the garden: colours come and go"; "who's most afraid of death? thou art of him"; "somewhere i have never travelled,gladly beyond"; "you shall above all things be glad and young" and "hate blows a bubble of despair into." Scores more of his poems parallel, and scores more again merely parody, these few, but that doesn't make the few vulnerable or the many extraneous. A slim selection of the best wouldn't be much help, since you need to be acquainted with a couple of hundred of the lesser poems to sort out the language difficulties in the thirty or so (counting in the satires) which are really tremendous. In short, Cummings needs real study—not the fake kind, but the kind with generosity built in. It's not enough to be able to trace Cummings's debts to Baudelaire, Flecker and *Krazy Kat*, although that helps.

Cummings's other poetry is mainly a defence of the thematic unity I have just described. Eliot once defined humour as the weapon with which intelligence defends itself: a profound statement in that it described the dynamics of the business by suggesting that humour moves always from a base. Cummings's humour (and his satire is usually funny enough to be dignified by this categorically superior word) moves from a base in his fertile territory of love, and by gruesomely specifying the enemy forces helps convince the reader that the home base is not Cloud-Cuckoo-land but the only viable actuality: you must live in love or else nowhere.

> take it from me kiddo
> believe me
> my country, 'tis of
>
> you, land of the Cluett
> Shirt Boston Garter and Spearmint
> Girl With The Wrigley Eyes (of you
> land of the Arrow Ide
> and Earl &
> Wilson
> Collars) of you i
> sing

And so on in a thousand details, all of them aimed at establishing the "real" as the false: politics, the army, the police, the academy, the science whose microscopes "deify one razor blade into a mountain range." None of this is literary news now, of course, but Cummings paved the way and nobody since has done the job better. The real objection to the bulk of the work of Ginsberg, Ferlinghetti and the rest is that the man who started it all could squeeze their scattered effects into a form and make the whole thing travel like a skilfully aimed custard-pie. The technical difference mirrors the difference in mental make-up, not to say mental intensity: Cummings isn't kidding. He really loathes what they are half in love with. His field of observation is broad enough and deep enough to get the detail right, but the detail is not *loving* detail: a concentration of Menckenese at its very best, his invective is a roar of pain. And again like Mencken's, Cummings's pain is founded on a knowledge of the past, of what has always been valuable. Cummings was superbly educated, he had his measures of excellence and he was not at sea. He knew exactly what he did not want. There is no element, in his condemnation, of complicity in what he condemns. Unlike his successors, he is deeply rational and it is only through complete trust in his own rationality that he is able to condemn intellect. There is not a trace of mysticism in him: he proposes no dualisms, but simply asserts the divine as the sole level of reality and perpetual revelation as the only mode of vision. Cummings, as well as bringing a tradition into being, was winding one up: a New England tradition, and hence a European tradition, and hence a tradition of civilization in the West. He is far closer to Catullus than he is to a man like Ginsberg. The old way was all *perizia,* and Cummings takes that to pretty near the limit. The new way is all *Dummheit:* a new start, a new rate of speaking for a world growing to look like Los Angeles—a speech clumsily spectacular, semi-constructed, half articulate, a bit thick. In this world the intensity, and above all the *velocity,* of an intelligence like Cummings's will be close to incomprehensible.

Cummings's love poetry is beautiful on the one hand, and his attacking poetry explosive on the other, because of a sense of form trained up high and punishingly maintained. He rewrote the sonnet form as a jazz solo in which the tag phrase jolts what you have been hearing into rhythmic intelligibility. Treating the whole sonnet as a rhythmic unit and using its traditional inner partitions only to lean against for a quick intake of breath, he avoided the usual caboose effect of squeaky couplets, quatrains or sestets tugged along behind. His sonnets finish so strongly that it is a fair guess to say he wrote them from the bottom up: certainly he hardly ever let the formal requirements trap him into a forced thought. Working for him always, in this and in any other form, was a strictly sensational capacity to propel a line: the special feature of Cummings's technique is not typography but kinetics.

> when every thrush may sing no new moon in
> if all screech-owls have not okayed his voice

—and any wave signs on the dotted line
or else an ocean is compelled to close

The packed stresses at the end of the first line are the knuckles of the hand
which unrolls the second like a bolt of cloth. Cummings's diction was
often self-indulgent (as Edmund Wilson pointed out at the beginning,
Cummings overworked the long "i"), his super-precise-looking adverbs
were often only padding, but the impetus of his line remained a miracle
from first to last. Except for some largish poems early on, he never used
a form bigger than he could control in a single rhythmic breath, but the
alterations of pace within that rhythmic unit were, in the jazzman's sense
of the word, ridiculous. In a sense he was *too* good. Able to move anything
at any pace, he was tempted to move hunks of nothing like a rocket, and
you come across fast-travelling assemblages which have velocity but no
momentum.

Cummings's true technical triumphs were all sonic. Except where they
freed him into new areas of audio effect, his typographical tricks—the
Apollinaire-raids—were an irrelevance. They gave courage to a generation
of bad poetry, they give courage to bad poetry still, but they came from
the graphic, merely talented side of his mind and were very limited in
their poetic usefulness. The "concrete" effects can always be related to
the theme, but only mechanically. "Moon" is just as suggestive a way as
"mOOn" of writing "moon." Cummings was dedicated to typographical
innovation all his life and set great store by meticulously indirect layout.
He will be remembered for little of this: he can no more be credited with
it as an invention than held responsible for the damage it has since caused.
Several of Cummings's pages of alphabet soup (now seen in this country
for the first time, since Faber & Faber, who handled his work here in
previous years, never took them on) are really exploded sonnets. Put them
back together and you quickly find they are not as good as the sonnets
he was careful to leave in one piece.

A more troublesome technical point concerns his syntactical effects,
which are numerous enough to constitute a private language and render
his poetry virtually untranslatable. One of Quasimodo's translations illustrates this point well. Cummings has written

the great advantage of being alive
(instead of undying)

and Quasimodo renders this as

> il grande privilegio di essere vivo
> (anzi che immortale)

exactly reversing the sense, since by "undying" Cummings doesn't mean "immortal" at all, but means the ordinary existence which everybody except his chosen people lead and (mistakenly in his view) dignify with the name "life." *Questa voce . . . potremmo paragonare a un canto a bocca chiusa o a un canto lontano di cui non si percepiscano le parole*, writes Quasimodo hopefully. In fact Cummings is quite clear and quite consistent in his untiring use of such effects, which are misleading only if you attempt to do a prac. crit. on single poems and neglect to read him entire. The real trouble with his syntax starts when whole poems are made up of nothing but negatively or tangentially defined concepts hemming in a falsely thrilling platitude. This poem is one of the neater examples:

> when god decided to invent
> everything he took one
> breath bigger than a circus tent
> and everything began
>
> when man determined to destroy
> himself he picked the was
> of shall and finding only why
> smashed it into because

The circus tent saves the day for the first stanza, but it takes more than a passing acquaintance with Cummings's work to make sense of the second, and by the time you have acquired a certain familiarity you are well aware that this is the side of Cummings which needs to be left alone to die off by itself. Probably it will be pummelled to death in brainless articles for *PMLA* circa 1990. But this is an extreme example and with steady reading his use of such devices becomes perfectly clear. As it becomes clear, it tends to become tedious. Like his typography, this component in Cummings's use of language did its work by making him feel special as he slogged on. Now that he is dead its importance should very much lessen. Young poets who admire him will always betray themselves by echoing this sort of thing, but really it is a mannerism and can't be followed. Caught up in his commitment to the unique, Cummings was often a mannerist—but at least it was his own manner.

Cummings's satirical poems, with their crazy-quilt diapering of billboard slogans, campaign buttons and patriotic clichés now long forgotten, have a receptivity to the emergent American idiom which reminds us that his vital development was contemporaneous with the gradual appearance of that great repository of informal poetry, Mencken's *American Language*. As Valéry once suggested, the language itself is the real poem. As a contributor to this poem, any bus-conductor with an authentic gift for swearing has the edge on the darling of the literary society. Cummings measured himself against the anonymous contributors to the language, to joy, to the traditions of skill: balloon men, good-time girls, strippers, whores, acrobats who climb on ladders of swords, dancing elephants. Of the small amount of his poetry which is perfect we can say that it is good enough for its author's name to be forgotten in safety. Of the large amount which is less so, we can say that it needs understanding in the light of its author's manifest intentions, and that these intentions were life-giving, basically sane, lyrically inspired and good. He also measured himself against the finest poets of the near and far past, prepared himself to join them, and is with them now.

(the Review, 1969)

D. H. Lawrence in Transit

If one were to take a wax pencil and trace Lawrence's travels on a globe of the world, the result would be an enigmatic squiggle: a squiggle that started off minutely preoccupied in Europe, was reduced still further to a fat dot formed by the cramped wartime movements within England, broke out, enlarged itself to a bold transoceanic zigzag which at one wild moment streaked right around the planet and then subsided again into more diffident, European vagaries—still restless, but listless, tailing off. The pencil should properly come to a halt at Vence, in the Alpes-Maritimes, although if we substituted for it another pencil of a different colour we might legitimately add one last, sweeping leg to the journey as Lawrence's mobility recovered in death and his ashes rode back mindlessly to New Mexico.

In a few minutes we could map the wanderings of nearly two decades. It wouldn't tell us much, apart from the obvious fact that he liked to move about. He was in search of something, no question of it. Headquarters, the fissure into the underworld—it had many names. But one is permitted to doubt whether it could ever have been found, the doubt being engendered less by the world's nature than by an assessment of Lawrence's insatiable hunger for meaning. There is a tendency, once Lawrence's odyssey has been identified as a spiritual quest, to suppose that Lawrence had a firm idea of his spiritual object: hence the notion that he was in revolt against twentieth-century society, or post-Renaissance Europe, or post-Columbian America, or whatever you care to name. Lawrence was in revolt all right, but the revolt encompassed almost everything he knew in the present and nearly all the past he ever came to know, and this ability to exhaust reality through intimacy shows up in his travels as much as in anything else he did.

It was not so much that familiarity bred contempt—and anyway, there were some familiarities of which he never quite tired—as that it bred unease. Never to find things important enough is the mark of a dreamer. Lawrence, thoroughly practical and business-like in matters large and small, was no ordinary dreamer: nevertheless he could get no lasting peace from his surroundings, and as time went by felt bound to look upon them as an impoverished outwardness implying a symbolic centre—and this despite an unrivalled ability to reflect the fullness of physical reality undiminished onto the page. Lawrence is beyond the reach of any other modern writer writing about what can be seen, since whatever could be seen he saw instantaneously and without effort—which is probably why he could regard it as nothing but the periphery of the real. If he had lived longer, his novels might well have lost any touch at all with worldly objects: the sense of actuality which other men serve long apprenticeships to attain was for him a departure point. And again if he had lived longer, he might well have exhausted the earth with travel. Had he not placed such an emphasis on turning inwards to the dark, fiery centre, we could by now have been tempted to imagine him turning outwards, away from the tellurian cultures depleted by the ravenous inquiry of his imagination and towards an uncapturable infinity that actually exists—orchestrations of dark suns, unapproachable galaxies peopled by Etruscans who stayed on top, nebulae like turquoise horses, the ocean of the great desire. Quetzalcoatl's *serape!* Sun-dragon! Star-oil! Lawrence was in search of, was enraged over the loss of, a significance this world does not supply and has never supplied. For a worldling, his symbolist requirements were inordinate. As a spaceman he might have found repose. Heaven knows, he was genius enough not to be outshone by the beyond. He could have written down a supernova.

Supposing, though, that this was what his journeyings were all in aid of—home. The supposition is at least part of the truth, although by no means, I think, the largest part. If home was ever anywhere, it was at the Del Monte and Flying Heart ranches in New Mexico— whose mountains seemed to be the place he could stay at longest without feeling compelled to move on. Yet there were still times when he missed Europe, just as, in Europe, there were so many times when he missed America, and just as, on either continent, there were troubled times when he missed England. Headquarters tended to be where Lawrence was not. Places abandoned because they did not possess the secret could be fondly remembered later on—perhaps they had had the secret after all. But it never occurred to Lawrence that there *was* no secret. Out of all the thousands of pages of his incredibly productive short life, the great pathos which emerges is of this extraterrestrial unbelonging—far more frightening, in the long run, than the social challenges which by now we have absorbed, or else written off as uninformative propositions. Critical unreason often occurs in creative genius, but creative unreason rarely does: for a talent to be as big as Lawrence's and yet still be sick is a strange thing. It's easily understandable that people equipped to appreciate his magnitude as a writer should take the intellectually less taxing course, declaring Lawrence to be a paragon of prophetic sanity and the world sick instead.

Lawrence's first travels were to London, Brighton, the Isle of Wight, Bournemouth. Readers of the early letters will be rocked back on their heels to find the same descriptive power turned loose on Brighton as later reached out to seize the dawn over Sicily, the flowers in Tuscany, the Sinai desert, the sperm-like lake in Mexico and the ranches after snow. Then, in 1912, the first run to Metz, in Germany: Waldbröl in the Rhineland, Munich, Mayrhofen in Austria. A walk over the Tyrol. Lake Garda. Back to England in 1913, then back to Bavaria. Lerici. England again. The war confined these short European pencil strokes to a fitfully vibrating dot within England, covering Sussex, Hampstead, Cornwall; an angry return to London after being hounded from the coast and possible contact with the High Seas Fleet; Berkshire, Derbyshire.

In 1919, free to quit England, he broke straight for Italy: Turin, Lerici, Florence, Rome, Picinisco, Capri. In 1920, Taormina, in Sicily. Malta. In 1921, Sardinia, Germany, Austria, Italy, Taormina again. (Taormina is a node, like—later on—Taos, and the Villa Mirenda at Scandicci, outside Florence.)

In 1922, the emboldened pattern struck outwards to Ceylon. Australia for two months. Then America: Taos, the Del Monte ranch, the mountains. In 1923 he was in Mexico City, New York, Los Angeles, Mexico again and . . . England. In 1924, France, Germany, New York, Taos. The Flying Heart ranch, alias the Lobo, alias the Kiowa. Oaxaca, in Mexico.

The year 1925 ended the period of the big pattern. After a wrecking illness in New Mexico he returned to London. Then Baden-Baden. Spotorno. In 1926, Capri, Spotorno and the Villa Mirenda in Scandicci—his last real place to be. Germany, England, Scotland. Italy.

In 1927 he toured the Etruscan tombs. A score of names cropped up in his itinerary: Volterra, Orvieto, Tarquinia—short strokes all over Tuscany and Umbria, the Etruscan places. Then to Austria and Germany, and in 1928 to Switzerland, with the Villa Mirenda abandoned. Gsteig bei Gstaad, Baden-Baden (the Kurhaus Plättig) and the Ile de Port-Cros, Toulon. From low-lying sun-trap to *Höhenluftkurort,* the short strokes moved trembling. Bandol, in the south of France. He was in Paris in 1929, then Palma de Mallorca, Forte dei Marmi, Florence, Bandol again. In 1930 Vence, and death.

Even in Vence he wasn't too sick to use his amazing eyes. There isn't a place on the list that he didn't inhabit at a glance. And yet as we read on and on through the magnificence of his travel writings, a little voice keeps telling us that the man was never there. The man, the spaceman, never travelled except in dreams. Dreaming, while dying, of India and China and everything else that lay beyond the San Francisco gate. Dreaming of altogether elsewhere, of an England that was not England, of a Europe that was never Europe.

It was a great day, Frieda said, when they walked together from the Isartal into the Alps. Lawrence wrote it down in a way that takes us straight there. But where was he? "We stayed at a Gasthaus," he wrote to Edward Garnett, "and used to have breakfast out under the horse-chestnut trees, steep above the river weir, where the timber rafts come down. The river is green glacier water." Compare this to one of the famous opening sentences of *A Farewell to Arms*—"In the bed of the river there were pebbles and boulders, dry and white in the sun, and the water was clear and swiftly moving and blue in the channels"—and we will find Lawrence's descriptive prose both more economical and less nostalgic, the effortless reportage of an infallibly observant visitor.

Still on the same descriptive trail, go south to Italy ("I love these people") and look at Lerici. "And in the morning," he wrote to Lady Cynthia Asquith, "one wakes and sees the pines all dark and mixed up with perfect rose of dawn, and all day long the olives shimmer in the sun, and fishing boats and strange sails like Corsican ships come out of nowhere on a pale blue sea, and then at evening all the sea is milky gold and scarlet with sundown." The fake-naïve rhythms, suitable for consumption by titled ladies, can't mask the searing power of that simplicity. "The mountains of Carrara are white, of a soft white blue eidelweiss, in a faint pearl haze—all snowy. The sun is very warm, and the sea glitters." It still does, even though polluted with a thoroughness which even Lawrence would have hesitated to prophesy. "The Mediterranean is quite wonderful—and when the sun sets beyond the islands of Porto Venere, and all the sea is like heaving white milk with a street of fire across it, and amethyst islands away back, it is too beautiful." It's small wonder that Lawrence could talk about art having characteristics rather than rules, and even disparage the idea of art altogether. He had it to burn.

Reality offered Lawrence no resistance. Mysticism did, and it was into mysticism that he poured his conscious energy. Turning to *Twilight in Italy*, we can find something on every page to match the descriptions in the letters. Here is Lake Garda at dawn:

> In the morning I often lie in bed and watch the sunrise. The lake lies dim and milky, the mountains are dark blue at the back, while over them the sky gushes and glistens with light. At a certain place on the mountain ridge the light burns gold, seems to fuse a little groove on the hill's rim. It fuses and fuses at this point, till of a sudden it comes, the intense, molten, living light. The mountains melt suddenly, the light steps down, there is a glitter, a spangle, a clutch of spangles, a great unbearable sun-track flashing across the milky lake, and the light falls on my face.

But superb as this is, it isn't what this book or any other Lawrence book is about. *Twilight in Italy* is about north and south, hill and dale—it is the tentative prototype for a great sequence of increasingly confident polarities, by which Lawrence the traveller was to go on splitting the world in two until there was nothing left of it but powder. The Bavarian highlanders, it appears, "are almost the only race with the souls of artists . . . their processions and religious festivals are profoundly impressive, solemn, and rapt." Again, they are "a race that moves on the poles of mystic sensual delight. Every gesture is a gesture from the blood, every expression a symbolic utterance." Your Bavarian highlander "accepts the fate and the mystic delight of the senses with one will, he is complete and final. His sensuous experience is supreme, a consummation of life and death at once." Whether drinking in the *Gasthaus*, or "hating steadily and cruelly," or "walking in the strange, dark, subject-procession" to bless the fields, "it is always the same, the dark, powerful, mystic, sensuous experience is the whole of him, he is mindless and bound within the absoluteness of the issue, the unchangeability of the great icy not-being which holds good for ever, and is supreme." Yes, it was all happening in Bavaria—or, rather, it was all to happen later on in Bavaria. But the thing to grasp here is that word "dark." Not only (as is well known) is it the key adjective in all of Lawrence, but Lawrence's travels can usefully be summarized as an interminable search for a noun it could firmly be attached to.

No sooner is Lawrence in Italy than we discover that the Italians have dark interiors too. "The Italian people are called 'Children of the Sun.' They might better be called 'Children of the Shadow.' Their souls are dark and nocturnal." A feature of the dark soul is unconsciousness, as in the spinning-woman, whose mind Lawrence can apparently read. "She glanced at me again, with her wonderful, unchanging eyes, that were like the visible heavens, unthinking, or like the two flowers that are open in pure clear unconsciousness. To her I was a piece of the environment. That was all. Her world was clear and absolute, without consciousness of self. She was not self-conscious, because she was not aware that there was anything in the universe except *her* universe."

But the darkly unconscious haven't got it all their own way. Much later in the book, during the fascinating passage that deals with the local production of *Amleto,* Lawrence spies a mountain-man in the audience: he is of the same race as the old spinning-woman. "He was fair, thin, and clear, abstract, of the mountains. . . . He has a fierce, abstract look, wild and untamed as a hawk, but like a hawk at its own nest, fierce with love . . . it is the fierce spirit of the Ego come out of the primal infinite, but detached, isolated, an aristocrat. He is not an Italian, dark-blooded. He is fair, keen as steel, with the blood of the mountaineer in him. He is like my old spinning-woman."

To reconcile this mountain-man with the spinning-woman, we must assume she was never dark-blooded, when a good deal of what we were told about her when we were reading about her suggested that she was. And indeed, looking back, we find that she *hasn't* been given a dark soul or dark blood—she is simply "the core and centre to the world, the sun, and the single firmament." Lawrence hasn't at this stage entirely identified the dark soul with the earth's centre, so it's still possible to combine abstractness with being at the centre of the world, and, presumably, dark-bloodedness with *not* being at the centre of the world. What's difficult to reconcile, however, even when stretching the idea of poetic consistency until it snaps, is a Bavarian highlander's dark-bloodedness with a mountain-man's clear abstractness: if these conditions are both different from an ordinary Italian's dark-bloodedness, are they different in different ways?

The awkward truth is that Lawrence left his Bavarian highlanders behind in his opening chapter and forgot about them while writing the bulk of the book, which even without them would still be extremely difficult to puzzle out. The confusion confesses itself in the passage about Paolo and Maria. Paolo is a native of San Gaudenzio, and therefore a hill-man—fair, eyes-like-ice, unalterable, inaccessible. Maria is from the plain—dark-skinned, slow-souled. "Paolo and she were the opposite sides of the universe, the light and the dark." Nothing could be clearer. "They were both by nature passionate, vehement. But the lines of their passion were opposite. Hers was the primitive, crude, violent flux of the blood, emotional and undiscriminating, but wanting to mix and mingle. His was the hard, clear, invulnerable passion of the bones, finely tempered and unchangeable." As an opponent to, or complement of, the passion of the blood, the passion of the bones was evidently judged by Lawrence to be somewhat unwieldy—it never again made such an unabashed appearance. Pretty soon, the blood's passion became the only kind of authentic passion you could have.

In *Twilight in Italy,* though the destructive mechanization of the world had already clearly been perceived, Lawrence still had something to say for abstractness, intellectuality and cognate non-dark attributes. In 1915, he wrote to Lady Ottoline Morrell from Ripley, in Derbyshire: "It is a cruel thing to go back to that which one has been. . . . Altogether the life here is so dark and violent; it all happens in the senses, powerful and rather destructive: no mind or mental consciousness, unintellectual. These men are passionate enough, sensuous, dark—God, how all my boyhood comes back—so violent, so dark, the mind always dark and without understanding, the senses violently active. It makes me sad beyond words." It's not the first time that the word "dark" is used like a comma, but it's one of the few times—all early—when Lawrence freely admitted the possibility that the dark soul could be as murderous on its own as intellect could. The emphasis was still on keeping a balance, on checking the word against the thing it was supposed to stand for. Lawrence's later history is the story of darkness being awarded a steadily more automatic virtue, the periodic calls for an equilibrium of forces degenerating into unfathomable proposals about establishing the correct relationship between the components of darkness itself.

Lawrence's "dash" (his word) to Sardinia produced a book—*Sea and Sardinia*—which clearly shows his untroubled ability to uproot all the attributes he has just so triumphantly detected in a place, move them on to the next place, and then condemn the first place for either not having them in sufficient strength or never having had them. In Cagliari the men "stood about in groups, but without the intimate Italian watchfulness that never leaves a passer-by alone." Looks as if the Italians' dark blood wasn't dark enough, an impression confirmed by the menacing loins of the Sardinian peasant, "a young one with a swift eye and hard cheek and hard, dangerous thighs. . . . How fascinating it is, after the soft Italians, to see these limbs in their close knee-breeches, so definite, so manly, with the old fierceness in them still. One realises, with horror, that the race of men is almost extinct in Europe. . . ." Plainly the war period has helped sour Lawrence on Europe altogether, but even taking that convulsive time-lag into account, it's still difficult to square up *Sea and Sardinia* with *Twilight in Italy*. The real difference, it appears, is that Italy is *connu* and therefore sterile, whereas Sardinia is unknown and therefore isn't. "There are unknown, unworked lands where the salt has not lost its savour. But one must have perfected oneself in the great past first."

Whether in the vegetable market near the start of the book or at the peasants' procession near the end, Lawrence's colour sense is at its sumptuous best, and in general *Sea and Sardinia* is a remarkable piece of visualization. "When we came up, the faint shape of land appeared ahead, more transparent than thin pearl. Already Sardinia. Magic are high lands seen from the sea, when they are far, far off, and ghostly translucent like icebergs." Beautiful writing, but no lasting pledge. Lawrence was in and out of Sardinia in a hurry, and spent a good half of 1921 sitting in Taormina getting sick of Europe, which can't be said to exclude Sardinia. Just as Sardinia had it over Italy, somewhere else had it over the whole of Europe. "I would like to break out of Europe," he wrote to Mary Cannan. "It has been like a bad meal of various courses . . . and one has got indigestion from every course." He was thinking of "something more velvety"—Japan, perhaps, or Siam. The south of Europe was better than the north, but there was no denying that even the south had gone off: "I can't get the little taste of canker out of my mouth," he told Catherine

Carswell. "The people—" A few days later he was telling E. H. Brewster that they were *canaille, canaglia, Schweinhunderei,* stinkpots. "A curse, a murrain, a pox on this crawling, sniffling, spunkless brood of humanity."

In his mind Lawrence was already embarked for Ceylon, and in another few days Mabel Dodge—by inviting him to Taos—had made it possible for him to project his mental journey right around the globe. Europe was promptly pronounced to be "a dead dog which begins to stink intolerably." England (in the same letter, written to S. S. Koteliansky) was declared "a dead dog that died of a love disease like syphilis." Bad news for Koteliansky, who was living in it at the time. (This letter also featured the Lawrentian pearl about "one of those irritating people who have generalized detestations. . . . So unoriginal.")

"I feel I can't come—" Lawrence wrote to Brewster in January 1922, "that the East is not my destiny." Later in the same month, destiny doubled back, and Lawrence decided to go via Ceylon after all. "I feel it is my destiny," he wrote to Mabel Dodge, "to go east before coming west." Destiny pulled another double-cross in Ceylon, where Lawrence found the velvety Orient inane. "The East, the bit I've seen," he told Mary Cannan, "seems silly." As he frequently did when off balance, he thought of England, telling Robert Pratt Barlow that "the most living clue of life is in us Englishmen in England, and the great mistake we make is in not uniting together in the strength of this real living clue—religious in the most vital sense—uniting together in England and so carrying the vital spark through . . . the responsibility for England, the living England, rests on men like you and me and Cunard—probably even the Prince of Wales. . . ." The Prince of Wales was indirectly responsible for Lawrence's "Elephant" poem, the most tangible result of the Singhalese sojourn apart from a disillusioning close-up of inscrutable platoons of dark people with dark eyes—"the vastness of the blood stream, so dark and hot and from so far off."

As far as the East went, darkness was a dead loss. Not that the contradiction with many things he'd said before, or with nearly everything he said later, ever slowed him down. The task was to push his mystical system around the planet until it clicked; there was no obligation to explain why it kept going wrong.

Australia was a country Lawrence couldn't characterize . . . "the spell of its indifference gets me." Mystical content, zero. "This is the most democratic place I have *ever* been in," he wrote to Else Jaffe. "And the more I see of democracy the more I dislike it. . . . You *never* knew anything so nothing, *nichts, nullus, niente,* as the life here." The situations in *Kangaroo* are mainly imported, and it's doubtful if Lawrence ever gave Australia much thought after the first few days. Nevertheless the settings in *Kangaroo* have small trouble in being the most acutely observed and evocative writing about Australia that there has so far been— bearing out my point that Lawrence could reproduce reality with no effort whatsoever. Trollope, Kipling, Conrad, Galsworthy and R. L. Stevenson all visited Australia at one time or another, but if any of them was capable of bringing off a piece of scene-setting like the opening chapter of *Kangaroo,* he didn't feel compelled to. The moment he got to Thirroul, Lawrence dispatched letters announcing his longing for Europe—the dead dog lived again. The central situation in *Kangaroo* looks to be about Italian Fascism—the Australian variety, which emerged much later, was very different. But *Kangaroo* is a bit more than a European play with an Australian set-designer. It has an interesting early scene in which Lawrence makes Lovat out to be a prig, reluctant to lend Jack Callcott a book of essays in case it bores him. " 'I might rise up to it, you know,' said Jack laconically, 'if I bring all my mental weight to bear on it.' " There is a hint here that someone might have shaken Lawrence by urging him to lay off the intensity. It's a rare moment of self-criticism, and almost *the* moment of self-deprecating humour. Lawrence was perhaps a touch less certain about the aridity of the Australian spirit than he let on.

America. Lorenzo in Taos—it was a giant step. It rapidly became clear that the most dangerous item of local fauna was Mabel Dodge, the hostess who favoured will over feeling—a priority always guaranteed to grate on Lawrence, whose will and feeling were united in Destiny. "My heart still turns most readily to Italy," he told Mary Cannan—a strong sign of unease—and "I even begin to get a bit homesick for England. . . ." A certain sign. At this stage Lawrence had decided that the Indians couldn't be copied. "And after all, if we have to go ahead," he wrote to Else Jaffe, "we must ourselves go ahead. We can go back and pick up some threads —but these Indians are up against a dead wall, even more than we are: but a different wall." And to Catherine Carswell: *"Però, son sempre Inglese."* Even after moving to the Del Monte, putting a helpful seventeen miles between himself and the Mabel-ridden Taos, Lawrence was detecting the same *innerlich* emptiness in his surroundings as had wasted his time in Australia. Mexico, however, worked differently, and he was soon telling the much-maligned Middleton Murry that if England wanted to lead the world again she would have to pick up a lost trail, and that the end of the trail lay in—Mexico.

The Plumed Serpent is a work of uncanny poetic force which manages to keep some sort of shape despite intense distorting pressures from Lawrence's now rampant mysticism. Kate, with her European blood and conscious understanding, is outdistanced by dark-faced silent men with their columns of dark blood and dark, fiery clouds of passionate male tenderness. In addition to the oppressive symbolic scheme, there are moments which lead you to suspect that the author might simply be cracked—as when he suggests that Bolshevists are all born near railways. Yet Chapter V, "The Lake," is one of Lawrence's supreme stretches of writing. The boatman "pulled rhythmically through the frail-rippling, sperm-like water, with a sense of peace. And for the first time Kate felt she had met the mystery of the natives, the strange and mysterious gentleness between a scylla and charybdis of violence: the small poised, perfect body of the bird that waves wings of thunder and wings of fire and night in its flight." Frail-rippling—what a writer. The transparent purity of the book's descriptions is inseparable from its symbolic structure, which is an opposition between principles which no ordinary mortal will ever be able to clarify, since Lawrence himself could only grope towards them with incantatory phrase-making.

The book's incandescent set pieces—the burning of the images, the execution of the traitors, and so on—are spaced apart by impenetrable thickets of unmeaning. "But within his own heavy, dark range he had a curious power," Kate learns of Cipriano. "Almost she could *see* the black fume of power which he emitted, the dark, heavy vibration of his blood . . . she could feel the curious tingling heat of his blood, and the heavy power of the *will* that lay unemerged in his blood." What the Bavarian highlanders and plains Italians had lost, the sons of Quetzalcoatl had gained.

Lawrence learned about Indians during the hiatus between writing Chapter X and Chapter XI of *The Plumed Serpent.* His mystical conclusions are distributed between the later part of that novel (e.g., the snake in the fire at the heart of the world) and *Mornings in Mexico,* a travel book of unusual difficulty, even for Lawrence. Certainly he no longer pleads for a balance between the disparate consciousnesses of the white man and the dark man. You can't, it appears, have it both ways. The most you can hope for is to harbour a little ghost who sees in both directions. Yet ghost or no ghost, Lawrence seems to be trying hard to belong to the Indian way, to the "abdomen where the great blood stream surges in the dark, and surges in its own generic experiences." What we seek in sleep, Lawrence says, the Indians perhaps seek actively, "the dark blood falling back from the mind, from sight and speech and knowing, back to the great central source where is rest and unspeakable renewal." Relieved by some of his most brilliant descriptive passages, the rhetoric is short of totally suffocating, but still fearsomely turgid. It takes the letters to remind us that he could write in an unfevered way during this period. "Here the grass is only just moving green out of the sere earth," he wrote to Zelia Nuttall, "and the hairy, pale mauve anemones that the Indians call owl flowers stand strange and alone among the dead pine needles, under the wintry trees. Extraordinary how the place seems *seared* with winter: almost cauterized. And so winter-cleaned, from under three feet of snow." A cold towel for the reader's forehead. Green glacier water.

Back in Europe to stay, Lawrence unpacked his mystical machine and set about applying it to the Etruscans. At the same time, and without any disabling sense of contradicting himself, he started rehabilitating Europe, even the long-forsaken north. "I am very much inclined to agree," he wrote to Rolf Gardiner in July 1926, "that one must look for real guts and self-responsibility to the Northern peoples. After a winter in Italy—and a while in France—I am a bit bored by the Latins, there is a sort of inner helplessness and lack of courage in them. . . ." Writing from Lincolnshire to E. H. Brewster, he claimed to have rediscovered "a queer, odd sort of potentiality in the people, especially the common people. . . ." The common English people, back in the running at long last! Whether or not the Prince of Wales qualified wasn't stated.

As a traveller through ordinary space, Lawrence got back on slanging terms with his repudiated Europe. Baden-Baden, for example, was a *Totentanz* out of Holbein, "old, old people tottering their cautious dance of triumph: *wir sind noch hier. . . .*" As a traveller through time and thought, he moved on a grander scale. *Etruscan Places* is a gentle book, endearingly characteristic in its handy division between Etruscan and Roman and disarmingly uncharacteristic in its emphasis on delicacy and humour: it's the book of a strong man dying. "We have lost the art of living," he writes, "and in the most important science of all, the science of daily life, the science of behaviour, we are complete ignoramuses." The

Etruscans weren't like that. Their art had the "natural beauty of proportion of the phallic consciousness, contrasted with the more studied or
ecstatic proportion of the mental and spiritual Consciousness we are
accustomed to." The contrast, as always, is asserted with a degree of
confidence which is bound to draw forth a preliminary nod of assent. It
remains a fact, however, that this kind of argument has practically nothing
to do with post-Renaissance art or pre-Renaissance art or any kind of art,
since art is more likely to depend on these two sorts of proportion being
in tension than on one getting rid of the other. Lawrence's binomial
schemes were useless for thinking about art, as those of his disciples who
tried to employ them went on to prove. Without them, though, we
wouldn't have had *his* art.

In January 1928, Lawrence told Dorothy Brett that he still intended
coming back to the ranch. "It's very lovely," he wrote to Lady Glenavy,
"and I'd be well there." But his seven-league boots were worn through,
and he was never to get out of Europe alive. We have only to read
"Reflections on the Death of a Porcupine" or the last part of *St. Mawr*
to realize that his ashes ended up on the right spot. The mountains were
a cherished place. They weren't home, though. Home was at the Source,
and the Source—he said it himself—is past comprehension.

(1972)

A Dinosaur at Sunset

Like the first, the second volume of what will eventually be a four-book set of Shaw's correspondence looks and handles like a doorstop from Valhalla. Nearly a thousand pages of it, most of them unskippable: the reader must forge on in a kind of despairing delight, overwhelmed by the abundance and vitality of what is on offer and secretly grateful that he knows only as a statistic what Professor Laurence knows for a fact—the complete set will contain a mere hundredth of the communications Shaw actually wrote. Compared with Shaw, Dickens is Ronald Firbank. Here is writing as a form of breathing, industry as a form of rest. In the last couple of weeks I have read both volumes and been convinced all over again that Shaw was out of this world, not least in his ability to understand the world so well. In this volume, covering the twelve years (1898–1910) in which he revolutionized the theatre, his grasp of affairs—big and little, world-wide and domestic—is as true as it is powerful. Not until a long time later did garrulity displace eloquence and brainwaves insight. For the present, he is making history, and so we read on with the unsettling certainty that he is helping to make us: a character-building experience, relieved by the high entertainment value of his style as a correspondent.

"All genuine intellectual work," he wrote to Florence Farr, "is humorous," and whatever the truth of that in general, in his own particular case he was at this time busy proving it. Apart from the pamphlet-length letters to his biographer Archibald Henderson, the book is marked by compression, cogency and a vivid epigrammatic *brio*. Gags abound, all of them emergent from a penetrating realism. "Like a greengrocer and unlike a minor poet," he tells the concussed Henderson, "I have lived instead of dreaming." Everybody knows about Shaw's ability to immerse himself in the detail of activity: it's the quality which provides the solid underpinning of *Music in London* and *Our Theatres in the Nineties*, securing those six volumes as the finest critical achievement in the language. And for years now there has been a growth industry in exploring Shaw's interests: books like *Shaw: The Chucker-Out* amplify the picture sketched in monographs and biographies by men like Chesterton, Pearson and (still a central book) Eric Bentley. But what this selection of correspondence uniquely provides is the feel and force of all Shaw's enterprises raging forward simultaneously from day to day: the Goethean artist-philosopher, the intellectual omnivore, is right there in front of you. By the beard of the prophet, was there nothing the man could ignore?

He goes up in a balloon, and within weeks is already an expert on balloons. He buys a car and becomes a leading authority on cars. He commences an international correspondence with photography fanatics: this lens, that lens, wet plates, dry plates. The virtues and failings of a new pianola are sorted out and communicated to fellow pedal-pushers. These minor themes of his intellectual formation multiply in a steadily more complicated counterpoint. Surging through them are the major themes, most of them developed in an earlier period but still involved in an endless process of receiving their final elaborations. His Socialism by this stage had become complex, tirelessly analytical and cleansed of utopianism. "Of course an artificial city, so to speak, is no more impossible than a canal is," he writes to Edward Rose in 1899, "but the thing should be kept clear of philanthropy and utopian socialism because people (the tenants) will not stand being kept in a nursery." It could be contended that his judgements are sound because he is relying on what he sees rather than on (as he did at a later stage, about Soviet Russia) what the Webbs thought they saw. But the contention won't quite do. Shaw in this period was able to make reliable generalizations about America, which he had never visited, and when the Fabians split over the South Africa question he put himself above the battle by providing an analysis of the situation prophetic in its clarity—in fact, South African history is now working itself out along lines which Shaw deduced from documents seventy years ago without setting foot outside London. Prophecy is not the test of analysis, but as supplementary evidence it's hard to ignore, and the reader of this volume will find himself encountering it every few score pages.

His power of generalization from detail—not only from observed detail, but from reported detail collated and pondered—is at its peak. It's only one of the ways in which he resembles Croce in the same period: one grows more and more convinced that they are the twin master-minds over that stretch of history. Like Croce, Shaw had read Marx before Lenin did, and again like Croce he had gone on to a vastly more complicated analytical position. Shaw's cyclic theory of history, in which events swung back and forth like a clock's pendulum but civilization went forward like a clock's tick, bore a piquant resemblance to Croce's, in which all occurrences ran in Viconian circles but the human spirit was carried forward by Providence. Both men had sought to discard the vulgarities of historicist metaphysics while retaining an ideal of progress. And to cap the resemblance, Shaw was as obviously (and remains to this day) the greatest prose stylist in English as Croce was and remains the greatest in Italian. Such a comparison isn't meant to imply that Shaw is Croce's equal as a philosopher: in fact, the difference between the two men is a precise demonstration of why the artist-philosopher is finally engaged in something other than philosophy. But it is meant to imply that this was the last modern period in which super-minds could grasp the world whole, with confidence of purpose as well as of ability. This purposive element is what now makes them look like dinosaurs—dinosaurs at sunset. Croce thought evil was simply error, and that no movement totally devoid of constructive ideas could possibly affect history. Shaw's view was perilously similar and ran into the same kind of difficulty. The arrival of totalitarianism settled the hash of their ideas of progress as effectively as they themselves had discredited the materialistic determinism of their predecessors —an irony compounded by the fact that the new callousness was a throw-back to those predecessors. The consensus now is that Shaw was a fool to understand totalitarianism so slowly. My point in bringing up Croce is that Shaw was not alone in being so unhorsed. It was the very magnitude of their minds that misled them. They thought that unreason could be reasoned out of countenance. A great, a truly great, mistake.

In these years occur the first productions of all Shaw's early plays. He was involved in the practicalities of theatrical business to the uppermost bristle of his eyebrows. There are brilliant letters to Ada Rehan on the changing character of the stage since Ibsen which show the kind of trouble he was prepared to take to convince actors that they were doing something serious. Ignore such instruction as they might, the actors were unlikely to brush lightly aside the accompanying bombardment of technical advice: the nuts and bolts of performance and production stick out tangibly everywhere in the volume, re-creating in the most abrasive way what a Shaw matinée at the Royal Court must have been like—an act of dedication, and not just because scarcely anybody got properly paid. These were the days before Shaw became the "overwhelming force in the theatre" that the Penguin blurbs were later to call him. Commercially, it was small-time: but the planning that went into the presentation was the full complement of the thought that went into writing the plays, and anyone who doubts that Shaw's humility was as endless as his conceit should look at the relevant letters and see the lengths that selfless toil can go to. A visionary, he was yet the opposite of a dreamer. He was responsibility incarnate. As a vestryman of St. Pancras he fights to keep the district's solitary free women's loo open; as a playwright he strives to convince his translator Trebitsch that arbitrary variations on words play havoc with construction; as an author he controls everything from the renting out of his own electrotypes to the width of his margins and the founts of his title-pages. Nothing, but nothing, is let slide. It will be a rare contemporary reader who contemplates this perfection of character without wishing a plague on the man's ashes.

Orwell somewhere calls Shaw an empty windbag and somewhere else confesses that he has read practically every word Shaw has written. Such ambivalence is inevitable. The superhuman is inhuman in the end, and only a dolt could admire it without misgivings. But that doesn't mean we should go on trying to cut Shaw down to size. It's widely supposed that Shaw wasn't capable of sex, but a less comfortable and more likely supposition is that he was above it, like Leonardo. He could certainly be an interfering busybody, but only because as a totally truthful man he couldn't readily conceive of someone intelligent not wanting to hear the truth. Poor Erica Cotterill was allowed to entertain her hopes of conquest too long, but one doubts whether it was because Shaw was toying with her affections; he probably believed that by an application of common reason he could fill her head with something else besides passion. Shaw's friendships were so disinterested as to be hardly recognizable as friendship. He lent money to acquaintances of good character but would never grant a loan to his friend Charles Charrington, whose bad character he would forgive but not abet. He supported Wells in the Fabian power struggle until the moment when Wells's reckless indolence was proved, whereupon he destroyed him overnight. Shaw can appear callous only to the selectively compassionate—i.e., to nearly all of us. Most of us love unreasonably, tell half-truths and favour our friends. The world is like that —which is what I mean by saying Shaw was out of it. He was a moral genius.

"His correspondence alone would fill many volumes," St. John Ervine wrote in his now reissued *Bernard Shaw,* "and the task of editing it will not be enviable." Enviable, perhaps not. Vital, certainly. Professor Laurence, half-way home, has already proved himself fully equal to the task.

(*The Listener,* 1972)

VISIONS
BEFORE MIDNIGHT

Tolstoy Makes
Television History

Dead ground is the territory you can't judge the extent of until you approach it: seen from a distance, it is unseen. Almost uniquely amongst imagined countries, Tolstoy's psychological landscape is without dead ground—the entire vista of human experience is lit up with an equal, shadowless intensity, so that separateness and clarity continue even to the horizon.

This creative characteristic is so powerful in Tolstoy that we go on regarding it as his most important distinguishing mark even when his progressively doctrinaire intellect imposes the very stereotypes and moralistic schemes which his talent apparently came into existence to discredit. The formal perfection and retributive plot of *Anna Karenina* don't, we feel, represent an artistic advance on *War and Peace*—quite the reverse. And yet we never call our reservations disappointments, any more than we are disappointed with Titian's last phase or the original, Great Fugue ending to Opus 1 30. If a great talent pushes on beyond what we have loved in it, it is usually because a great mind has things it feels forced to do.

Besides, Tolstoy's gift remains so obviously the *same* gift, from first to last, that it does our criticism for us: in *War and Peace* Napoleon is an unsatisfactory characterization according to the standards set by Tolstoy himself (in Kutuzov, for example) and even in the most inflexible of the moral parables ("How Much Land Does a Man Need?" or—to go the whole hog—*Resurrection*) we are obviously in the presence of the same all-comprehending vision that brought back its clinically objective reports from the bastions at Sebastopol. Any aesthetic experience obliterates all other aesthetic experiences for as long as it lasts, and with Tolstoy it lasts for days and days, so that the reader may feel—as he feels with Shake-speare and Dante—that his life is being remade.

The technique of the novel, or even the medium of prose, has no separate conceptual meaning in such a context: there can be no question of transposing Tolstoy from the page to the screen, since he is not on the page in the first place. He is like Michelangelo and Mozart in that the attempt to grasp him entails a sacrifice of comprehension. Universal genius is its own medium and transpositions out of it are impossible—it's one of genius's defining characteristics. That Verdi re-created Othello in music doesn't make Othello a transferable asset. It simply means that Verdi is in Shakespeare's league.

So far, the BBC's *War and Peace* has done nothing like a good enough job of being not as good as the book, and instead of driving the viewers to read Tolstoy—which is the best, I think, that a TV adaptation could hope to do—might well lull them into thinking that Tolstoy is Russia's answer to Mary Renault. Marianne Moore wanted her poems to be artificial gardens with real toads in them. This production reverses that desirable order: the sets and costumes are as real as research and technol-ogy can make them, while the people who inhabit them are of an artificial-ity no amount of good acting—and there is plenty of appalling acting on tap—can defeat.

Working together as fatally as Laurel and Hardy trying to climb a wall, the script and the direction do a brilliantly thorough job of boiling Tol-stoy's complexity of dialogue, commentary and revealed action down to a simple narrative line which simultaneously faithfully reproduces and utterly betrays the novel's flow of events. "Papa's arranged a little dinner for my name day," breathes Hélène, her piercing boobs heaving in a frock closely resembling a two-car garage: "I hope . . . you'll be there." Pierre, valiantly played by Anthony Hopkins, can only goggle, bemused. Except when the occasional voice-over supplies a brief stretch of interior mono-logue, goggling bemused is what Pierre goes in for full time. At Hélène's party, during which her sensational norks are practically on the table among the sweetmeats, Pierre is asked to do a worried version of the bug-eyed act Sid James turns on when he is abruptly shoved up against Barbara Windsor in those unspeakable *Carry On* films.

Hopkins would be the ideal Pierre if the part were nearer half-way to being adequately written, but all he can do, given the material to hand, is project the necessary inner confusion without transmitting the bashful radiance which Tolstoy stunningly insists that Pierre and Hélène share:

there is no such thing as *mere* passion in Tolstoy, and even while racked by doubts Pierre is supposed to experience in his contemplation of Hélène the kind of *visione amorosa* which helps drive Anna Karenina into the arms of Vronsky. What I'm saying is, he's not just hung up on a pair of knockers, right? So those tight shots of Pierre peeking sideways through his prop specs at where his companion's lungs pulsate off-screen might look like clever direction but are in fact graffiti.

The hamming contest between the marriage-mongering old Princes is a groan-inspiring trial, but in the long run not so debilitating as principal casting that has gone wrong. Given, which one doesn't give, that the characters are types, it would have been better to cast *against* type than to cast to type—at least complexity would have been hinted at, if not embodied. Alan Dobie's whole screen persona is confined by his face and voice to the band between melancholy and preoccupation, with occasional joyful leaps upward into apprehensiveness. Putting him into uniform and calling him Andrey Bolkonsky gives us one aspect of the character while instantly eliminating all the others. As for Morag Hood's Natasha—well, I am not in the business of baiting actresses for errors of casting they did not commit and can do little to overcome. Miss Hood has been excellent in other things and will be excellent again, once she has got over being told to jump up and down rapidly on the spot, lithp with her sinuses, skip on to the set like Rebecca of Sunnybrook Farm and declare with a jaw well-nigh dislocated by youthful vitality that she is Natasha Rostov. Poor mite, can she help it if she arouses throughout the country an unquenchable desire to throw a tarpaulin over her and nail down the corners?

This is not to say that a few things have not gone right. As Princess Maria, for instance, the delicate Angela Down is turning in one of her customary elegantly modulated performances, and some of the wide-open location spaces capture your imagination for the brief time before a sequence of restricted camera movements forcibly reminds you that even the most expensive television is a very cheap movie when the cathode tube is pre-empted by emulsion. Like most people, I'll go on watching, but I won't be gripped. It's no use saying that a chance has been lost. The chance was never there. The series could have been a lot better, but my point is that it would still not have made television history. Television history is made out of television, not out of Tolstoy.

(22 October 1972)

Drained Crystals

On *Star Trek* (BBC1) our galaxy got itself invaded from a parallel universe by an alien *Doppelgänger* toting mysterioso weaponry. These bad vibes in the time-warp inspired the line of the week. "Whatever that phenomenon was," piped Kirk's dishy new black lieutenant, "it drained our crystals almost completely. Could mean trouble."

In our house for the past few years it's been a straight swap between two series: if my wife is allowed to watch *Ironside,* I'm allowed to watch *Star Trek,* and so, by a bloodless compromise possible only between adults, we get to watch one unspeakable show per week each. (My regular and solitary viewing of *It's a Knock-Out* and *Mission Impossible* counts as professional dedication.)

How, you might ask, can anyone harbour a passion for such a crystal-draining pile of barbiturates as *Star Trek*? The answer, I think, lies in the classical inevitability of its repetitions. As surely as Brünnhilde's big moments are accompanied by a few bars of the Valkyries' ride, Spock will say that the conclusion would appear to be logical, Captain. Uhura will turn leggily from her console to transmit information conveying either (a) that all contact with Star Fleet has been lost, or (b) that it has been regained. Chekov will act badly. Bones ("Jim, it may seem unbelievable, but my readings indicate that this man has . . . *two hearts*") will act extremely badly. Kirk, employing a thespian technique picked up from someone who once worked with somebody who knew Lee Strasberg's sister, will lead a team consisting of Spock and Bones into the *Enterprise*'s transporter room and so on down to the alien planet on which the Federation's will is about to be imposed in the name of freedom.

The planet always turns out to be the same square mile of rocky Californian scrubland long ago over-exposed in the Sam Katzman serials: Brick Bradford was there, and Captain Video—not to mention Batman, Superman, Jungle Jim and the Black Commando. I mean like this place has been *worn smooth*, friends. But the futuristic trio flip open their communicators, whip out their phasers and peer alertly into the hinterland, just as if the whole layout were as threateningly pristine as the Seven Cities of Cibola. *Star Trek* has the innocence of belief.

It also has competition. On the home patch, an all-British rival has just started up. Called *Moonbase 3* (BBC1), it's a near-future space opera plainly fated to run as a serial, like *Dr. Who*, rather than as a series. In this way it will avoid the anomalies—which I find endearing—that crop up when one self-contained *Star Trek* episode succeeds another. In a given episode of the *Enterprise*'s voyages (Its Mission: To Explore Strange New Worlds), the concept of parallel universes will be taken for granted. In the next episode, the possibility will be gravely discussed. Such inconsistencies are not for *Moonbase 3*, which after one instalment has already turned out to possess the standard plot of the bluff new commander setting out to restore the morale of a shattered unit: i.e., *Angels One Five* or *Yangtse Incident* plus liquid oxygen.

Moonbases 1 and 2 belong to the United States and the U.S.S.R. Moonbase 3 belongs to Europe, so it looks as if ELDO got into orbit after all. Being European, the base's budget is low, but its crew can supply zest and colour when aroused. The ambitious second-in-command, Lebrun, says things like "Zoot" to prove that he is French. The in-house quack, Dr. Smith, is a lushly upholstered young lady with a grape-pulp mouth who is surely destined to drain the new commander's crystals at an early date.

In the revived *Softly, Softly* (BBC1), Harry the Hawk leapt back to form by cocking up within the first ten minutes, thereby opening the way for a sequence of pithy sermons from Frank Windsor. The Hawk externalized his frustrations in the usual manner, opening and closing every door in sight. Evans has lost two stone and Snow has now reached the final stage of *Angst*-ridden taciturnity, staring at his superiors like Diogenes when Alexander blocked the sun. The dirigible-sized question hanging over the series is whether Barlow will return.

Spy Trap (BBC1) is back, but Commander Anderson has moved on, being replaced by a narrow-eyed wonder-boy called Sullivan, who in the first episode successively penetrated HQ's security, uncovered Commander Ryan's secret, tortured a heavy and ripped off the cap of a ball-point with his teeth.

One of those BBC2 linkmen specially chosen for their inability to get through a typewritten line of the English language without fluffing announced "another in this series of nothing ventured, nothing win adventures starring noo, nah, George Plimpton."

The male voice-over on the new Make-a-Meal commercial said: "If you're a woman, you're a meal-maker for someone." Keep a hand over your crystals, brother: if a women's libber catches you, they'll be drained for sure. One of the art directors on the old Vincent Price movie *The Fly* (ITV) bore the name Theobold Holsopple. Beat that.

(16 September 1973)

Anne and Mark Get Married

Niggle as they might through the days leading up to the main event, the iconoclasts cut little ice.

Switching on *The Frost Show* (LWT) late, as part of my usual preparation for switching it off early, I found Alan Brien declaring that it was nonsense to treat the Royals as something special and that what he had recently done for Anne he would have done for any girl—i.e., travel to Kiev and position himself beside a difficult fence in order to describe her as bandy-legged when she fell off her horse. Angus Maude, M.P., then gave the hapless Brien what small assistance he still needed in alienating the audience's sympathies, and with a healthy sigh of anticipation we entered the period of curfew, or purdah: from here until lift-off the tone would be affirmative, *nem. con.* It was hard to see why this should not be so. Though nobody out there in the videospace knew very much about Anne's personality or anything at all about Mark's, the wish to see them properly spliced was surely very widely shared.

On the Monday night the BBC and ITV both screened the same interview with the betrothed twain. Andrew Gardner, wearing the discreet grin and the cheery twinkle, represented commercial television. Alastair Burnet, wearing the awestricken pallor and the beatified smile, incarnated the spirit of Establishment broadcasting. The Princess immediately proceeded to run deeply incised rings around both of them. Anne, it was suddenly apparent, was perfectly at ease, more than a tinge larky, smart as a whip and not disposed to suffer fools gladly. To help her prove this last point, Gardner and Burnet did everything but dress up in cap and bells: whether because their lines of inquiry had previously been checked and vetted into inanity, or because both had fallen prey to a shattering attack of *folie à deux*, they served up questions the like of which had not been heard before in the history of the human race. It was a mercy when an embarrassing point was abandoned so that a fatuous one might be taken up.

Anne had an opinion on everything except the political role of the monarchy—an understandable lacuna. Mark's views were not so easily elicited. Here was Beatrice, but where was Benedick? Still, Benedick himself had been a stumbler for love: for these fellows of infinite tongue, that can rhyme themselves into ladies' favours, they do always reason themselves out again. Much more inhibiting was the problem of impersonal speech: second nature to Anne, it was as yet an obstacle to Mark, who had still to grasp the principle that the whole art of making oneself understood when one is confining oneself to the one pronoun is just to bash on regardless even when one's ones threaten to overwhelm one. His shy charm there was no denying, although the piercing Colortran lights gave him blushes that were younger than his years. The theme by which his life was linked to hers, it inexorably emerged, was horses. From this rich deposit of equine subject-matter, one guessed, would exfoliate much of the media-men's symbolism on the magic day. And so, with a head full of Piesporter fumes and the first bars of the overture to a Wagnerian dose of flu, your reporter flamed out into the flea-bag.

The Day dawned over Islington in the form of a flawless canopy of *pietra serena* rubbed with crushed roses—a spectacle which gradually transmuted itself into the palest of pure Wedgwood as one fed a hot lemon drink to one's throat-load of streptococci. The Beeb led off with the official photos and a daring, jauntily suitable use of the Beatles' "When I'm Sixty-four." Fyffe Robertson was on hand, reading with undiminished verve from what might possibly have been a steam-powered autocue. *Nationwide* reporters were everywhere among the citizenry. Asked how tall she thought Anne was, a little girl guessed three feet. Ursula Bloom, purportedly the author of five hundred books, and lately the perpetrator of something called *Princesses in Love*, gave an interview in which it was pretty thoroughly established that Anne is good with animals. Astrologers were called in: Anne's Fourth Node was in the Fifth House of Creative Love so the whole deal was already sewn up tight, no sweat. A woman had been to ten thousand weddings.

At 8 a.m. Alastair Burnet came on, still radiating a nimbus while dutifully flogging the tone of portent. "And no doubt, if the bride is awake and has peeped out through the curtains . . . ," he speculated tweely. Valerie Singleton promised that in the course of the next hour we would be shown what the dress might look like, to tide us over the further two hours before we would be shown what the dress did actually look like. Another astrologer gratuitously proclaimed that Mark wasn't as dreary and ineffectual as one might imagine—Leo and Virgo had complementary strengths. Bob Wellings talked to Mark's tank crew. "Is he, is he, does he, is he . . . *popular?*" "Yes." Film of Mark protruding staunchly from the reverse-parked turret of a Chieftain belting along a road in Germany indicated that Virgo came not unarmed to the combat with Leo.

Valerie Singleton talked to Richard Meade. Meade alleged, sensationally, that Mark was very shy. In Belfast, Mr. and Mrs. Monahan were interviewed. Married for seventy years, they were as sweet-natured as they were unintelligible. Burnet chaired a discussion with some Miss World contestants. My compatriot Miss Australia, the current title-holder, ventured intrepidly into the nether levels of depth psychology: "I think, arm, it must be a nerve-racking experience for both of them." "I oper," said Miss Belgium, "I oper we will be seeing it on Belgian television." She could rest assured: 500,000,000 people would be plugged in by the time the real action started.

Alison Oliver, Anne's trainer, was interviewed up-country. "What's the atmosphere like before a big event?" Mrs. Oliver explained persuasively that it could be quite tense. At 9 a.m. Pete Murray was shown coaxing record requests from people lining the route. A bystander, Julie Granchip, thought the wedding was great, and the reason she was here was to see the wedding, because the wedding, she thought, would be great. "Julie, thanks for talking to us."

To the West Country, where Mark's village, Great Somerford, has slept through the centuries awaiting its encounter with Cliff Michelmore. The local bell-ringers thought the programme of 5,000-odd changes scheduled for the Abbey was a breeze: they aimed to double it. "You're goana doublet?" bellowed Cliff. "I doan believe ya." The Red Arrows performed to the music of Buddy Rich—the most gripping imagery of the morning.

"A lot of people, perhaps," intoned Burnet, "are wondering why Captain Phillips is not the Earl of Somerford." The Richmond Herald said that a title had been withheld for political reasons. Richmond, you could see, thought that democracy was getting out of hand. In the Abbey the carpets had been cleaned and covered with druggets. The druggets were being cleaned.

Michele Brown talked to a little girl. Why was she here? "Wedding." "Japan," said a Japanese, "has a loyal famiry rike you have." Too tlue. A résumé, in stills and film, of Mark's career, showing how he rode before he could walk. One got the impression that he had trampled the midwife.

"Do you think she's a typical young girl?" Michele Brown asked a typical young girl. "No." "Do you think she's got too many privileges?" "Yes." "What privileges?" "Horses." Ann Monsarrat, a mine of royal information, told us that James I's daughter had had the most expensive gown and that Henrietta Maria's train had a man underneath it. Dimbling suavely, Tom Fleming introduced the scene in the Abbey and environs. "And here is the bride's home," he jested, over a shot of Buckingham Palace. "Perhaps he's there in spirit . . ." he conjectured, over a shot of George VI's statue. Fleming flannelled devotedly for some time, being particularly careful, in the early stages, to keep us in ignorance of who the guests shown to be arriving might in fact be. Janey Ironside extemporized a commentary, with mixed results, on the range of hats available. It was a suitable time for the bored viewer to switch over to ITV, discover it to be screening a Profile of Princess Anne, and switch back again. The Household Cavalry rode out of the Palace gates. "For a bride and groom who have an interest in horses," ventured Fleming, "this must be a thrilling sight." Mark's parents arrived at the Abbey. "A few weeks ago," announced Fleming, with that peculiar combination of awe and vulgarity which the BBC needs so acutely to be rid of, "people might have said, who are *they?*"

Blues, Royals . . . Glass Coach! She was on the way. Cut back to the Abbey, where Mark stood poised before the altar—the final fence for a clear round. What did Stendhal say about the novel, that it's a mirror going down a road? The British Constitution is a Princess going down an aisle. As the Dean and the Archbishop begin to read their text, the prattle of the media-men perforce ceases, and for a while the resplendent poetry of the marriage service lifts the proceedings beyond the grasp of straining hacks, before the demented chanting and the kapok-voiced lesson-reading of the minor clerics haul it back down to drugget-level.

No less buoyant than its hallowed cargo's hearts, the Glass Coach spins back to the Palace, where Fleming's voice awaits them with the completion of the week's recurring theme. "I'm sure," he sings, "these horses know that they're home."

(18 November 1973)

A Pound of Flash

Admiring Olivier past extravagance, I was little pleased to discover that his Shylock (*The Merchant of Venice*, ATV), infected by the nervous bittiness of the surrounding production, crumbled to the touch.

The British theatre rations itself to one intellectual at a time and currently Jonathan Miller is the one. Being an intellectual is all right by me, and I sincerely hope that Miller will be allowed to go on having ideas until doomsday. It would be nice, though, if his ideas were all as good as most of them are big.

The Big Idea of setting *The Merchant of Venice* in the nineteenth century—apparently to underline the commercial aspects—used itself up in the first few minutes, leaving the viewer to contend with several hours of top hats, three-piece suits and bustles. Julia Trevelyan Oman did her usual fanatical-meticulous job in re-creating the nineteenth-century Venetian interiors, thereby proving that nineteenth-century Venetian interiors bore a lulling resemblance to nineteenth-century Cromwell Road interiors: a few ceilingsful of reflected water-lights might have made a difference, but strangely they were not forthcoming, so all depended on a quarter of an hour's worth of location footage. It had never been clear in the first place that the nineteenth century was at all an appropriate period in Venetian terms. The city was already far gone in decline by then, and Shakespeare manifestly wrote the play on the assumption that Venice was a fabulously wealthy maritime power.

The temporal dislocation was a big fault. As often with Miller, small faults abounded too. Portia and Nerissa left for Venice in a carriage. Upon returning they were to be seen toiling (or rather Nerissa was to be seen toiling while Portia, free of luggage, walked—a nice touch) for miles through the grounds of their house. So what happened to the carriage? Perhaps the horse drowned.

With all that, though, the production had Mind. This is the quality one is grateful for to Miller: it's the chief reason why his productions, when they reach television, are less of a piece but hold more of interest than the common output of classic drama. To show, in their first scene together, Antonio and Bassanio acting *friendly* to Shylock was to bring out the tension of the gentile/Jewish relationship far better than with the normal postures of ill-concealed hostility. Spitting on the gaberdine had been translated to a more gentlemanly but still intolerant ambience, where Shylock was welcome in the boardrooms but somehow never got elected to the clubs.

A lot more such transforming thought, and the evening might have been saved. But alas, the supply was thin, leaving Olivier to create a whole world on his own. It had been said of the stage production that he took refuge in impersonating the George Arliss portrayal of Disraeli, but any fan of Walt Disney comics could turn on the set and see at a glance that he had modelled his appearance on Scrooge McDuck.

Whatever Olivier had done to his front teeth left his long top lip curving downwards in a fulsome volute on each side, producing a ducky look to go with his quacky sound, since for reasons unknown he had chosen to use a speeded-up version of his Duke of Wellington voice. When he put a top hat on over all this, the results were Disney's canard zillionaire to the life, and one couldn't refrain from imagining him diving around in Money Barn No. 64 while bulldozers stacked dollars and the Beagle Boys burrowed through the wall. In a way he's still too young for the role: his energy gave the lens a gamma-burn in the close-ups, and at one point of anger he broke into the hyena-walk of Hamlet heading for the platform or Richard looking for a horse.

Crippled, the evening slogged bravely on. The Prince of Morocco did a coon turn: "As much as ah deserb! Wah, dat's de lady." Two terrible sopranos sang to Bassanio. A good giggle, but why would Portia have them in the house? There are no indications in the text that she is meant to be tasteless—only that she is meant to be hard, snobbish and dull. There is nothing to be done with Portia, a point upon which Joan Plowright lavished abundant proof.

(17 February 1974)

Hermie

Over the past five years television has been instrumental in convincing humanity that unless it has a vasectomy and learns to recycle its non-biodegradable flotsam, it will be smothered by a rising tide of empty detergent containers on or about April 1979. This impression being by now well ground in, the new fashion is to set about reversing it.

Broadly, the shift is from the gloomwatch mood of Professor Ehrlich back to the good old dependable zest and bounce of Bucky Fuller, who cheerily regards energy crises as the merest blockages in Spaceship Earth's fuel-lines, easily cleared by the whirling Dyno-rod of the human intellect.

Embodying this change of emphasis on a massive scale is fat-man futurologist Herman Kahn, hugely in evidence this week in a *Horizon* called "The Future Goes Boom!" (BBC2). Roly-poly Herman first reached fame as a Thinker About the Unthinkable, dreaming up Scenarios for the conduct of nuclear war. In the Pentagon his message went down like a 50-megaton bomb, since thinking about the unthinkable was an indispensable preliminary requirement to financing it. Inspired by this success to an ever more panoramic view of the future, Herman went into business as a panoptic clairvoyant. Gradually the negative aspects (e.g., the prospect of total devastation) got played down. More and more it turned out that the years ahead were viable, even rosy. He saw the future, and it worked.

Like Enoch Powell, Kahn has the knack of convincing people who in the ordinary way know nothing about what constitutes intellectual distinction that he is intellectually distinguished. His purported I.Q. of

200 is bandied about like Powell's Greek. Bernard Levin—than whom, usually, no man rates higher for acerbity and gorm—has been seen arriving at Kahn's feet by helicopter and nodding thoughtfully at the very kind of *ex cathedra* folderol which in the normal course of events he would greet with a penetrating raspberry. And if Kahn fooled Levin, he made a turkey of Brian Gibson, who in producing this programme put a glaring dent in his track record as a documentary whizkid. Renowned for his programmes on Venice and Charing Cross Hospital, Gibson should have been smart enough to lay on some opposition that would pin Kahn down. As it was, the fat man was left free to toddle.

The really fascinating thing about Kahn's predictions is their predictability. With the aid of his colleagues in the Hudson Institute—an outfit which hires itself out on a global basis as an ecosystematic Haruspex—Kahn is able to focus a divining eye on a country rich in natural resources and predict that it will get rich. Similarly he is able to glance at the figures for a country poor in natural resources and predict that it will get poor. But genius is nothing if not flexible, and the Institute is proud of having discovered, all of ten years ago, that Japan would become a leading world Power. The true marvel, of course, would have been to discover anybody who ever thought anything else, but you can't expect miracles. Kahn's boys don't claim to be infallible: merely prescient.

Kahn speaks a personal language featuring units of time and distance otherwise unknown to science. In particular, the auto-extruding temporal unit "fivetenfifteentwennytwennyfiveyearsfromnow" crops up often enough to be worthy of a name. On the analogy of the Fermi (the diameter of an electron), I propose it should be called the Hermie. Kahn's First Law of Ecodynamics can then be simply stated. In the space of one Hermie, anything that is happening now will still be happening only more so, unless something stops it. (The Second Law states that the fee for being told the First Law will be very large.)

Apart from their predictability, Kahn's predictions are also notable for their vulgarity, as in his notion that future wealth will allow everybody two cars and a helicopter each, plus access to free-fall sex. A sociologist from the University of Kent was allowed just enough screen time to point out that Kahn's preachings constituted an ideology, but not enough to outline which ideology it was. The producer's hope, I suppose, was that Kahn would condemn himself out of his own mouth. The hope was pious, placing too much trust in the efficacy of self-revelation. A quick salvo of incisively expressed disbelief would have done wonders.

(10 March 1974)

Wisdom of the East

Even the most healthy Westerner has only to think back over his own medical history to start suspecting that there ought to be, has to be, another way, or Way: all those powders and needles and gases, all that helpless waiting while the white witch-doctor decides how much he dares tell you. Think what it would be like to run your own organism, instead of it running you! In the face of Yoga no one can afford to feel superior. It was with a proper humility, then, that I tuned in to Hugh Burnett's documentary *The Roots of Yoga* (BBC1). Already hushed by the shock of hearing from a reviewer that I was "over-bright," I was determined from now on to be over-dumb. Un-smart, non-clever, receptive.

"I shrink to the size of an atom and reach out to the moon," a man said almost immediately. The type of Yoga under examination was Hatha Yoga. The man was sitting in a position that looked fiercely difficult. A friend of mine, who can do the same position, says that there are even harder ones up the line, culminating in a number where your legs double back under your tail and you sit comfortably on your ankles with your feet cupping your behind. The attitudes these chaps could get into were undeniably impressive. For the benefits of getting into them, however, we had to take verbal assurances. Such-and-such a position was good for hookworm and tapeworm.

There was a doctor on hand to say that Hatha Yoga really could deal with arthritis, bronchial asthma, colitis, dysentery and things like that. It seemed more than possible. That someone who could wrap his legs around his head would be an unlikely candidate for arthritis seemed a truism.

What about hookworm, though? Perhaps the hookworms can't stand the activity: they pack up and quit.

Water was poured in one nostril and came out the other. A piece of thread, good for adenoids, was introduced into the nose. This was also good for hair and eyes: "all the organs it is affecting." It also improved your eyesight. A man swallowed twenty-nine feet of white bandage. "Yes, but first you have to practise for two days." This was good for stomach ailments, helped you reduce, and dealt with eighteen different types of skin disease. Since the man had not a blemish on him, he could have said 180, or 1,800—or rather the man talking on his behalf could have. The man himself was full of cloth.

It was somewhere about here that Hugh Burnett succumbed to a mild panic—induced, I think, by the deadly Eastern combination of visual miracle and verbal tat. When his guide assured him that after the appropriate training the adept would soon be "sucking the water through the rectum," Burnett, instead of saying, "Show us, show us," said "How? How?" Apparently the stomach makes a vacuum and the liquid rushes in through the sphincter to fill the gap. I have no doubt that this happens, but it would have been nice to see a beaker of water marked "Before" and "After" held by somebody—Burnett would have been the ideal candidate —who had actually been there when the man sat on it. And the same goes double for the bloke who can suck air through the penis. Not only air, but milk, honey and mercury. "Mercury!" shouted Burnett, "why *mercury?* Isn't that dangerous?" "No," came the all-wise answer, "it is not dangerous."

A man bent a steel bar with his eyelid, but I was still thinking about the mercury. I stopped thinking about it when a much older man smashed a milk bottle and lay down in the pieces while they put a heavy roller over him. There was a fulsome crunching as the small pieces of glass became even smaller pieces. The man rose to his feet long enough to brush a few slivers from his unmarked skin and win a tug-of-war with an elephant. Then he lay down again and they drove a Mercedes truck over him.

Plainly this skill would come in handy any time you fell asleep on a broken milk bottle in the middle of an autobahn. Apart from that, its only function can be to convince the sceptical that Hatha Yoga gives you power over the body. No arguments, although I would like to know if there is a limit to how much the old man can stand. Suppose you wheel away the Mercedes and bring on, say, a Volvo Thermo-

King juggernaut: would he still be lying there, or would he go off and meditate?

The programme wound up by visiting an *ashram* with 120 inmates, half of them Westerners. The *ashram* was meditationsville, and whenever Westerners meditate you have to wear a snorkel, else the rhetoric will drown you. One girl adores her Baba Yogi so much she just likes to stand near him, "to feel his vibrations. Which, as he is a Perfect Master, are very pure."

Here was the universe being solved in personal terms, with the Americans being the most self-obsessed of all. "He knows *everything* . . . and yet he has retained his physical form out of pure compassion, because he wants to help us." The girl's face was lit up like a torch. But it was another girl who took the biscuit.

"My meditations are so intense . . . I start doing really *strange things* . . . it used to hurt me when I meditated . . . it cleansed me, completely cleaned me out. . . . I can't get enough of my meditations . . . because my meditations have taken over my life. . . . I feel his vibrations coming into me . . . it makes me feel love."

(9 June 1974)

Hi! I'm Liza

Bad Sight and Bad Sound of the Week were twin titles both won by *Love from A to Z* (BBC1), a river of drivel featuring Liza Minnelli and Charles Aznavour. Right up there beside the Tom Jones specials in the Bummer Stakes, this grotesque spectacular was fascinating for several reasons, none of them pleasant.

To begin with (and to go on with and end with, since the phenomenon was continuous), there was the matter of how Charles had contrived to get himself billed above the normally omni-dominant Liza. Not only was his name foremost in the opening titles, but the between-song lectures, instead of being delivered by Charles on the subject of Liza's talent, were mainly delivered by Liza on the subject of Charles's genius. "Hi!" Liza would yell intimately, her features suffused by that racking spasm of narcissistic coyness which she fondly imagines looks like a blush, "I'm Liza." (Such a coup is supposed to stun you with its humility, but in the event it is difficult to choke back the urge to belch.) She would then impart a couple of hundred words of material—supplied by someone going under the name of Donald Ross—on the topic of Charles Aznavour, with particular reference to his creativity, magnanimity and vision.

This would be followed by a lengthy and devastating assault on "My Funny Valentine" by Charles himself, in which the song's subtlety would be translated into the standard emotional intensity of the French cabaret ballad, leaving the viewer plenty of opportunity to note how the tortured singer's eyebrows had been wrinkled by hard times, lost loves and the decline of the franc. Or else, even worse, Liza in person would pay a tribute to Lorenz Hart by singing "My Romance" as if her task were to put significance into the lyric instead of getting it out. "You know," she announced at one point, and I had a sinking sensation that I did, and didn't agree, "the most that you can ever hope for as an entertainer is to *touch* people."

Liza, who can't even walk up a flight of stairs sincerely (a flight of stairs was wheeled on for the specific purpose of allowing her to prove this), is more touching than she knows. She began her career with a preposterous amount of talent, the shreds of which she still retains, but like her mother she doesn't know how to do anything small, and, like almost every other young success, she has embraced the standards of excellence proposed by Showbiz, which will agree to love you only if your heart is in the right place —where your brain should be.

Liza can't settle for being admired for her artistry. She wants to be loved for herself. Charles, to do him the credit he's got coming as the composer of the odd passable song in the relentlessly up-and-down-the-scale French tradition, is less innocent. In fact he's so worn by experience he's got bags under his head. He knows the importance of at least feigning to find his material more interesting than his own wonderful personality —a key trick for prolonged survival, which Liza will have to learn, or go to the wall. The show was recorded at the Rainbow. It was pretty nearly as bad as anything I have seen in my life, and deepened the mystery of why it is that it is always the BBC, and not ITV, which brings us these orgies of self-promotion by dud stars: package deals which consist of nothing but a wrap-up.

(14 July 1974)

Mission Unspeakable

No-no news report of the decade came from ITN, who speculated darkly about whether the Lizard Peninsula would be hit by pieces of the Saturn rocket making its flaming return to Earth. Cub reporter Stephen Matthews was in position at the threatened site. "People around the Lizard Peninsula don't seem at all worried about being hit by bits of the American rocket." He turned dramatically to look at the aforementioned geographical feature while the camera zoomed in to show the rocket not hitting it.

In the current series of *Mission Impossible* (BBC1), the Master of Disguise role is played by Leonard Nimoy, alias Mr. Spock from *Star Trek*. For Trekkies this is a disturbing duplication, since it becomes difficult to watch the Impossibles in action without being assailed by suspicions that a leading member of that well-drilled team is suffering from atrophy of the ears. Last week the Impossibles were once again in contention against an Eastern European people's republic, called the Eastern European People's Republic.

The plot hardly varies from episode to episode. A disembodied voice briefs the taciturn chief of the Impossibles about the existence—usually in the Eastern European People's Republic—of a missile formula or nerve-gas guidance system stashed away in an armoured vault with a left-handed chromosympathetic ratchet-valve time-lock. The safe is in Secret Police HQ, under the personal protection of the E.E.P.R.'s Security Chief, Vargas. The top Impossible briefs his black, taciturn systems expert and issues him with a left-handed chromosympathetic ratchet-valve time-lock opener.

The Master of Disguise taciturnly adopts a rubber mask which transforms him into Vargas. A tall, handsome Impossible, who is even more taciturn than his team-mates (and who possesses, like James Garner, a propelling-pencil skull), drives the team to the E.E.P.R., which is apparently located somewhere in Los Angeles, since it takes no time at all to get there by road and everyone speaks English when you arrive. A girl Impossible—who has no detectable function, but might possibly be making out with the top man—taciturnly goes along for the ride.

After a fantastically elaborate deception in which the Secret Police end up handing over the plans of the vault and placing themselves under arrest, the systems expert disappears into the air-conditioning duct and gets to work. A great deal of sweat applied to his forehead and an abundance of music applied to the sound-track combine to convince us that the tension is mounting. A succession of reaction shots shows each of the Impossibles grimly checking his watch. Can the left-handed chromosympathetic ratchet-valve time-lock opener do its thing before the real Vargas blasts his way out of the broom-cupboard and rumbles the caper? Click. The nerve-gas guidance system is in black but trustworthy hands. The Impossibles pile taciturnly into their truck and drive back to America, leaving the contented viewer with just one nagging question: *what on earth has gone wrong with Spock's ears?*

Mission Impossible is glop from the schlock-hopper. *Columbo* (Anglia) tries harder—which in my view makes it less interesting, since although I would rather have art than schlock, I would rather have schlock than kitsch. Here again the plot is invariable. A high-toned heavy commits a fantastically elaborate murder, whereupon Columbo drives up in a pile of junk and is almost arrested as a vagrant by the young cop on duty. (That Kojak can dress so well and Columbo so badly on what must basically be the same salary is one of the continuing mysteries of American television.) Gradually the murderer—last week it was Robert Culp—crumples under the pressure of Columbo's scruffy scrutiny. The plot is all dénouement, thereby throwing a lot of emphasis on Columbo's character. As often happens, the character element is not as interesting as the programme's creators would have you believe. *Kojak,* for instance, rates as the No. 1 imported fuzz opera mainly because Telly Savalas can make bad slang sound like good slang and good slang sound like lyric poetry. It isn't what he is, so much as the way he talks, that gets you tuning in.

Barlow, currently re-emergent on BBC1, is what he is, alas. Despite the

Radio Times articles on the alleged miracles of its making, the series is in fact tedious to the last degree. The complexity of Barlow's character would have to rival that of Dostoevsky's if we were to stay interested while he concerned himself—as he did last week—with washing up, making coffee and listening to the radio. When he sets his jaws against the foe, the foe dutifully turn pale with terror, but it is difficult to believe. Stratford Johns partly disarmed criticism on this point by cramming himself into the same studio with William Hardcastle on *In Vision* (BBC2) and hinting that he might conceivably be sending the role up.

(12 January 1975)

Thatcher Takes Command

"It's a team game we're playing, if it's a game. It's not a game. But we're a team." This remark, delivered by Colin Shepherd, M.P., on *Midweek* (BBC1) the week before last, struck me at the time as an apposite motto for the current period of Tory confusion. Its neatly circular argument generates a runic impenetrability: the maximum semantic chaos with the minimum effort.

I've got witnesses to prove that my money was on the broad all along. In one addled mind at least, Mrs. Thatcher was always a serious candidate. Obviously *World in Action* (Granada) thought so too, since they profiled her last Monday night, a whole day before she established wide credibility by running away with the first ballot. Since Mrs. Thatcher probably ranks somewhere near the Chilean junta in *WIA*'s scale of affection, it seemed possible that they were examining her as a toxic phenomenon, like nuclear proliferation. An air of objectivity, however, was strenuously maintained. Perhaps it was assumed that mere exposure would suffice, and that the sprightly lady would stand self-condemned. It wasn't going to be as easy as that, as events later proved.

But even at that stage, the jaundiced professional eye could detect ample evidence that Mrs. Thatcher was working on her screen image with a view to improvement. All political figures try this, but usually they take the advice of their media experts—men disqualified simply by the fact of being available, since nobody of ability would take such a lickspittle appointment.

It was an expert who told Harold Wilson that he should smile during his speeches, and another expert who told Heath to take his coat off and relax. The respective results were of a corpse standing up and of a corpse sitting down. In America at this very moment it is an expert who is busily convincing President Ford that his speeches will gain resonance if he illustrates them with diagrams drawn in the air. Mrs. Thatcher, as far as I can tell, has declined such help, and set about smoothing up her impact all by herself.

Visually she has few problems. The viewer, according to his prejudices, might or might not go for her pearls and twin-sets, and the hair-styles are sheer technology. But the camera loves the face and the face is learning to love the camera back. She is rapidly becoming an adept at helping a film crew to stage a fake candid. While her excited daughter unleashes a hooray bellow in the background and her husband, Mr. Mystery, vaults out of the window or barricades himself into the bathroom, the star turn is to be seen reading the newspapers with perfect casualness, right in focus.

The hang-up has always been the voice. Not the timbre so much as, well, the *tone*—the condescending explanatory whine which treats the squirming interlocutor as an eight-year-old child with personality deficiencies. It has been fascinating, recently, to watch her striving to eliminate this. BBC2 *News Extra* on Tuesday night rolled a clip from May 1973, demonstrating the Thatcher sneer at full pitch. (She was saying that she wouldn't *dream* of seeking the leadership.) She sounded like a cat sliding down a blackboard.

In real life, Mrs. Thatcher either believes that everybody can help himself without anybody getting hurt, which means she is unhinged; or else believes that everybody who can help himself ought to do so no matter who gets hurt, which means she is a villain—a sinister prospect either way. On the tube, though, she comes over as a deep thinker: errors of judgement like the food-hoarding goof will probably disappear with experience, and are by no means as damaging as the blunders the men perpetrate in quest of screen warmth. ("You know me, Robin, I'm a pretty human sort of chap," I caught William Whitelaw saying a couple of months ago.) She's cold, hard, quick and superior, and smart enough to know that those qualities could work for her instead of against. "Like any winner's dressing-room after the big fight, the champagne flowed," said *News at Ten*, its grammar limp with admiration.

In *Taste for Adventure* (BBC1), a man of incredible strength, bravery and stupidity called Sylvain Saudan skied down the Eiger. "My head hurt," he declared Pythonically. In *Inside Story* (BBC2), a cow called Celia was impregnated by a jaded Lothario of a bull called Cliftonmill Olympus II. Cliff produced 5,000,000,000 sperm at a stroke, but never got the girl. The stuff was deep-frozen and transported to the site in a white VW driven by Mr. Ray Cod, who donned elbow-length gloves and socked it to Celia with minimal foreplay. Meanwhile Cliff was presumably reading *Penthouse* and preparing himself for further triumphs. Brief encounter.

(9 February 1975)

The Higher Trash

Its fourth anxious episode having been duly transmitted to the nation, the Bergman blockbuster *Six Scenes from a Marriage* (BBC2) stands nakedly revealed as the Higher Trash. After more than fifteen years of joyless cohabitation, Ingmar and I are through.

Instead of being equipped with subtitles, a device presumably eschewed as being too off-putting for the hordes of proletarians the Beeb hoped to snare with Bergman's Scandinavian magic, the series has been dubbed, in a fashion so comprehensively disastrous that the reeling viewer suspects the television set of having developed a split personality. Has the tuning mechanism ruptured a rheostat and started picking up an old Lana Turner movie playing on the commercial channel? Certainly no such voices, in this day and age, can be heard anywhere else than in the cocktail lounge of the daily Pan Am jumbo from Heathrow to Boston as it trails its lumbering shadow across the stratocumulus over mid-Atlantic. Marianne sounds like a well-stoned fashion correspondent blowing bubbles through a dry martini. Johan sounds like the bloke who bought it for her. Separate, they're amazing. Together they're incredible.

The voices violate the dialogue, but since the dialogue is a corpse the crime is necrophilia rather than rape. I imagine, however, that Bergman's heftily deployed sentiments evinced a hint more snap in the original Swedish. The English translation (which for those with a taste for calcified prose can be obtained in a Calder & Boyars paperback at £1·95) is muesli without milk. A single mouthful would be quite sufficient to choke any actor in the world. Guess what Marianne said to Johan in Episode Two, when they were driving along together in the morning? "What fun it is driving along together in the morning!" And the word "for" is consistently employed in place of "because"—a usage hitherto confined to formal poetry and *Daily Express* editorials.

Nobody has ever talked the way these two talk in the whole of English history. The translation is the merest transliteration, which it would have been a matter of elementary competence—requiring about two days of an averagely endowed writer's time—to work up into a speakable text. You don't have to be able to speak Swedish to change "What fun it is" into something an actress can *say*. All you have to be able to do is speak English.

That the chat clouds the issue, however, should not be allowed to obscure the fact that the issue is dead. The real trouble with the alliance between Marianne and Johan—a trouble which Bergman hasn't begun to examine, being too busy with focussing his pitiless analytical glance—is that they could have no possible reason for being interested in each other in the first place. Liv Ullmann is hardly the earth mother she is cracked up to be (a few weeks ago in this very newspaper A. Alvarez was to be seen promoting her as a combination of Eleanora Duse, Sieglinde in *Die Walküre* and Edwige Feuillère), but the awkward truth that she fades on the mind's eye almost as fast as Monica Vitti or Jeanne Moreau doesn't make her entirely weightless: she has more than enough substance to give the diaphanous role she is playing the pulse of real blood. How, though, did Marianne ever see anything in Johan? And Johan being Johan, how could he have seen anything in her, or anyone?

Johan, functionary of something called a Psychotechnical Institute and failed poet (striving devoutly to distance his own personal experience, Bergman can get only as far as foisting it on a *failed* artist: a non-artist is beyond his powers), finds after years of keeping up appearances with Marianne that his passion for another girl commands him away. So he lets Marianne in for a burst of the bitter truth. "I'm trying to be as honest as I can—but by God it's not easy."

What made this scene (the core of Episode Three) unintentionally laughable was Bergman's innocent failure to realize that Johan's sudden cruelty, far from revealing him as a passionate rebel, merely branded him as a perennial zombie.

It is difficult to over-emphasize sex, but very easy to over-isolate it, and Bergman's whole effect is of a puritanical hedonism in which sex includes all possible means of contact instead of being the most important of several. That his characters do not amuse each other is not surprising, since Bergman—despite *Smiles of a Summer Night* and his early grounding in comedy—has a sense of humour considerably inferior to that of F. R. Leavis. But they have nothing else to offer each other either.

In this context, it is natural that sexual gratification should be thought to equal happiness and that happiness should be sought as an end—a monomaniacal defiance of the axiom that happiness is not a worthwhile aim in life, and can exist only as a by-product of absorption. And Bergman's continuing problem is that he is not quite enough of an artist to imagine what people who are not artists could possibly be involved *with*. "What will I say to the children?" wails Marianne as Johan stomps out. "Say what you like," growls Johan, and Bergman honestly believes that he is showing us the interplay of real emotions, instead of putting on a carbolic-soap opera. "If all the people who live together were in love," says Baptiste in *Les Enfants du Paradis,* "the earth would shine like the sun." Nobody is ever going to call Jacques Prévert, who wrote that film, a fearless investigator of marriage—yet compare the shattered pleadings of Maria Casares with anything that Bergman can provide for Liv Ullmann, and ask yourself which is the explorer, the romantic or the realist.

(2 March 1975)

Schmlittering Prizes

The first in a series of six plays about 1950s Cambridge written by Frederic Raphael under the collective title of *The Glittering Prizes* (BBC2), "An Early Life" starred Tom Conti as an energetic, sensitive, witty and passionate student, singled out by his Jewishness and alacrity of mind.

From the ample pre-publicity there were good reasons to think that Frederic Raphael had based this central character on himself. Whatever the truth of that, Adam Morris (for so the pivotal figure in the play was named, "Frederic Raphael" having presumably been judged too direct) was certainly a good subject for a *Bildungsroman*—or would have been, had he not arrived in Cambridge with his *Bildung* already completed.

Normally there is no juicier topic than a bright young man coming up to university and getting his education. But Adam Morris seemed to have got his in the sixth form, leaving him nothing to do with his Cambridge days except (a) make the odd pardonable mistake, and (b) lose his virginity. The odd pardonable mistake lay in underestimating the nasty-looking aristocratic mother of his dying room-mate; from her he learned a lesson in self-denial. He lost his virginity, with enviable lack of fuss, to a beautiful student teacher.

Apart from these events, which were doubtless formative in their different ways, Adam was already uncannily intact—sardonic, wise, mature. He was crass about attacking people's religious faith, but you could see his reasons. Otherwise he had the aphoristic subtlety of Montaigne. There seemed small reason for his being a student at all. He should have been doing the teaching. Cambridge, for better or for worse, is a place where young people grow and change. Adam was above that. Tom Conti played Adam in a style reminiscent of Peter Sellers pretending to be a lounge lizard. So tentative and inwardly giggling a manner half-worked when Conti was being Madame Bovary's husband last year, but didn't work at all when he was being energetic, sensitive, witty and passionate, singled out by his Jewishness and alacrity of mind. When not emitting one of the clever things Frederic Raphael once said (or else *would* have said, but thought of too late, and so is saying now), Conti conveyed introspection by encouraging his eyes to glisten wetly, while smiling with secret knowledge.

The hard-to-take hero would have mattered less if the play built around him had given you more idea of what Cambridge in that period was actually like. Doubtless future episodes will. But here, in the instalment that was meant to set the tone, there was precious little sense of anything special going on—and fifties Cambridge, after all, was the time and place when all the hot-shots who have since dominated the media were getting to know one another. They were, or if they weren't they are, self-consciously a Generation.

Only the contemporary habit of imitating Bluebottle's voice gave us a sense of time, which was promptly undone by showing us a list of names on a St. John's College staircase done in Letraset instead of hand-painted. The sense of place was most conspicuously given by inviting the mastaba of the University library, the most hideous building in Cambridge, to loom in the background. (E. M. Forster has an excellent essay listing all the vantage points from which it can't be seen.)

Nor were the epigrams any great shakes. Reviewing a book by Michael Frayn, Mr. Raphael once talked about the Cambridge trick of smiling to recruit someone's intellectual assent, and being intelligent to recruit his affection. This might have been a pseudo-observation (why isn't it an Oxford trick, or an Aberystwyth trick?), but I could have stood for a few like it in the script. And instead of conflating and disguising the real-life illuminati, it might have been more evocative simply to name them, or even give them identity tags. A dull start.

Clayhanger (ATV) is so-so: better than bad, but less than a knock-out. A lot of it takes place around the dinner table. People like to watch actors eat (Ferenc Molnár wrote a whole play based on this principle), but there are limits. When the action moves elsewhere, the series looks under-budgeted: the Five Towns are less grimy than tatty, with lanes and alleys laid suspiciously flat and walls that shake if you lean against them. Until Janet Suzman arrived in Episode Three, Harry Andrews as old Darius Clayhanger had to carry the burden, or can, of being the salient figure. A doddle for him, since all he had to do was rant, but tiresome for us. Young Edwin, even though by Episode Four he had grown up enough to be played by Peter McEnery, was never in the running as the centre of excitement. It was from Hilda Lessways that the boost had to come if the show was to achieve orbit.

It hasn't happened. Janet Suzman can work every miracle except looking callow. Trying to be that, she is arch. As the series progresses through time, she will become more credible, but at the moment we have to watch the most womanly of women pretending to be girlish, which she does by crooking her elbows and talking with a coy trill. If she had less presence, she might get away with it.

On *Read All About It* (BBC1), A. J. Ayer indulged his bad habit of saying "Mm, mm" impatiently while other people spoke, as if their points were too obvious to require putting. I found this wonderfully unendearing. Lord Chalfont, fronting *Who Says It Could Never Happen Here?* (Anglia), was also on characteristic form. Aided by Anthony Lejeune, Lord Shawcross and similar deep thinkers, he warned of the Communist threat to democracy. The warnings sounded like a threat to democracy in themselves. Lord Shawcross said that the next "five or fifteen years" would see a totalitarian Government installed in Britain—probably a Communist one. So in four or fourteen years it'll be time to get your skates on.

(25 January 1976)

Unintelligibühl

"If we ate what we listened to," said the pianist Earl Wild (BBC2), "we'd all be dead." He meant Muzak, but his observation applied equally well to the English language, which in this week's television received a fearful bashing from more than one direction.

For example, there was NATO Supreme Commander General Alexander Haig, talking to Robin Day on *Newsday* (BBC2). General Haig looks the way a general ought to look, with a Steve Canyon countenance, shoulders like an armoured personnel carrier, and rows of medal ribbons running down one side of his chest and out of the picture. Unfortunately he sounds like nothing on earth. It is almost impossible to understand him, since he crams so many polysyllabic abstractions into a sentence that he forgets the beginning before he reaches the end.

Quizzed by Robin on the Soviet military buildup, General Haig squared his jaw and talked of the restructured multi-capable inter-parity situation of the SALT ceiling. Robin adjusted his glasses and rephrased his question. General Haig squared his jaw even further and rephrased his answer, talking of how the shortfall in assessment of the balanced triad necessitated that he participate in the evolution of viable agreement postures.

Apart from hitting General Haig in the face with a custard-pie, there wasn't a lot Robin could do except plough on. If the West was going broke, how could it meet the Russian threat? General Haig squared his jaw to the point of crystalline fatigue failure and gave answer. The United States no longer wielding hegemonial power in the tightly interdependent global strategic environment, the NATO allies in the present socio-economic crisis situation would require to keep their perspectives clear.

Robin, looking as if he had been wrestling a mattress full of treacle, retired defeated. General Haig looked triumphant. Now for the Russians.

"John Curry pulled out *everything!*" screamed Alan Weeks in *Olympic Grandstand* (BBC1). So did the BBC commentators. For them, Innsbruck was a kind of apotheosis. What would the Winter Olympics be without them?

To start with, it would be literate—but let's not carp. We've done that before. In the sweet instant of an unarguable British victory, it behoves us to be proud, and that includes being proud of Alan Weeks, Ron Pickering, David Vine and David Coleman. Vine, especially, is a changed man. Not once did he lapse into a repetition of the unforgettable moment when he predicted that an athlete would shortly "pull out the big one." He left that to Alan Weeks, who on the evening of the pairs figure-skating final duly delivered himself of a classic. "This might well be the night," mused Alan, "when Rodnina pulls everything out." Thereby confirming our suspicions about Russian female athletes.

Coleman, Weeks, Pickering and Vine all made copious use of this year's official BBC demonstrative adjective, "this." "This man," "this is the man," "this girl," "this is the girl." The skiing ability of Klammer was referred to as "the brilliance of this man." There were several instances of last year's "the man who," as in "The man who was injured last year," but they were overwhelmed by the popularity of "this is the man who," as in "This is the man who challenged Thoeni at Burble Valley."

"This is the man who" was sometimes shortened to "this the man who," as in "This the man who leads the commatition." For some reason, this advanced form was never used when referring to women, who were still sometimes "the girl who" (as in "The girl who lives in the tiny village of Unintelligibühl"), were very often "this is the girl who" (as in "This is the girl from Gruntstadt in Mumblestein who fractured an ovary at Grenoble") but were never "this the girl who."

Why this should be was a difficult question. This the question that was difficult to answer. While you were working on it, there were some nice things to watch. I liked the American pairs skaters, anglo Randy Gardner and ethnic Tai Babilonia. Super-Wasp and the Half-Breed! As usual, Irina Rodnina carried on like a ballbreaker, incinerating Zaitsev with her beetle-browed hate-stare when he got his blades tangled. It will be a relief when those two retire from commatition, since for all their technical razzle-dazzle they are unpoetic to the last degree. Not that Rodnina lacks femininity compared to some other members of the Russian team. One of their speed-skating persons bore a startling resemblance to Johnny Weissmuller. Perhaps it was thinking about her which led Reginald Bosanquet on *News at Ten* (ITN) to mention an event called "the 500 kilometres women's speed-skating."

If you can accept the fact that *Bouquet of Barbed Wire* (LWT) is the house of Atreus transferred to Peyton Place on a long low loader, there are worse serials to get hooked on. It won't rot your brains like *The Brothers*. Nor will you see—as in so many other series currently on the screen—the roof of a coal-mine fall on the hero's father. Instead there is plenty of solid middle-class adultery and incest. Sheila Allen is having a whale of a time as the Older Woman who has welcomed her daughter's husband into her bed, which is roughly what her husband (Frank Finlay) would like to do with the daughter, and perhaps will, or even perhaps once did, or perhaps both.

I have been unfair to *When the Boat Comes In* (BBC1), which has really been far too good to ignore. James Bolam is quite superb in the leading role. But I was sad to see, in the latest episode, the roof of a coal-mine fall on the hero's father.

I hate to go on and on about *The Brothers* (BBC1), but it's turning into a very freaky scene. It looks as if Jenny is scheduled for the funny farm. That's where Brian went when they wrote him out for a whole series. When he came back, he had a moustache. When Jenny comes back, will she have one too? If there is no room at the asylum, she could always become one of the presenters of *Terra Firma* (BBC2): there are three already, and might as well be four, since the main interest of this new magazine programme's first instalment lay in watching the cooks crowd round the broth.

Ned Sherrin, a genuinely sharp character, could easily have run the whole show on his own, but had been burdened with help. Alasdair Clayre, fronting a thrill-a-minute story about canals, spoke in the tones of someone contemplating taking holy orders. Nemone Lethbridge was in charge of the standard item about stud bulls. There was a certain *frisson* in listening to her ritzy accent while her elegant hand patted a bull's bum, but the news was stale—which didn't, of course, stop *Nationwide* (BBC1) covering the same topic all over again a few nights later.

(15 February 1976)

Solzhenitsyn Warns the West

In a week's television not otherwise notable for moral content, Aleksandr Solzhenitsyn (*Panorama*, BBC1) bulked large. He was interviewed by Michael Charlton, who probably did as good a job as was possible, considering that there is no way of extracting Solzhenitsyn's message in condensed form.

The interview was preceded by a lightning tour of Solzhenitsyn's career. A measure of his success in writing books which evoke recent Russian history in its full horrific force is that such summaries now seem hopelessly inadequate. In the interview proper, Solzhenitsyn spoke Russian, with a translation dubbed over. This intensified, I found, the already slightly other-worldly feeling induced by his appearance, so evocative of both Lincoln and Dickens—men who spoke roundly on ethical issues, a largely vanished practice. That Solzhenitsyn should engage in such an old-fashioned activity is a reminder, difficult to assimilate, that the Soviet present branches off from somewhere in our past—it is a parallel universe, different and inimical. Talking to us about moral regeneration, he sounds like Dr. Arnold of Rugby. A bit dated. After all, we've got beyond all that. We're all the way up to Hugh Hefner.

The question of Solzhenitsyn's pride in his mission was raised when he told Charlton that his personal experience was vital to the West but won't be understood by it. Knowing Solzhenitsyn's books reasonably well, I believe that he is being humble when he speaks like this, but I can easily see how he might appear the opposite, especially to those who will be basing their opinions of him on watching *Panorama* rather than knuckling down to the admittedly formidable task of reading his collected works.

What Solzhenitsyn means here, I think, is not that he is some lofty exemplar of a difficult principle (later in the interview he repeatedly rejected Charlton's suggestion that he might see himself as a redeemer, an anti-Lenin) but that historical lessons can't be transmitted intact. He makes it clear in *Gulag Archipelago* Volume I that he has no faith in the ability of the truth to propagate itself automatically, even under ideal conditions of freedom. His remarkable humility consists in addressing himself with such heroic resolve to a task of which he has no false expectations.

Solzhenitsyn declared himself unable to comprehend how the West can possess freedom and not value it. This was a telling rhetorical point, but as a tenet in his position—which it is, recurring throughout his work—it has some awkward logical consequences. For example, if freedom is valued most when it is nearest to being extirpated, and least when it is most prevalent, then perhaps freedom needs to be threatened in order to be conscious of itself. It's a high price to pay for consciousness.

There is no possibility of over-valuing freedom, but there is the possibility of valuing it wrongly, and I think that to a certain extent Solzhenitsyn does so. He is on sure ground when he warns against tyranny but weak ground when he laments that liberty has not made us morally aware. Liberty can't do that: political freedom means nothing unless it is extended to those who are incapable of valuing it. Warning the West against the East, Solzhenitsyn can hope to be of some effect. Warning the West against itself, he is surely addressing himself to the wrong object. The West lacks a common moral purpose *because* it is free, so there is no point in his attacking our lack of moral purpose unless he attacks freedom too.

Similarly, his doctrine concerning the undividable nature of freedom has awkward consequences for his line of argument about what the West should do. It might well be that the Soviet Union will attempt to dominate the world. But that doesn't mean we should allow ourselves to be repressed by our own leaders in order that the threat might be countered —not if we believe that freedom is undividable. For the West, the political meaning of the Vietnam war lay in the refusal of an American generation to let its Government subvert the Constitution by suppressing specific freedoms in the name of an allegedly greater good. In the eye of history, which does not take sides, this might well prove to have been part of a disastrous chain of events in which the West destroyed itself by trying to preserve its free institutions.

But my point is that Solzhenitsyn can't have it both ways. One of the great lessons of his life and work is that the only thing ensured by giving up freedoms for a greater good is that the greater good will be evil when it arrives and the freedoms will be impossible to retrieve. To be worried about the K.G.B. doesn't mean that we should stop being worried about the C.I.A. In fact being worried about the C.I.A. is probably the most effective way of being worried about the K.G.B., since the West will never be able to defeat totalitarianism by going totalitarian—it will always arrive second—but might possibly stand a chance by remaining liberal.

Talking of the West's imminent collapse, Solzhenitsyn is paradoxically enrolling himself in a millenarian tradition which includes Marx. He is likely to be no better than his forerunners at predicting history. Solzhenitsyn's strength—his majestic strength—lies in his capacity to recover the past. He is the survivor of an historical catastrophe so violent that it would be understandable if he were no longer sane. And yet when you look at what he has achieved, the first thing that strikes you is the human tone, the lack of messianic rant.

Primus inter pares in what he called on *Panorama* the "fight for our memory," he is at one with comparably brave writers like Eugenia Ginzburg and Nadezhda Mandelstam in being true to what he knows, and beyond them in being able to extend that personal awareness to what he did not himself experience. He has given facts the force of imagination and made history a work of art, while being aware that a work of art is the most intense possible revelation of the assumptions which inform it. As he said in his Nobel Lecture, "conceptions which are devised or stretched do not stand being portrayed in images, they all come crashing down, appear sickly and pale, convince no one. But those works of art which have scooped up the truth and presented it to us as a living force —they take hold of us, compel us, and nobody ever, not even in ages to come, will appear to refute them."

(7 March 1976)

The *QB VII* Travesty

Spreading over two evenings, *QB VII* (BBC1) was a mammoth American opus about Hitler's destruction of the European Jews. Done from the heart, with no expense spared—everybody from Lee Remick to Sir John Gielgud walked through—this was a television programme which was not afraid to plumb the depths of the human spirit. Not afraid, and not qualified.

The title was a tip-off. Big bad novels often have numbers for titles, market research having revealed that browsing yokels respond to figures rather than to letters when seeking out an easy read. Hence *Butterfield 8, Catch-22, Slaughterhouse-Five, Mila 18*—the last being the work of Leon Uris, who indeed also wrote the novel *QB VII*, from which one Edward Anhalt drew the tele-play for the programme under discussion. QB VII is apparently the standard abbreviation for Queen's Bench No. 7 of the Law Courts, London, where Uris and Anhalt pretended that a Dr. Sir Adam Kelno sued a Jewish novelist called Abraham Cady for libel after Cady had imputed that Kelno performed hideous operations on Jews in concentration camps. With many excursions through time to explore the personalities of Kelno and Cady, the story-line unfolded in the courtroom.

Shorn of the flashbacks, the trial scenes would have worked well enough. In fact they had done so once before, when a much smaller programme on the same subject was made in England, its script based closely on a trial which actually took place, with Uris involved. Uris and Anhalt took the same real-life event as their departure point, but in adding their own explanations did a far more effective job than their less ambitious predecessor of leaving the matter in the dark.

The script throughout was worthy and giftless, like the dialogue put into the actors' mouths in the star-strewn film *Judgment at Nuremberg*, another big bad production on the same theme, with an equally strident sense of mission. And just as, at the time, it was inadvisable to point out that *Judgment at Nuremberg* was a big bad movie without first laboriously establishing that you were not necessarily pro-Nazi, so now it is perhaps not wise to argue that *QB VII* was a big bad programme without also insisting that one is far from indifferent to the subject of the Holocaust. In fact one would like to believe oneself even more passionate on the topic than *QB VII*'s authors, who, if they really understood its importance, would have had the grace to leave it alone, since their talents were patently not up to treating it.

From the first few minutes of the show, when the inmates of the concentration camps liberated in 1945 were described as "pathetic scarecrows of human beings," you knew that nobody concerned with the production could write for nuts. However exalted in its aims, this was going to be hack-work. The casting was adequate in the leading roles— Ben Gazzara, who played Cady, and Anthony Hopkins, who played Kelno, are both good actors, although Hopkins increasingly took refuge in mannerism as the script left him high and dry—but the conceptions of character which the players were asked to embody were hopelessly cliché-ridden, despite everything the director, producer and writers could do to make them profound. *Because* of everything they could do.

For the student of schlock (and schlock-merchants *always* produce schlock, especially when they try to be sincere), the role of Abraham Cady, successful Jewish novelist, was especially revealing. Whether or not Mr. Uris identified with him, Cady was a classic example of the Hollywood writer's fantasies about Integrity and Talent. For much of the first part of the show he was to be seen barging about spilling drinks, consumed with self-disgust at writing bad books. It is *de rigueur* in this fantasy for the writer to suppose that he writes bad books through choice, and that if he could only reject the swimming-pool and recover his Integrity he would be able to write good ones. It rarely occurs to him—certainly it never seemed to occur to Cady—that he writes bad books because he is a bad writer.

At the end of Part I, Cady, consumed by self-loathing and shattered by the collapse of his marriage, went to Jerusalem, where he visited the

Yad Vashem Memorial, at last grasped what the Nazis did to his people, and recovered his Integrity along with his faith. "I know what I have to write about now," he gritted, with the sub-*Exodus* sound-track music welling in the background. "I want the reader to be there when they haul up the Star of David over Jerusalem and rekindle the Sacred Flame. I pray that God gives me the Talent to do it." In Part II, God came through with the goods.

The problem was left in abeyance of how we could possibly respect Cady as a writer if he had to recover his faith before he found out what Nazi Europe had been like. What on earth had he thought before? The universal catastrophe of ideological genocide was reduced to a specious conflict in the mind of a Hollywood mediocrity. The few powerful scenes could only emphasize this central inadequacy, although they did lift the show a notch above *Judgment at Nuremberg,* which left a generation of young cinema-goers with the impression that the Nazi regime did bad things to Judy Garland.

Chronicle (BBC2), hosted by Magnus Magnusson, featured a Danish family voluntarily returning to Iron Age conditions. "A box of matches was the only concession to the twentieth century," Magnus explained, as the Bjornholts squatted around the quern and ground the draves with a splon. The nubile Bjornholt daughters glumly bared their bosoms to the Iron Age breeze, thereby supplying the male viewer with an alternative centre of interest while their father chipped splinths. "They settled into an Iron Age routine of making food and making fire," said Magnus. The routine couldn't have been routiner. Killing a chicken counted as heavy action.

We were shown the uncannily well-preserved bodies of people who had supposedly been ritually slain and dumped in the bogs, although the possibility was hard to rule out that they had suicided to escape the Iron Age tedium. Then it was back again to Dad, striding purposefully around in hair pants on the trail of edible klud. It helped to fight off sleep if you counted how many other concessions there were to the twentieth century besides the matches, although perhaps Mum's dark glasses were authentic Iron Age artefacts, obtained from one of those caravans that blew in from Rome once every ten years with a cargo of beads.

(2 May 1976)

Onward to Montreal

The gymnastics and the swimming having finally been got out of the road, the *Olympics* (BBC1 recurring) settled down to the task of boring you rigid with the track and field events.

For the Beeb's harassed commentators it was hard to know how to follow that climactic moment at the swimming-pool when David Wilkie won a gold medal and Alan Weeks had an orgasm. So loud was the shouting from the commentary box that it was sometimes difficult to sort who was screaming what. Hamilton Bland, Alan's new technical assistant, is not very quiet even when he is talking normally. "But tonight the Union Jack is raised and is being waved very proudly indeed!" "A proud Scot!" "And so the big moment has arrived!" "The Flying Scotsman!" "We have a certain gold medallist!" All these were among the things yelled, but the loudest bellow of all was unmistakably Alan's: "David Wilkie is absolutely superb!" And so he was. It was a proud moment for England. Well, Britain. All right, Scotland. What? Oh yes, and the University of Miami.

But when the focus shifted to track and field our patriots found themselves starved of material. Ron Pickering tried to ward off the encroaching void by co-opting new words, of which his favourite was "absolutely," as in "We're absolutely short of medals." And we absolutely were. Nor did the Canadian television people seem to care very much about our plight. Ron was clearly distressed when we weren't even allowed to see Geoff Capes being red-flagged on his last put, the director having cut away to watch a Russian girl getting nowhere in the javelin. And in the 10,000 metres Brendan Foster ("We had such high hopes of Brendan Foster") barely got into shot during the final stages, leaving Ron to speculate that he might be "thinking of that plane-load of supporters from Gateshead."

What Frank Bough constantly referred to as "Britain's medal-tally" depended absolutely on whether our athletes lived up to our high hopes when it came to "the big one." Although "the big one" is more David Vine's term than Ron's, nevertheless Ron is apt to help himself to it in the heat of the moment, as he did in the women's javelin, where one of the competitors was commended for having managed to "pull out the big one." A variation was "the longer one," as in "He's got a longer one out." And one of the pole-vaulters called forth a burst of eroticism verging on the lyrical. "Just before he slots it in, you'll see him whip it up around his ears . . . keeping his left arm absolutely firm . . . carrying it parallel to the ground. . . ."

Even before the Olympics started, David Coleman was already grappling with the problem of how to describe East Germany's Renate Stecher. "The big girl, Renate Stecher" and "East Germany's powerful Renate Stecher" were two of the devices he resorted to then. By the time of the Games proper, he was obsessed. "Stecher really *very* squarely built." "Really square. Very, *very* strong." "The bulky figure of Renate Stecher." With regard to Renate, the age of chivalry is dead. The erstwhile attempts to establish that she is really quite feminine off the field have been given up, and nobody now pretends that she wouldn't roll straight over you like a truck.

As in the Winter Olympics, there was heavy use of "this," "the man" and "the man who," with perms and combs of all three. Thus we heard about "The man they said couldn't win the big one," "This the girl we've seen before," "This the technique to follow," "This the race," "The man who's writing a thesis on the psychological effects of world-class sprinting" and "This the man who didn't want to compete in this." As a recompense, "situation" was largely eschewed, except when Ron said that a race was "getting pretty close to the middle situation," meaning that it was almost half over.

But if "situation" was on its way out, "a lot to do" was plainly on its way in. "Jenkins has a lot to do" was a new way of saying that our man, of whom we had such high hopes, was not going to pull out the big one. A variation was "an awful lot to do," as in "and Ovett's got an awful lot to do," meaning that our man was about to finish an awful long way behind the man who didn't want to compete in this.

Another term in vogue was "Olympic history," which differs from ordinary history in being rewritten from minute to minute, so that "the fastest man in Olympic history" can become "the second fastest man in Olympic history" in just the time it takes someone to pull a longer one out. But all these new locutions paled into insignificance beside the sudden importance of "hamstring" and "Achilles tendon."

With the possible exception of the Queen, everybody at the Olympic Games pulled a hamstring or an Achilles tendon. Sonia Lannaman, of whom we had such high hopes, pulled a hamstring and was unable to compete in her two sprint events. Alan Pascoe failed to recover fully from his pulled hamstring. Maria Neufville fell in her event, having had "a lot of trouble . . . with Achilles tendons." Lucinda Prior-Palmer's horse went lame after a clear round. One Spanish horse went lame from merely looking at the first fence. The logical conclusion was that everybody concerned—man, woman or beast—was trying to do more than nature permits.

To agonize about our medal-tally is absurd. If our medal-tally were larger, there would be real reason for worry, since it would mean that Britain was more concerned with sporting prestige than any free nation of its size ought to be. In the Olympic Games it is neither important to win nor important to have taken part. Sport is just something people who feel like doing it do, up to the point where the effort involved becomes inhuman. Beyond that point, politics takes over. Politically, the Olympic Games are a farce on every level. It is grotesque that in 1976 the BBC commentators should still be sounding like old Pathé Pictorials, desperately cherishing an illusion of British influence which would be fatuous even if it were real.

(1 August 1976)

AT THE PILLARS
OF HERCULES

Farewelling Auden

I. ON *EPISTLE TO A GODSON*

"You don't need me to tell you what's going on:" writes W. H. Auden in his latest book's first piece, "the ochlocratic media, joint with under-the-dryer gossip, process and vent without intermission all to-day's ugly secrets. Imageable no longer, a featureless anonymous threat from behind, to-morrow has us gallowed shitless: if what is to happen occurs according to what Thucydides defined as 'human,' we've had it, are in for a disaster that no four-letter words will tardy."

This passage is highly interesting prose, detectable only in its lexical intensity as the work of a poet: Hazlitt, right on this point as on so many others, long ago laid down the word about that give-away proneness to local effect. An ochlocracy is mob rule; the O.E.D. last noticed "joint" being used that way in 1727; to gallow is an obsolete form of to gally, which is itself a way of saying to frighten that hasn't been heard for a long time anywhere except in a whaling station; "tardy" as a verb staggered on a few years past its moment of glory in *A Winter's Tale* only to disappear in 1623. But let's start again.

In the title poem of *Epistle to a Godson*, W. H. Auden writes:

> . . . You don't need me to tell you what's
> going on: the ochlocratic media,
>   joint with under-the-dryer gossip,
>   process and vent without intermission
> all to-day's ugly secrets. Imageable
> no longer, a featureless anonymous
>   threat from behind, to-morrow has us

gallowed shitless: if what is to happen
occurs according to what Thucydides
defined as "human," we've had it, are in for
a disaster that no four-letter
words will tardy.

This passage is highly interesting poetry, but only within the confines of Auden's strictly prosaic later manner. Paying lip-service to some dimly apprehensible classical metre, sentences wriggle intricately and at length down the syllabic grid.

Blessed be all metrical rules that forbid automatic responses,
force us to have second thoughts, free from the fetters of Self.

The greatest modern verse technician, Auden long ago ran out of metrical rules needing more than a moment's effort to conform to. Technically, his later manner—which involves setting up a felt rhythmic progress inside an arbitrary syllabic convention—is really a way of restoring to the medium some of the resistance his virtuosity earlier wiped out. This technical mortification is closely allied with the ethical stand forbidding any irrationalities, all happy accidents. No automatic responses, no first thoughts. Helping to explain the omission of certain poems from his *Collected Shorter Poems 1927–1957*, Auden wrote in 1966:

A dishonest poem is one which expresses, no matter how well, feelings or beliefs which its author never felt or entertained. For example, I once expressed a desire for "New styles of architecture"; but I have never liked modern architecture. I prefer *old* styles, and one must be honest even about one's prejudices. Again, and much more shamefully, I once wrote:

History to the defeated
may say alas but cannot help nor pardon.

To say this is to equate goodness with success. It would have been bad enough if I had ever held this wicked doctrine, but that I should have stated it simply because it sounded to me rhetorically effective is quite inexcusable.

Glumly reconciling themselves to the loss of *September, 1939,* in its entirety and favourite fragments from other poems engraved in the consciousness of a generation, critics respectfully conceded Auden's right to take back what he had so freely given. It was interesting, though, that no strong movement arose to challenge Auden's assumption that these youthful poetic crimes were committed by the same self being dishonest, rather than a different self being honest. Auden was denying the pluralism of his own personality. It was his privilege to do so if he wanted to, but it was remarkable how tamely this crankily simplistic reinterpretation of his own creative selfhood was accepted.

More remarkable still, however, was the virtual silence which greeted the spectacle of a great modern talent disallowing the automatic response, proclaiming the virtues of knowing exactly what you mean against the vices of letting the poem find out what *it* wants to mean. Auden had apparently worked his way through to the last sentence of the *Tractatus Logico-Philosophicus. Wovon man nicht sprechen kann,* Wittgenstein had written, *darüber muss man schweigen.* What we cannot speak about we must pass over in silence. It was piquant to find the poet who above all others seemed to command the secret of modern magic occupying this position so very long after the philosopher who thought of it had moved out. Here was a man attacking the validity of his own serendipity, discrediting his own trick of setting up a bewitching resonance. Long before, combining with Louis MacNeice in preparing that seductive lash-up of a book *Letters from Iceland,* Auden had written:

> And the traveller hopes: "Let me be far from any
> Physician"; And the poets have names for the sea;

But on the way to press this was accidentally transformed into

> And the traveller hopes: "Let me be far from any
> Physician"; And the ports have names for the sea;

Noting straight away that "ports" suggested more than "poets," Auden let the slip stand. The names that ports have for the sea are likely to be functional as well as mythical, mistrustful as well as admiring, many-rooted rather than casually appropriate—in a word, serious. Or so we guess. Or so the unexpected ring of the word, its unpredictability in that context, leads us to conjecture—gives us *room* to conjecture. And this thinking-space, the parkland of imagination that existed in Auden's earlier manner, was what marked it out—and what he annihilated in forming his later manner. There have been artists who possessed some of Auden's magic and who went on to lose it, but it is hard to think of anyone who deliberately suppressed it. All conscious artists feel the urge to refine what is unique in their work, but few interpret this call to refine as a command to eliminate. Unless we are dealing with a self-destructive enthusiast—and Auden on the face of it can scarcely be categorized as one of those—then we are up against that most disciplined of all artistic adventurers, the man who gets sick of his own winning streak.

Pick up a photostat of the 1928 *Poems* and read it through (it takes about twenty minutes): was there ever a more capacious young talent? It goes beyond precocity.

> We saw in Spring
> The frozen buzzard
> Flipped down the weir and carried out to sea.
> Before the trees threw shadows down in challenge
> To snoring midges.
> Before the autumn came
> To focus stars more sharply in the sky
> In Spring we saw
> The bulb pillow
> Raising the skull,
> Thrusting a crocus through clenched teeth.

Hindsight lends us prescience, but it is permissible to claim that merely on the basis of this passage's first three lines we would have pronounced the writer capable of virtually anything. The way the turn from the second line into the third kinetically matches the whole stated action is perfect and obviously instinctive—what other men occasionally achieve was all there as a gift.

> The sprinkler on the lawn
> Weaves a cool vertigo, and stumps are drawn . . .

Elated by the effortless lyricism of a coup like this, we need to remember not just Auden's age, but the time. Yeats had not yet finished forming the compact musicality of his last phase, and the authoritative clarities of the first of Eliot's *Quartets* were still years away. Auden got this sonic drive absolutely from out of the blue. The plainest statement he could make seemed to come out as poetry:

> Nor was that final, for about that time
> Gannets blown over northward, going home . . .

It was a Shakespearian gift, not just in magnitude but in its unsettling —and unsettling especially to its possessor—characteristic of making anything said sound truer than true. In all of English poetry it is difficult to think of any other poet who turned out permanent work so early—and whose work seemed so tense with the obligation to be permanent. In his distinguished essay on Auden, John Bayley penetratingly pointed out that it was not in Auden's creative stance ever to admit to being young. What has not yet sufficiently been noticed is that it was not in the nature of Auden's talent to win sympathy by fumbling towards an effect—to claim the privileges of the not yet weathered, or traffic in the pathos of an art in search of its object. Instant accomplishment denied him a creative adolescence.

As always in Auden, ethics and techniques were bound up together. Barely out of his teens, he was already trying to discipline, rather than exploit, the artistic equivalent of a Midas touch. It is for this reason that the *Scrutiny* group's later limiting judgements and dismissals of Auden were wrong-headed as well as insensitive: they were branding as permanently undergraduate the one major modern gift which had never been content with its own cleverness for a moment. They missed the drama of Auden's career in the 1930s and 1940s, never realizing that the early obscurity and the later bookishness were both ways of distancing, rather than striving after, effect. The moral struggle in Auden was fought out between what was possible to his gift and what he thought allowable to it: the moralists, looking for struggles of a different kind, saw in his work nothing but its declarative self-assurance. The more he worked for ironic poise, the more they detected incorrigible playfulness. Subsequent critical systems, had they been applied, would not have fared much better. Suppose, for example, that our standards of the desirable in poetry are based on the accurate registration of worldly things. We would think, in that case, that a man who had come from the frozen buzzards of 1928 to the etymological fossicking of 1972 had moved from the apex of an art to the base. But suppose the ability to send frozen birds flipping over the mind's weir came too easily to be gone on with? What then?

> Doom is dark and deeper than any sea-dingle.
> Upon what man it fall
> In spring, day-wishing flowers appearing,
> Avalanche sliding, white snow from rock-face,
> That he should leave his house,
> No cloud-soft hand can hold him, restraint by women;
> But ever that man goes
> Through place-keepers, through forest trees,
> A stranger to strangers over undried sea,
> Houses for fishes, suffocating water,
> Or lonely on fell as chat,
> By pot-holed becks
> A bird stone-haunting, an unquiet bird.

Quoted from the first public edition of *Poems,* this stanza was the kind of thing which made Auden the hero of the young intelligentsia. Noteworthy, though, is the way in which the enchanting declarative evocation discussed above is painstakingly avoided. The stanza's rhythmic progress is as dazzlingly erratic as a sky-rocket toppled from its bottle. The switchback syntax, the Hardyesque hyphenated compounds—they pack things tight, and the reader is never once allowed to draw an inattentive breath. One of the many triumphs of Auden's first public volume was that this difficult verse came to be regarded as equally characteristic with the simpler felicities that were everywhere apparent.

> Beams from your car may cross a bedroom wall.
> They wake no sleeper; you may hear the wind
> Arriving driven from the ignorant sea
> To hurt itself on pane, on bark of elm
> Where sap unbaffled rises, being spring . . .

Merely to mention the headlight beams crossing the wall was enough to create them for the reader's dazzled eye. But Auden's maturity had already arrived: he was well aware that such moments were not to be thought of as the high points of poetry—rather as the rest points. Take, for example, these lines from "Prologue," the opening poem of his 1936 collection, *Look, Stranger!*

> And make us as Newton was, who in his garden watching
> The apple falling towards England, became aware
> Between himself and her of an eternal tie.

The apple falling towards England is superb, but poetry which had such effects as a *raison d'être* would be a menace. This very instance has in fact come under critical attack—an accusation of decadence has been levelled. But it should be obvious that Auden had no intention of allowing such facility to become fatal. Set against it were the inhibitors: syntactical, grammatical, lexical. And with them they brought ambiguity, resonance, areas of doubt and discovery—all the things his later poetry was to lose. The suggestiveness of Auden's poetry lay in the tension between his primal lyricism and the means employed to discipline it. The suggestiveness couldn't survive if either term went missing. And eventually it was the lyricism that went.

As we look through the individual collections of Auden's poems, each in succession strikes us as transitional. On each occasion there seems to be a further move towards paraphrasable clarity. Even at the height of his bookish phase (in, say, *New Year Letter*), Auden is still being more narrowly clear than he was before. Gradually, as we read on to the end, we see what kind of progress this has been. It has been a movement away from excitement and towards satisfaction.

Epistle to a Godson is like *About the House* and *City Without Walls* in being utterly without the excitement we recognize as Audenesque. And yet it, like them, gives a peculiar satisfaction: the patriarch grunts, having seen much and come a long way. The book is flat champagne, but it's still champagne. Part of Auden's genius was to know the necessity of chastening his talent, ensuring that his poetry would be something more enduring than mere magic. The resource and energy he devoted to containing and condensing his natural lyricism provide one of the great dramas in modern literary history. Pick up *Look, Stranger!* or *Another Time*—they read like thrillers. Every poem instantly establishes its formal separateness from all the others. Through Auden's work we trace not just themes but different ways of getting something unforgettably said: the poem's workings are in the forefront of attention. Finally the contrast between the early and the late manners is itself part of the drama. To understand Auden fully, we need to understand how a man with the capacity to say anything should want to escape from the oppression of meaning too much. Late Auden is the completion of a technical evolution in which technique has always been thought of as an instrument of self-denial. What Auden means by the fetters of Self is the tyranny of an ungoverned talent, and his late poetry is a completed testament to the self-control which he saw the necessity for from the very start—the most commendable precocity of all.

(*Times Literary Supplement*, 12 January 1973)

II. ON HIS DEATH

For a long time before his death, the fact that a homosexual was the greatest living English poet had the status of an open secret: anybody with better than a passing knowledge of W. H. Auden's writing must have been in on it, and in his later essays (one thinks particularly of the essays on Housman and Ackerley) he was teetering on the verge of declaring himself outright. During E. M. Forster's last decades the intelligentsia was similarly privy to covert information. At Forster's death, however, the obituaries—many of them written by old acquaintances—didn't hesitate to let the cat spring from the bag and dash about among a wider public. It isn't recorded that anybody died of shock at this revelation. One would have thought that a precedent for plain dealing had at long last been set. With Auden's demise, though, there has been a retreat into coy mummery—perhaps to protect his dedicatees still living, but more probably because no respectable literatus wants the responsibility of firing the gun that will set the young scholars off on their plodding race to re-explicate what any sensitive reader has long since seen to be one of the more substantial poetic achievements of the modern age. Poor scorned clericals, they will find that their new key turns with bewitching ease, but that it might as well be turning in a lake as in a lock. Auden is a long way beyond being a crackable case.

Nevertheless, the truth helps. It was an often-stated belief in Auden's later essays that knowledge of an artist's personal life was of small relevance in understanding his work. Insatiably and illuminat-

ingly inquisitive, Auden transgressed his own rule on every possible occasion. The principle was the right one, but had been incorrectly
stated. He was saying that to know the truth will still leave you facing
a mystery. What he should have said was that to know the truth will
leave you with a better chance of facing the *right* mystery. And it
quickly becomes evident, I think, that to accept the truth about
Auden's sexual nature does nothing to diminish his poetry—quite the
opposite. Acceptance leads in the very short run to the realization
that the apparent abstractness of Auden's expressed sensuality is really
a lyricism of unique resonance, and in the long run to the conviction
that Auden's artistic career, taken as a whole, is a triumph of the
moral self living out its ideal progress as a work of art. Auden's first
poems instantly revealed an unrivalled gift for luminous statement.
Simply by naming names he could bring anything to life:

> Who stands, the crux left of the watershed,
> On the wet road between the chafing grass
> Below him sees dismantled washing-floors,
> Snatches of tramline running to the wood
> An industry already comatose. . . .

After the withering of 1930s illusions it became fashionable to laugh at
"Pylon" poetry, but even though intentions do not make deeds there was
always something honourable in the intention of domesticating a techno-
logical imagery, and anyway Auden himself had only to intend and the
deed was done. So formidable a capacity to elevate facts from the prosaic
to the poetic had been seen rarely in centuries, and such fluent gestures
in doing it had almost never been seen. Auden's poetry possessed the
quality which Pasternak so admired in Pushkin—it was full of things. And
yet in an epoch when homosexuality was still a crime, this talent was the
very one which could not be used unguarded to speak of love.

For that, he was forced from the concrete to the abstract, and so moved
from the easy (for him) to the difficult. As Gianfranco Contini defini-
tively said when talking of Dante's dedication to the rhyme, the departure
point for inspiration is the obstacle. The need to find an acceptable expression for his homosexuality was the first technical obstacle to check
the torrential course of Auden's unprecedented facility. A born master
of directness was obliged to find a language for indirection, thus becoming immediately involved with the drama that was to continue for the

rest of his life—a drama in which the living presence of technique is the antagonist.

> Doom is dark and deeper than any sea-dingle.
> Upon what man it fall
> In spring, day-wishing flowers appearing,
> Avalanche sliding, white snow from rock-face,
> That he 'should leave his house,
> No cloud-soft hand can hold him, restraint by women;
> But ever that man goes
> Through place-keepers, through forest trees,
> A stranger to strangers over undried sea,
> Houses for fishes, suffocating water,
> Or lonely on fell as chat,
> By pot-holed becks
> A bird stone-haunting, an unquiet bird.

In this first stanza of Poem II in *Poems* (it was entitled "The Wanderer" only later, in *Collected Shorter Poems 1930–1944*), the idea of the homosexual's enforced exile is strongly present, although never explicit: the theme lies hidden and the imagery is explicit instead, thereby reversing the priorities of the traditional lyric, and bodying forth an elliptical suggestiveness which rapidly established itself as the new lyricism of an era. But already we are given a foretaste of the voyage that came to an end in Oxford forty years later—a wanderer's return to the Oxford of *Another Time*, the centre of anger which is the only place that is out of danger. Auden never looked for cloistered safety until very late on the last day. The danger and fatigue of his journey were too much of an inspiration.

> There head falls forward, fatigued at evening
> And dreams of home,
> Waving from window, spread of welcome,
> Kissing of wife under single sheet;
> But waking sees
> Birds-flocks nameless to him, through doorway voices
> Of new men making another love.

Only tiredness could make the doomed traveller dream the banalities of hearth and wife: awake, he is once again involved with real love. And real love is a new love, with all political overtones fully intended. Auden's radicalism, such as it was, was at one with his sexuality, with the subsequent result that he spent the thirties experiencing Communism as sensual and sex as political.

As Brecht found his politicized lyricism in sophistication *(In der Asphaltstadt bin ich daheim)*, Auden found his in innocence: masturbation in the dormitory, languishing looks between prefects and blond new boys, intimate teas and impassioned lollings on grassy hillsides. The armies and the political parties of the thirties were the thrillingly robust continuation of school rugger and cricket teams, being likewise composed of stubborn athletes and prize competitors. Bands apart, they were all-male and Hellenic—and the neo-Hellenism of the thirties was all Teutonic. Auden's political and intellectual spectrum in the thirties is mainly German, and it's harder than the gullible might think to pick his emotional allegiance between the two sets of muscle-packed shorts, Communist or Nazi. Intellectually, of course, he didn't fool with Fascism for a moment; but to his sexual proclivities the blond northern hero made an appeal which only a poetic embodiment could resolve— it took pearl to silence the irritation set up by those vicious specks of grit.

> Save him from hostile capture
> From sudden tiger's leap at corner;
> Protect his house,
> His anxious house where days are counted
> From thunderbolt protect,
> From gradual ruin spreading like a stain;
> Converting number from vague to certain,
> Bring joy, bring day of his returning,
> Lucky with day approaching, with leaning dawn.

Towards the glamour of the opposing teams—the chaps—Auden's feelings were ambiguous. So were his feelings towards his own homosexuality. Like many homosexuals, he seems to have experienced homosexual congress as the only clean kind, and thus had no reason to hesitate in identifying homosexuality with a new political order. Nevertheless guilt remained. In the thirties it was a cultural residue (later on, when Auden returned to Christianity, it became a religious precept), but was no less powerful for that. Just as, in another poem, the "ruined

boys" have been damaged by something more physical than the inculca-
tion of upper-class values which Left readers delightedly assumed, so in
this last stanza of "The Wanderer" the spreading ruin is something
closer to home than the collapse of Europe. There was fear in Auden's
pride about his condition. Fear of the police and fear that the much-
trumpeted corruption might be a fact. He thought that heterosexual
people could enjoy security but that only homosexuals could enjoy danger; that the intensity of the homosexual's beleaguered experience was
the harbinger of a new unity; but that, nevertheless, the homosexual was
unlucky. In the last line of this most beautiful of young poems, he doesn't really expect luck to be granted or his kind of day to dawn. It's yet
another mark of Auden's superiority that whereas his contemporaries
could be didactic about what they had merely thought or read, Auden
could be tentative about what he felt in his bones. (It was marvellous,
and continues to be marvellous, that the *Scrutiny* critics never detected
in Auden his unwearying preoccupation with the morality of his art, nor
realized that a talent of such magnitude—the magnitude of genius—
matures in a way that criticism can hope to understand but not pre-
scribe.)

It will be useful, when the time comes, to hear a homosexual critic's
conjectures about the precise nature of Auden's sexual tastes. It seems to
me, who am no expert, that Auden's analysis of Housman's guilt feelings
(he said Housman was so convinced a Hellenist that he felt ashamed of
being passive rather than active) was an indirect admission that Auden
was passive himself. Even in the earliest poems he seems not to be taking
the lead. All too often he is the forsaken one, the one who loves too much
and is always asking his beloved to share an impossibly elevated conception of their union.

> You whom I gladly walk with, touch,
> Or wait for as one certain of good,
> We know it, we know that love
> Needs more than the admiring excitement of union,
> More than the abrupt self-confident farewell,
> The heel on the finishing blade of grass,
> The self-confidence of the falling root,
> Needs death, death of the grain, our death,
> Death of the old gang . . .

But as Auden half-guessed that it might turn out, the old gang wouldn't go away: oppression would always be a reality and homosexual lovers would continue to live in fear and fragments. Out of this insecurity as a soldier in a lost army, it seems to me, emerged Auden's unsettling obsession with the leader principle—a version of *Führerprinzip* which was in fact no more Hitlerite than Stalinist, but was simply Auden's dream of a puissant redeemer.

> Absence of fear in Gerhart Meyer
> From the sea, the truly strong man.

The Truly Strong Man, the Airman, the Tall Unwounded Leader/Of Doomed Companions—he occurs and recurs throughout Auden's younger work, forever changing form but always retaining the magic power to convert fear into peace. A tall white god landing from an open boat, a laconic war-bitten captain, the Truly Strong Man is a passive homosexual's dream of equitable domination. He is the authentic figure of good in early Auden just as his half-brother, the Dictator, is the authentic figure of evil, the man swifter than Syrian horses who can throw the bully of Corinth and is seeking brilliant Athens and us.

In the Strong Man's embrace Auden achieves release from terror and a respite from his own admitted ugliness—his post-coital death at the hands of his Hellenic aggressor would appear to have a close visual affinity with the Dying Warrior.

> Acquire that flick of wrist and after strain
> Relax in your darling's arms like a stone.

In this Owenesque half-rhymed couplet the schoolboy vocabulary of mutual masturbation snuggles up with dainty boldness to the image of the narrator coiled in the tall leader's massive embrace. We could be excused for assuming that Auden spent half of his most productive decade fainting dead away: he returns to the image of orgasm over and over, as the lolling bridegroom droops like a dying flower or lapses into a classic fatigue.

Auden's butch hero flying fast aeroplanes or roping his weaker companions up F6 bears an ineluctable resemblance to the Aryan demigod break-

ing records in his Bf.109 or pounding skywards at forty-five degrees into
the white hell of Pitz Palu. As with heterosexuals, so with homosexuals,
sexual fantasizing is the mind's dreariest function. The scholars, when
they finally do get started on this tack, would do well to refrain from
waxing ecstatic when nosing truffles of ambiguity. Auden started supplying a sardonic critique of his physical ideal almost from the moment of
its creation. All generalized desire leads to banality. Auden staved off
bathos by transcendence on the one hand and by foolery on the other.
It needs always to be understood that the British schoolboys of his generation saw too much homosexuality ever to think of its mere mechanism as
a mystery. Auden planted an abundance of gags for the lads.

> Out of the reeds like a fowl jumped the undressed
> German,
> And Stephen signalled from the sand dunes like a wooden
> madman. . . .

Those were the days. Penned during his early time as a schoolmaster,
frolicsome lovesick odes to the rugger team are similarly self-aware. Their
presence in *Poems* edifyingly reminds us that Auden's exaltation of the
third sex (soon to have its internationalism recognized by being sneeringly
branded "the homintern") as a political paradigm was innocent only
politically—sexually it was self-analytical to an extent that made Auden's
achievement of chaste lyricism a double triumph.

In *Look, Stranger!*, the wonder book of Auden's poetry, the lyricism
was carried to its height. On the one hand, there was the perfection of
his abstract sweetness—*dolcezza* so neutralized that it could be sung as
plighting music for lovers everywhere.

> Moreover, eyes in which I learn
> That I am glad to look, return
>   My glance every day;
> And when the birth and rising sun
> Waken me, I still speak with one
>   Who has not gone away.

On the other hand, there was a deepening admission of vulnerability, of
a fateful strangeness which no amount of bravado could usher into its
inheritance.

> Whispering neighbours, left and right,
> Pluck us from the real delight;
> And the active hands must freeze
> Lonely on the separate knees.

All lust, Auden now complains, is at once informed on and suppressed: the new political forces will offer outlaws no place. Throughout *Look, Stranger!* the heterosexuals are characteristically pictured as the tireless sentries guarding those lonely roads on which lovers walk to make a tryst, unpitying soldiers

> Whose sleepless presences endear
> Our peace to us with a perpetual threat.

It's the threat which makes the homosexual's peace more poignant than the heterosexual's freedom, as Auden had already stated in *Poems,* XXVI:

> Noises at dawn will bring
> Freedom for some, but not this peace
> No bird can contradict: passing, but is sufficient now
> For something fulfilled this hour,
>   loved or endured.

In *Look, Stranger!,* with the thirties barely half over and the big battles yet to be fought, Auden already knew that for him and his kind the new age, if it ever came, would not come easily. Love would go on being a thing of glances meeting in crowded pubs, risky whispers in lavatories, one-night stands in cheap rooms, partings on railway stations, persecution and exile. Rhetorically he still proclaims his confidence; realistically he hints at a maturing doubt; poetically he creates from this dialectic some of the great love poetry of the century. To Poem IX in *Look, Stranger!* (called "Through the Looking Glass" in *Collected Shorter Poems 1930–1944*) only Lorca's "Llanto por Ignacio Sánchez Mejías" is even an approximate rival. For his compactness, for his mastery of lyricism as a driving force rather than a decoration, for his unstrained majesty of movement, Auden in this phase of his writing is without an equal. The poetry happens like an event in nature, beautiful because it can't help it.

Your would-be lover who has never come
In the great bed at midnight to your arms . . .

Imperfect, ruggedly rounded out, and in places appearing almost uncorrected, the poem creates its effects with a monstrously skilled carelessness that is in every sense superb, as if the mere details had been left to a team of assistants and the haughty master's attention reserved for passages like

Such dreams are amorous, they are indeed:
But no one but myself is loved in these,
And time flies on above the dreamer's head,
Flies on, flies on, and with your beauty flies.

How can we tell the intoxicator from the intoxicated? Lines like these are the loose scrawl of genius in its cups, the helpless, incandescent finale of Auden's meteorite making contact with the atmosphere of realism. Gorgeous fires of defeat.

But Auden's clairvoyant withdrawal into loneliness was pained as well as plangent, as we see in the hard-edged bitterness of *Look, Stranger!*, XXVIII:

Dear, though the night is gone
The dream still haunts today
That brought us to a room,
Cavernous, lofty as
A railway terminus

In this enormous room crowded with beds, Auden's lover turns towards someone else. The clarity of the setting belongs less to Lorca's branch of surrealism than to something colder and more northern. The presiding spirits at Lorca's lament are those of Buñuel and Dali. With Auden, it's Magritte.

Poem XXX in *Look, Stranger!* starts with the famous line "August for the people and their favourite islands" and is dedicated to Christopher Isherwood. In *Collected Shorter Poems 1930–1944* it is called "Birthday Poem," and in *Collected Shorter Poems 1927–1957* it does not appear at all—one of that volume's several shattering omissions. The line about the spy's career gains luminosity once we have accustomed ourselves to the close identification in Auden's mind of homosexuality with clandestine activity and all its apparatus of codes and invisible inks. There are lines between the lines of Auden's younger poems which will come to life in the mild heat of knowledge. Beginning far back in the schoolboy mythology of Mortmere, such symbolic cloak-and-dagger men as the Adversary and the Watcher in Spanish defeat all scholarly attempts to place them as political exemplars, but are easily apprehended as madly camp star turns at a drag ball. They are there to brighten the lives of secret men. As Auden wrote years later in "The Fall of Rome," all the literati keep an imaginary friend. Auden's artistic indulgence in the 1930s vocabulary of espionage—a vocabulary which was a matter of life and death to those from whom he borrowed it—seemed then, and can still seem now, trivial beyond forgiveness. It's worth remembering, though, that Auden was in a war too, and needed to hide himself just as deep. And his war had been going on since time out of mind.

To use his own phrase, the wicked card was dealt: in the face of totalitarianism, homosexuality was no longer a valid image for collective action. The world was not a school and adolescence was at long last over. Auden's exile began in earnest. In *New Year Letter* we learned that those hunted out of ordinary life are "wild quarry," but are granted the privilege of themselves becoming hunters—hunters of the past. *New Year Letter* is one of the synthetic works by which Auden accepted the responsibility of comprehending European culture—an acceptance which was to lead him in the course of time to his position as the most variously erudite poet since Goethe. The Strong Man had faded out and the Dictator was in control, leaving

> Culture on all fours to greet
> A butch and criminal élite

which is as clear, and personal, an image of violation as you could wish.

The innocence of young love retained its purity through knowledge, of itself and of the multiple past which justified the pluralist political dream—now solely an ideal, and more radiant for that—of the Just City.

White childhood moving like a sigh
Through the green woods unharmed in thy
Sophisticated innocence
To call thy true love to the dance.

In *Another Time,* his collection of lyrics from that period, Auden ushered in the new decade with a reiteration of his solitude:

Ten thousand soldiers marched to and fro:
Looking for you and me, my dear, looking for you and me.

The sentries were still walking the ridges. During the long decade of warfare and recovery they gradually and mysteriously grew fewer and less imbued with missionary zeal. In the decade between *Another Time* and *Nones* Auden seems to have faced the fact that art, politically speaking, has no future, only a past. Whatever Auden the person was up to, Auden the poet had begun to accept and love the world. He no longer thought of homosexuality as newness—just a permanent apartness. From *Nones* the diligent stylistic analyst will deduce that the poet's studies of the Oxford English Dictionary had got as far as the letter "C." The lover of his poetry will find that the period of dialectical tension has come to an end. Often taken as a gratuitous glibness, Auden's later insistence that all his poetry put together had not saved a single Jew was already a plain fact. Poetry, he had said even before the thirties were over, makes nothing happen. In *Nones* there was sardonic realism about love, but any idealism about it had been banished. What idealism there was was all about art, and the eternal order which art formed outside history.

As a mind, Auden curved away from the purely Germanic culture and developed a growing kinship with the all-embracing Latin one, of which he is indeed the true modern representative in English after Eliot. Despite his domicile in Austria and his involvement with German opera, his final affinity appears to have been with the thought of Valéry—whose shelf of N.R.F. paperbacks is the closest contemporary parallel to Auden's preoccupations with the aphorism and the ideal order of creativity.

In Christianity Auden found forgiveness for sin. But to redeem the luxuriance of his early cleverness he had to work out his own cure, and as with Dante the cure was *technical.* Holding his art to be a sacrament, Dante acted out his penitence in the form of technical behaviour. For the early sin of rhyming Christ's name with a dirty word he makes recompense in the *Divine Comedy* by never rhyming it with anything except itself—the only word to be so treated. The triadic symmetries of the *Divine Comedy* are a set of disciplines so strict that lyricism has no freedom to indulge itself: when it happens, it happens as a natural consequence of stating the truth. For the educated man, there is a moment of his early acquaintanceship with Dante when he realizes that all he has slowly taught himself to enjoy in poetry is everything that Dante has grown out of. A comparable moment of fear is to be had with Auden, when we understand that his slow change through the forties entails a renunciation of the art-thrill, and that the Audenesque dazzle is forever gone. For a poet to lose such a talent would have been a misfortune. For a poet to give it up was an act of disciplined renunciation rarely heard of in English.

A brief recapitulation of Auden's innovations in technical bravura is worth making at this point. Unlike Brecht, who wrote both "Die Moritat von Mackie Messer" and "Die Seeräuber-Jenny" in the year of Auden's first privately printed booklet, Auden never met his Kurt Weill. He met Britten, but the results were meagre. It is no denigration of Isherwood to say that if, of his two admired artistic types, Auden had teamed up with the Composer instead of the Novelist, modern English musical history would have been transformed. As it was, Auden's talent as a lyricist was never developed: the songs for Hedli Anderson had the melody-defeating line-turnovers of ordinary poems, and his activities as a librettist—whether writing originals for Stravinsky or translating *The Magic Flute*—seem to me frustrating in the recognizable modern English manner. Auden had command of a linear simplicity that would have suited the lyric to perfection. As it was, however, he stuck mainly to poetry; and anyway it's probable that the pressure of his homosexual indirectness would have distorted his linear simplicity as thoroughly as, and less fruitfully than, it dislocated his pictorial integrity. Alone with pencil and paper, Auden was free to explore his technical resources. They were without limit, Mozartian. Auden mastered all the traditional lyric forms as a matter of course, bringing to some of them—those which had been imported from rhyme-rich languages and for good reasons had never flourished—the only air of consummate ease they would ever possess. At the same time, he did a far more thorough job than even *vers libre* had done of breaking down the last vestiges of the artificial grip the lyric still had on the written poem. He produced apprehensible rhythmic unities which were irregular not only from line to line but within the lines themselves. Finally he penetrated within the word, halting its tendency toward slur and contraction, restoring its articulated rhythmic force. This is the technical secret behind his ability to sustain the trimeter and tetrameter over long distances, driving them forwards not along a fixed lattice-work of terminal and internal rhymes but with an incessant modulation across the vowel spectrum and the proliferating concatenated echoes of exploded consonantal groups.

Hazlitt said that Burke's style was as forked and playful as the lightning, crested like the serpent. Everybody sensitive to poetry, I think, has known the feeling that Auden's early work, with its unmatched technical brilliance, is an enchanted playground. The clear proof of his moral stature, however, is the way he left the playground behind when all were agreed that he had only to keep on adding to it and immortality would be his.

Auden's later books are a long—and sometimes long-winded—penitence for the heretical lapse of letting art do his thinking for him. In *Homage to Clio, About the House, City Without Walls* and *Epistle to a Godson,* he fulfils his aim of suppressing all automatic responses. A blend of metres and syllabics, his austere forms progressively empty themselves of all mesmeric flair. Auden conquers Selfhood by obliterating talent: what is left is the discipline of mechanical accomplishment, supporting the salt conclusions of a lifetime's thinking—cured wisdom. At the same time, Auden claimed the right to erase any of his early works he now thought were lies. A generation's favourites fell before his irascible, Tolstoyan scythe. His friend Louis MacNeice had once written that after a certain time the poet loses the right to get his finished poems back. Auden didn't agree with MacNeice's humility, just as he had never agreed with MacNeice's sense of usefulness: MacNeice had tired himself out serving the BBC instead of the Muse.

It is a common opinion among the English literati that Auden's later work is a collapse. I am so far from taking this view that I think an appreciation of Auden's later work is the only sure test for an appreciation of Auden, just as an appreciation of Yeats's earlier work is the only sure test for an appreciation of Yeats. You must know and admire the austerity which Auden achieved before you can take the full force of his early longing for that austerity—before you can measure the portent of his early brilliance. There is no question that the earlier work is more enjoyable. The question is about whether you think enjoyability was the full extent of his aim. Auden, it seems to me, is a modern artist who has lived out his destiny as a European master to the full, a man in whom all cultural history is present just as the sufferings of all the past were still alive in his lover's eyes:

> A look contains the history of Man,
> And fifty francs will earn the stranger right
> To warm the heartless city in his arms.

Famed stranger and exalted outcast, Auden served a society larger than the one in which he hid. In his later work we see not so much the ebbing of desire as its transference to the created world, until plains and hills begin explaining the men who live on them. Auden's unrecriminating generosity towards a world which had served him ill was a moral triumph. Those who try to understand it too quickly ought not to be trusted with grown-up books.

I was born in the month after Auden wrote "September 1, 1939," and saw him only three times. The first time, in Cambridge, about five years ago, he gave a poetry reading in Great St. Mary's. The second time, on the Cambridge-to-London train a year later, I was edging along to the buffet car when I noticed him sitting in a first-class compartment. When the train pulled in, I waited for him at the barrier and babbled some nonsense about being privileged to travel on the same train. He took it as his due and waved one of his enormous hands. The third time was earlier this year, in the Martini Lounge atop New Zealand House in London, where a reception was thrown for all of us who had taken part in the Poetry International Festival. Auden shuffled through in a suit encrusted with the dirt of years—it was a geological deposit, an archaeological pile-up like the seven cities of Troy. I don't think anybody of my generation knew what to say to him. I know I didn't. But we knew what to think, and on behalf of my contemporaries I have tried to write some of it down here. I can still remember those unlucky hands; one of them holding a cigarette, the other holding a brimming glass, and both trembling. The mind boggled at some of the things they had been up to. But one of them had refurbished the language. A few months later he was beyond passion, having gone to the reward which Dante says that poets who have done their duty might well enjoy—talking shop as they walk beneath the moon.

(*Commentary*, October 1973)

Robert Lowell's
Marble Chips

Of the three new books by Robert Lowell—all of them consisting, like their antecedent *Notebook,* of unrhymed sonnets—only *The Dolphin* contains entirely fresh material. It is dedicated to Lowell's new consort, Caroline, and deals with the life they are now leading together. *For Lizzie and Harriet* deals exclusively with the life Lowell has left behind: it isolates and reworks those poems concerning his ex-wife and daughter which were earlier scattered through *Notebook.* The central and bulkiest volume of the current three, *History,* is an extensive reworking and thoroughgoing reordering of all the remaining poems in *Notebook,* with eighty extra ones mixed in.

When we consider that *Notebook* itself had two earlier versions before being published in Britain, it is clear that there is a great deal going on. If mere bustle were creativity, then later Lowell would be the most creative thing in modern poetry. Daunted, the critic is tempted to hand the whole problem directly to the scholar and get the work of collating done before any judgements are hazarded. Unfortunately judgement will not wait—not least because these recent works offer an invitation to scholarship to start up a whole new branch of its industry, an invitation which will be all too eagerly accepted if criticism neglects to mark out the proper, and reasonably discreet, size of the job. Lowell is a giant, but his perimeter is still visible: there is no need to think that he fills the sky.

In so far as it had one, *Notebook*'s structure was rhapsodic—an adjective which, in its technical sense, we associate with the Homeric epic. As the poet stumbled in circles of crisis and collapse, digressions could occur in any direction, sub-sequences of the proliferating sonnets form round any theme. These sequences constituted rhapsodies, and it was easy to sense that the rhapsodies were intent on forming themselves into an epic. At that stage, the Lowell epic resembled John Berryman's *Dream Songs:* its digressions had shape, but there was no clear line of progress initiating them—no simple story for which they could serve as complications. The story was mixed in with them. All of human history was there, and Lowell's personal history was there too. Both kinds of history jumped about all over the place.

The new books have simplified everything, while simultaneously making a claim to universality that takes the reader's breath away. "My old title, *Notebook,* was more accurate than I wished, i.e., my composition was jumbled," writes the poet in a foreword. "I hope this jumble or jungle is cleared—that I have cut the waste marble from the figure." Cutting away the marble until the figure is revealed is an idea that reminds us— and is probably meant to remind us—of Michelangelo. As we realize that not even these new books need bring the matter to an end, the idea that the figure need never fully emerge from the marble also reminds us of Michelangelo. Lowell seems intent on having us believe that he is embarked on a creative task which absolves his talent from wasting too much time polishing its own products. He does a lot to make this intention respectable, and we soon see, when reading *History,* that although thousands of details have been altered since *Notebook,* the changes that really matter are in the grand structure. It is at this point that we temporarily cease thinking of marble and start thinking about, say, iron filings. *Notebook* was a random scattering of them. In *History* a magnet has been moved below, and suddenly everything has been shaken into a startling linear shape.

As rearranged and augmented in *History,* the sonnets begin at the dawn of creation and run chronologically all the way to recent events in the life of the poet. We have often thought, with Lowell, that history was being incorporated into the self. Here is the thing proved, and the pretension would be insupportable if it were not carried out with such resource. The information which Lowell commands about all cultures in all ages found a ragged outlet in *Notebook.* Deployed along a simple line of time, it gains in impressiveness—gains just enough to offset the realization that it is Lowell's propensity for reading his own problems into anything at all which makes him so ranging a time-traveller. *History* is the story of the world made intelligible in terms of one man's psychology. It is a neurotic work by definition. Nobody reasonable would ever think of starting it, and the moment Lowell begins to be reasonable is the moment he will stop. There is no good cause to assume, however, that Lowell any longer thinks it possible to be reasonable about history. Stephen Dedalus said history was a nightmare from which he was trying to awake. Raising the stakes, Lowell seems to believe that history is something you cannot appreciate without losing your sanity. This belief releases him into realms of artistic effect where reason would find it hard to go. That the same belief might bring inhibition, as well as release, is a separate issue.

Broadly, *History*'s progression is first of all from Genesis through the Holy Land to the Mediterranean, ancient Greece and Rome, with diversions to Egypt at the appropriate moments. Medieval Europe then gives way to the Renaissance and the Enlightenment, tipping over into the French Revolution. Through the complexities of the nineteenth century, strict chronological sequence is manfully adhered to, whether in painting, letters, music or ante- and post-bellum American politics. French symbolism sets the scene for the twentieth-century arts, while the First World War sets the tone for the modern politics of crisis and annihilation. The Russian Revolution throws forward its divisive shadow, which later on will split the New York intelligentsia. By this time Lowell's family history is active in all departments, and soon the poet himself arrives on stage. Everything that has happened since the dawn of humanity has tended to sound like something happening to Lowell. From here on this personal tone becomes intense, and those named—especially if they are artists— are mainly people the poet knows. By now, unquestionably, he is at the centre of events. But the book has already convinced us that all events, even the vast proportion of them that happened before he arrived in the world, are at the centre of him.

History is a long haul through places, things and, pre-eminently, names. Helen, Achilles, Cassandra, Orestes, Clytemnestra, Alexander, Hannibal, Horace, Juvenal, Dante, Villon, Anne Boleyn, Cranach, Charles V, Marlowe, Mary Stuart, Rembrandt, Milton, Pepys, Bishop Berkeley, Robespierre, Saint-Just, Napoleon, Beethoven, Goethe, Leopardi, Schubert, Heine, Thoreau, Henry Adams, George Eliot, Hugo, Baudelaire, Rimbaud, Mallarmé, Lady Cynthia Asquith, Rilke, George Grosz, Hardy, Al Capone, Ford Madox Ford, Allen Tate, Randall Jarrell, John Crowe Ransom, F. O. Matthiessen, Roethke, Delmore Schwartz, T. S. Eliot, Wyndham Lewis, MacNeice, William Carlos Williams, Robert Frost,

Stalin, Harpo Marx, Ché Guevara, Norman Mailer, Dwight Macdonald, Adrienne Rich, Mary McCarthy, Eugene McCarthy, Elizabeth Schwarzkopf, Martin Luther King, Robert Kennedy, de Gaulle, Lévi-Strauss, R. P. Blackmur, Stanley Kunitz, Elizabeth Bishop, I. A. Richards, John Berryman, Robert Lowell and many more: a cast of thousands. The range they cover, and the pertinent information Lowell is able to adduce when treating each one—these things are little short of astonishing. But they were already startling in *Notebook*. What makes these qualities doubly impressive now is the new effect of faces succeeding faces in due order. Leaving, of course, a thousand gaps—gaps which the poet seems understandably keen to set about filling.

Lizzie and Harriet's retributive presence in *Notebook* has been eliminated from *History* and given a book of its own. *The Dolphin* likewise enshrines a portion of Lowell's experience which is plainly not going to be allowed to overbalance the future of *History*. It is possible to suggest, given the dispersal of foci represented by these three volumes, that Lowell's "confessional" poetry is no longer his main thing. The *History* book now embodies his chief effort, and in relation to this effort the ordinary people inhabiting his life don't make the weight. *History* is full of public names, rather than private ones—public names united not so much by prestige as in their undoubted puissance in shaping, exemplifying or glorifying historic moments. In *History*, Lowell, alone, joins the great.

And the number of the great grows all the time. Instructive, in this respect, to take a close look at the *History* poem called "Cleopatra Topless," one of a short sequence of poems concerning her. Where have we seen it before? Was it in *Notebook*? But in *Notebook* it is untraceable in the list of contents. Where was it, then? The answer is that the poem *is* in *Notebook* but is called simply "Topless" and has nothing to do with Cleopatra. In the *Notebook* poem she's just a girl in a night-club:

> She is the girl
> as Renoir, Titian and all full times have left her

To convert her into Cleopatra, it is only necessary to get rid of the inappropriate Renoir and Titian, filling the space with a line or so about what men desire. Throughout *History* the reader is continually faced with material which has apparently been dragged in to fill a specific chronological spot. Nor does this material necessarily have its starting-point in

Notebook: the fact that it appears in that volume, if it does appear, doesn't preclude its having begun its life in an earlier, and often far earlier, Lowell collection. For example, a version of Valéry's "Hélène" is in *Imitations,* with the inspiration for it credited to Valéry. By the time it arrives in *History,* it is credited to no one but Lowell. It is true that the drive of the verse has been weakened with over-explanatory adjectives:

> My solitary hands recall the kings
> *(Imitations)*
> My loving hands recall the absent kings
> *(History)*
> Mes solitaires mains appellent les monarques
> (Valéry)

But this is incidental. As we can see abundantly in other places, Lowell's minor adjustments are just as likely to impart point as detract from it. Fundamentally important, however, is the way the imitation has been saddled with extraneous properties (Agamemnon, Ulysses) in order to bolster it for the significance it is being asked to provide in its new slot. Though making regular appearances in the early sections of *History,* Agamemnon and Ulysses are nowhere mentioned in Valéry's poem. But then, the poem is no longer Valéry's: in *History* the source is uncredited.

Trusting to the itch of memory and ransacking the library shelves in order to scratch it, the reader soon learns that Lowell has been cannibalizing his earlier works of translation and imitation—cutting them up into fourteen-line lengths and introducing them with small ceremony first of all into *Notebook* and later, on the grand scale, into *History.* Usually the provenance of the newly installed sonnet is left unmentioned. There are exceptions to this: the "Le Cygne" of *Notebook,* which the gullible might have attributed to Lowell, has a better chance of being traceable to its origins now that it is called "Mallarmé 1. Swan." It is in fact the second of the "Plusieurs Sonnets" in *Poésies* and is called—after its first line—"Le Vierge, le vivace et le bel aujourd'hui." In *Notebook,* Lowell had "blind" for *vivace,* an inscrutable boldness which in *History* has been softened to "alive." Other improvements in the new version are less welcome: "the horror of the ice that ties his wings" is a reversal of Mallarmé's sense, which in the *Notebook* version had been got right. Mallarmé is saying that the swan *accepts* the ice. Here Lowell seems to have been improving his first version without reference to the original. On the other hand, he has now substituted "wings" for "feet" and thereby humbly returned much closer to *plumage.* The key phrase, *l'exil inutile,* which is ringingly present in the *Notebook* version, is now strangely absent. Anyone who attempts to trace poems back through *Notebook* to their sources in foreign literatures is fated to be involved in these niggling questions at all, times. But at least, with such a clear signpost of a title, there is a hint that this particular poem *has* such a history. In many cases even this tenuous condition does not obtain.

When a bright young American scholar produces a properly indexed Variorum Lowell—preferably with a full concordance—it will be easier to speak with confidence about what appears in *History* that is not in *Notebook.* A good few poems appear in both with different titles, and it is difficult for even the keenest student to hold the entire mass of material clearly in his mind. But if *History*'s "Baudelaire 1. The Abyss" is not in *Notebook,* it was in *Imitations,* where it was billed as a version of "Le Gouffre." There it reduced Baudelaire's fourteen lines to thirteen. Now it is back to being a sonnet again, and the *Êtres* are now rendered as "being" instead of "form," which one takes to be a net gain. One is less sure that the poem's provenance would be so recognizable if it were not for the memory of the *Imitations* version. The question keeps on cropping up—are we supposed to know that such material started out in another poet's mind, or are we supposed to accept it as somehow being all Lowell's? Is it perhaps that Lowell is putting himself forward as the representative of all past poets? It should be understood that one is not questioning Lowell's right to employ allusion, or to embody within his own work a unity of culture which he feels to be otherwise lost. The ethics are not the problem; the aesthetics are. Because none of these poems carries the same weight when presented as ordinary Lowell as it does when its history is clearly seen to be still surrounding it.

"Baudelaire 2. Recollection" was called "Meditation" in *Imitations* and is thus a revision of a version of "Recueillement." It is interesting to see that *va cueillir des remords* now means "accumulating remorse" rather than the previous and unfathomable "fights off anguish." Minor satisfactions like that can be clung to while the reader totals "Baudelaire 1. The Abyss" and "Baudelaire 2. Recollection" and glumly reconciles himself to the fact that that's his lot on Baudelaire—two revamped imitations.

Rimbaud does better. Five sonnets. But all five turn out to have been in a sequence of eight versions printed in *Imitations*. "Rimbaud 1. Bohemia" was called "On the Road" and is a version of "Ma Bohème"; "Rimbaud 2. A Knowing Girl" was called "A Knowing Girl" and is a version of "La Maline"; "Rimbaud 3. Sleeper in the Valley" was more expansively called "The Sleeper in the Valley" and is a version of "Le Dormeur du val"; "Rimbaud 4. The Evil" was less expansively called "Evil" and is a version of "Le Mal"; "Rimbaud 5. Napoleon After Sedan" was called "Napoleon After Sedan," is a version of "Rages de Césars" and was the only one of the five to have made an intermediary appearance in *Notebook*, where it was called "Rimbaud and Napoleon III." With this last poem, then, we have three separate texts to help send us cross-eyed, but if we can concentrate long enough we will see a characteristic change. The *Imitations* version is shaped like the original and confines itself to the original's material, plus a few scraps of interpolated elucidatory matter (where Rimbaud just said "Compère," Lowell tactfully adds some explanatory horses) and of course the inevitable intensifying of the verbs. The *Notebook* version is no longer readily identifiable as an imitation: the stanza-breaks have been eliminated, the first four lines are a piece of scene-setting which have nothing to do with the original, and Robespierre's name has been introduced, answering a question—*"quel nom sur ses lèvres muettes/Tressaille?"*—which Rimbaud had left unanswered. The *History* version gets the fidgets, throwing out Compère but leaving the horses. By this time, you would need to be pretty thoroughly acquainted with Rimbaud if you were to spot the poem as anything but neat Lowell.

Of the other Rimbaud poems, "La Maline" is now closer to the way Rimbaud wrote it than the *Imitations* version, but Lowell's "Ma Bohème" misses by just as far as it used to, though in a different way:

> September twilight on September twilight.
> *(Imitations)*
> September twilights and September twilights
> *(History)*

A minor alteration to a major aberration: the repetition is not in Rimbaud and does nothing for his meaning whichever way Lowell puts it.

Material which had its starting-point in *Imitations* can be changed to any extent from slightly to drastically on its way to a fourteen-line living-space in *History*. Lowell's version of "L'Infinito" is squeezed by three lines but is otherwise the poem we have come to recognize as probably the least sympathetic translation of Leopardi ever committed. "Hugo at Théophile Gautier's Grave" is a rearrangement of an *Imitations* version of Hugo's "A Théophile Gautier" which had already cut the original by more than half. "Sappho to a Girl" was in *Notebook* as just "Sappho," and is a mosaic of bits and pieces which can be seen in *Imitations* still mounted in their original settings—i.e., versions of the poem to the bride Anactoria (No. 141 in the *Oxford Book of Greek Verse*) and that tiny, lovely poem to Night (No. 156) which contains the line about the Pleiads. In his *Imitations* version Lowell left the Pleiads out. In the *Notebook* version they were still out. In the *History* version he put them back in. The card-player, who is in all three versions, seems not to belong to Sappho, but could conceivably belong to Cézanne.

Imitations, however, is not the only source of workable stone. *Notebook/History* is Lowell's Renaissance and like the Renaissance in Rome it doesn't question its right to use all the monuments of the ancient city as a quarry. *History*'s "Horace: Pardon for a Friend" started life, at twice the length, as a version of Horace's *Odes* II, 7, in *Near the Ocean*. In the same collection first appeared "Juvenal's Prayer," which at that stage constituted the last nineteen lines of a version of Juvenal's tenth *Satire*. And to return briefly to Cleopatra, "Nunc est bibendum, Cleopatra's Death" is (as the title this time allows) another imitation, or at least a fragment of one—Horace's *Odes* I, 37, which in *Near the Ocean* can be found imitated in full.

And still they come, racing out of the past to find their new home. *History*'s "Caligula 2" is part of a much longer Caligula in *For the Union Dead*. And from as far back as *Lord Weary's Castle*, "In the Cage" is an acknowledged reworking, with the attention now turning from the observed to the observer. But other material from the same early period is less easily spotted. The sonnet "Charles V by Titian," for example, was called "Charles the Fifth and the Peasant" in *Lord Weary's Castle*, where it was subtitled "After Valéry" and appeared to be a version of his "César" in which almost every property, Titian included, was an interpolation. *History*'s "Dante 3. Buonconte" goes back to a poem in *Lord Weary's Castle* called "The Soldier," which was modelled on the Buonconte da Montefeltro episode in *Purgatorio* V. Here we have a clear case of the way Lowell's wide learning has matured with the years: he nowadays quietly and correctly renders *la croce* as Buonconte's hands folded on his chest, rather than as a crucifix—a subtly rich textual point of the kind which Lowell at his best is brilliantly equipped to bring out. Restored from an unwieldy third person to the direct first person of the original, this poem is easily the best of those devoted to Dante: "Dante 4. Paolo and Francesca" is a copy-book example of how Lowell's irrepressible extremism of language is unable to match the flow of lyrical Italian—and unabashed lyricism is a good half of Francesca's self-deluding personality. Lowell takes Francesca's side against the oppressors of her flesh. If it has occurred to him that Dante didn't, he doesn't say so. In the Dante rhapsody as a whole, we are able to see that below the uniform intensity of Lowell's language there is a uniform intensity of psychology—a certain monotony of feeling. Dante's love for Beatrice is presented rather as if the relationship between work and love bore strong resemblances to that same relationship in the life of Robert Lowell. Could Lowell find means, we wonder, to convey the fact that with Dante the consuming, disabling passion was just as likely to be for philosophy as for sex?

For all the examples cited above, elementary sleuthing suffices to trace the origins—either the title gives a clue or else the poem is more or less intact and can't fail to jog the reader's memory. But it's doubtful if the cannibalizing process stops there, and at this stage it's probably safer to assume that Lowell regards none of his earlier work, whether imitative or original, as exempt from requisitioning and a reconstruction ranging from mild to violent. For example, in a *History* poem called "The Spartan Dead at Thermopylae" the lines about Leonidas are lifted straight from the *Imitations* version of Rilke's "Die Tauben." Pretty well untraceable; if these lines weren't original Lowell then, they are now.

Lowell's discovery of a linear historical structure for *History* has opened the way to a poet's dream—the simple line allowing infinite complication. The sudden insatiable demand for material has sent him raiding back over all his past poetry—not necessarily just the translations—in a search for stuff that fits. A great deal does. On the other hand, isn't there something Procrustean about carving up all that past work into fourteen-line chunks? To get back to Michelangelo and the marble, it's as if Michelangelo were to pick up a power-saw and slice through everything from the Madonna of the Stairs to the Rondanini Pietà at a height of fourteen inches.

Whatever Procrustes might have thought, trimming things to fit an arbitrary frame is not a discipline. And without its rhyme-schemes, the sonnet is an arbitrary frame. There are many times in *Notebook/History* when the reader thrills to the impact of an idea achieving a formal measure almost in spite of itself:

> I hear the catbird's coloratura cluck
> singing fuck, fuck above the brushwood racket.
> The feeder deals catfood like cards to the yearling
> salmon in their stockpond by the falls.

The singing power of the mimesis, the clashing couplings of the shunting assonance, the muscle of the enjambement: if there were a single sonnet wholly assembled with such care, then one would not even have to set oneself to learn it—it would teach itself. But fragments are the most we get. Lowell's later method might allow some parts of his talent free play but it allows his technique only child's play. "I want words meat-hooked from the living steer," he writes in the course of rebuking Valéry for preferring six passable lines to one inspired one. He gets what he wants: meat-hooked words and inspired lines. But what one misses, and goes on missing until it aches, is form.

Still, within the limits he has now set for it—the liberating limits, as he sees them—Lowell's talent is still operating, and still majestic. There are times when nothing has happened except language yet you must helplessly concede that the vitality of his language is unique:

> Man turns dimwit quicker than the mayfly
> fast goes the lucid moment of love believed;

And there are times when the language subsides into nothing special, but the visualizing faculty reveals itself for the hundredth time as a profound gift:

> coming back to Kenyon on the Ohio local—
> the view, middle distance, back and foreground, shifts,
> silos shifting squares like chessmen—

What an idea! But in all the vast expanse of *Notebook/History* there are not many times when both things come together, and none at all when a poem sustains itself in the way to which Lowell once made us accustomed. There is no doubt that Lowell has abandoned his old course deliberately. Nor is there any doubt that he has opened up for himself an acreage of subject-matter which could never have been reached in the old way. But we still have to decide if what we are being given is poetry or something else. Of some comfort here is that Lowell appears to be still undecided himself.

If we set aside the decisive alteration of structure which turned the circularity of *Notebook* into the linear stride of *History,* all the minor changes seem to have been made with the fidgeting lack of direction that you might expect from a writer who somehow feels compelled to refurbish the deliberately formless. Most of the attention has been expended on points of language: it's too late by now to go back to fourteen passable lines, but apparently there is still hope of drumming up the odd inspired one. All too frequently, the striving for intensity results in a further, incomprehensible compression of an idea already tightened to the limit. In the *Notebook* version of "In the Forties 1":

> Green logs sizzled on the fire-dogs,
> painted scarlet like British Redcoats. . . .

Whereas the *History* version has:

> greenwood sizzling on the andirons,
> two men of iron, two milk-faced British Redcoats.

Without a knowledge of the first version, it would be hard to guess what the second might mean; the idea of the red paint has become familiar to Lowell, and he has got rid of it without pausing to reflect that we will have trouble following the idea unless it is spelled out to some extent. Scores of these changes for the worse could be adduced. Other changes are simply neutral. In *Notebook*'s "Harriet 2," the fly is like a plane gunning potato bugs. Appearing again in the sonnet "Summer 2" in *For Lizzie and Harriet,* the fly is like a plane dusting apple orchards. The second version is perhaps preferable for its verb being the more easily appreciated, but on the other hand potato bugs have more verve than apple orchards. It's a toss-up.

Another kind of change is incontestably for the better. In *History* Robert Frost's voice is "musical and raw" rather than, as in *Notebook,* "musical, raw and raw." One had always wondered why the repetition was there, and now one finds that Lowell had been wondering the same thing. In *Notebook* Frost was supposed to have inscribed a volume "Robert Lowell from Robert Frost, his friend in the art." In *History* this becomes "For Robert from Robert, his friend in the art." Much chummier. Was Lowell, for modesty's sake, misquoting the first time? Or is he, for immodesty's sake, misquoting now? It is impossible to tell, but grappling with the implications of these minor shifts is one of the involving things about reading all these books together.

The comparison between *Notebook* and *History* could go on for ever, and probably will. Discovering that the *Notebook* poem for Louis MacNeice is reproduced in *History* with one of its lines doubled and another line dropped—a really thunderous printer's error—one wonders distractedly if anybody else knows. Does Lowell know? It's large territory to become familiar with, even for him. Finally one decides that getting familiar with it is as far as appreciation can go. To recognize details is possible; but there is small hope of remembering the whole thing. Like Berryman's *Dream Songs*, Lowell's *Notebook/History/For Lizzie and Harriet* defeats memory. Perhaps *The Dolphin* is heading back to the way things were, but on examination it starts yielding the kind of names— Hölderlin, Manet—which make us think that most of it is fated to end up in the next version of *History*. In *The Dolphin* the only human, unhistoried, unsignificant voice occurs in the quoted parts of Lizzie's letters. If Lowell wrote them, he should write more. But there isn't much point in saying "should." The outstanding American poet is engaged in writing his version of the poem that Pound, Williams and Berryman have each already attempted—The Big One. Lowell thinks he is chipping away the marble to get at the statue. It's more likely that he is trying to build a statue out of marble chips. Who cares about history if poetry gets thrown away? Perhaps he does. And anyway the poetry was his to throw.

(*Times Literary Supplement*, 10 August 1973)

Don Juan in Hull:
Philip Larkin

Larkin collections come out at the rate of one per decade: *The North Ship*, 1945; *The Less Deceived*, 1955; *The Whitsun Weddings*, 1964; *High Windows*, 1974. Not exactly a torrent of creativity: just the best. In Italy the reading public is accustomed to cooling its heels for even longer. Their top man, Eugenio Montale, has produced only five main collections, and he got started a good deal earlier. But that, in both countries, is the price one has to pay. For both poets the parsimony is part of the fastidiousness. Neither writes an unconsidered line.

Now that the latest Larkin, *High Windows*, is finally available, it is something of a shock to find in it some poems one doesn't recognize. Clipping the poems out of magazines has failed to fill the bill—there were magazines one hadn't bargained for. As well as that, there is the surprise of finding that it all adds up even better than one had expected: the poems which one had thought of as characteristic turn out to be more than that —or rather the *character* turns out to be more than that. Larkin has never liked the idea of an artist Developing. Nor has he himself done so. But he has managed to go on clarifying what he was sent to say. The total impression of *High Windows* is of despair made beautiful. Real despair and real beauty, with not a trace of posturing in either. The book is the peer of the previous two mature collections, and if they did not exist would be just as astonishing. But they do exist (most of us could recognize any line from either one) and can't help rendering many of the themes in this third book deceptively familiar.

I think that in most of the poems here collected Larkin's ideas are being reinforced or deepened rather than repeated. But from time to time a certain predictability of form indicates that a previous discovery is being unearthed all over again. Such instances aren't difficult to spot, and it would be intemperate to betray delight at doing so. Larkin's "forgeries" (Auden's term for self-plagiarisms) are very few. He is more original from poem to poem than almost any modern poet one can think of. His limitations, such as they are, lie deeper than that. Here again, it is not wise to be happy about spotting them. Without the limitations there would be no Larkin—the beam cuts *because* it's narrow.

It has always seemed to me a great pity that Larkin's more intelligent critics should content themselves with finding his view of life circumscribed. It is, but it is also bodied forth as art to a remarkable degree. There is a connection between the circumscription and the poetic intensity, and it's no surprise that the critics who can't see the connection can't see the separation either. They seem to think that just because the poet is (self-admittedly) emotionally wounded, the poetry is wounded too. There is always the suggestion that Larkin might handle his talent better if he were a more well-rounded character. That Larkin's gift might be part and parcel of his own peculiar nature isn't a question they have felt called upon to deal with. The whole fumbling dereliction makes you wonder if perhaps the literati in this country haven't had things a bit easy. A crash-course in, say, art criticism could in most cases be recommended. Notions that Michelangelo would have painted more feminine-looking sibyls if he had been less bent, or that Toulouse-Lautrec might have been less obsessive about Jane Avril's dancing if his legs had been longer, would at least possess the merit of being self-evidently absurd. But the brainwave about Larkin's quirky negativism, and the consequent trivialization of his lyrical knack, is somehow able to go on sounding profound.

It ought to be obvious that Larkin is not a universal poet in the thematic sense—in fact, he is a self-proclaimed stranger to a good half, *the* good half, of life. You wonder what a critic who complains of this imagines he is praising when he allows that Larkin is still pretty good anyway, perhaps even great. What's missing in Larkin doesn't just tend to be missing, it's glaringly, achingly, unarguably *missing*. But the poetry is all there. The consensus about his stature is consequently encouraging, even if accomplished at the cost of a majority of its adherents misunderstanding what is really going on. At least they've got the right man.

The first poem in the book, "To the Sea," induces a fairly heavy effect of *déjà lu*. Aren't we long used to that massive four-stanza form, that conjectural opening ("To step over the low wall . . .") in the infinitive? Actually we aren't: he's never used them before. It's the tone that's reminiscent, and the tactics. The opening takes us back to the childhood and the lost chance of happiness, the shots that all fell wide—

> The miniature gaiety of seasides.

In the familiar way, sudden brutalities of diction bite back a remembered sweetness—

> A white steamer stuck in the afternoon.

Alienation is declared firmly as the memories build up—

> Strange to it now, I watch the cloudless scene:

Details well up in the mind with Proustian specificity—

> . . . and then the cheap cigars,
> The chocolate-papers, tea-leaves, and, between
> The rocks, the rusting soup-tins . . .

The mind, off guard, unmanned by recollection, lets slip the delicately expressed lyrical image—

> The white steamer has gone. Like breathed-on glass
> The sunlight has turned milky.

Whereupon, as in "Church-Going" or "The Whitsun Weddings," the poem winds up in a sententious coda.

> . . . If the worst
> Of flawless weather is our falling short

It may be that through habit these do best,
Coming to water clumsily undressed
Yearly, teaching their children by a sort
Of clowning; helping the old, too, as they ought.

The happiness we once thought we could have can't be had, but simple people who stick to time-honoured habits probably get the best approximation of it. Larkin once said that if he were called in to construct a religion he would make use of water. Well, here it is, lapping at the knobbled feet of unquestioning plebs. Such comfort as the poem offers the reader resides in the assurance that this old habit of going to the seaside is "still going on," even if reader and writer no longer share it. A cold comfort, as always. Larkin tries, he has said, to preserve experience both for himself and for others, but his first responsibility is to the experience.

The next big poem is the famous three-part effort that appeared in the *Observer*, "Livings." A galley proof of it is still folded into the back of my copy of *The Less Deceived*. I think it an uncanny piece of work. The proof is read to shreds, and I can still remember the day I picked it up in the office. Larkin had the idea—preserved, in concentrated form, in one of the poems in this volume, "Posterity"—that a young American Ph.D. student called Jake Balokowsky is all set to wrap him up in an uncomprehending thesis. The first part of "Livings" is full of stuff that Balokowsky is bound to get wrong. The minor businessman who annually books himself into "the ——— Hotel in ——ton for three days" speaks a vocabulary as well-rubbed and subtly anonymous as an old leather couch. Balokowsky will latch on well enough to the idea that the poem's narrator is a slave to habit,

> wondering why
> I keep on coming. It's not worth it. Father's dead:
> He used to, but the business now is mine.
> It's time for change, in nineteen twenty-nine.

What Jake will probably miss, however, is the value placed on the innocuous local newspaper, the worn décor, the ritual chat, the non-challenging pictures and the ex-Army sheets. It's dependable, it's a living; and "living" is not a word Larkin tosses around lightly. Judging the narrator is the last thing Larkin is doing. On the contrary, he's looking for his secret. To be used to comfort is an enviable condition. Beer, whisky, cigars and silence—the privileges of the old mercantile civilization which Larkin has been quietly celebrating most of his life, a civilization in which a place like Leeds or Hull (see "Friday Night in the Royal Station Hotel") counts as a capital city. There *is* another and bigger life, but Larkin doesn't underestimate this one for a minute.

In fact he conjures it up all over again in the third part of the poem. The setting this time is Oxford, probably in the late seventeenth century. The beverage is port instead of whisky, and the talk, instead of with wages, tariffs and stock, deals with advowsons, resurrections and regicide. Proofs of God's existence lie uncontested on dusty bookshelves. "The bells discuss the hour's gradations." Once again the feeling of indoor warmth is womb-like. Constellations sparkle over the roofs, matching the big sky draining down the estuary in Part I.

The central poem of the trio squirms like a cat caught between two cushions. Its narrator is conducting a lone love affair with the sea.

> Rocks writhe back to sight.
> Mussels, limpets,
> Husband their tenacity
> In the freezing slither—
> Creatures, I cherish you!

The narrator's situation is not made perfectly clear. While wanting to be just the reverse, Larkin can on occasion be a difficult poet, and here, I think, is a case of over-refinement leading to obscurity. (Elsewhere in this volume, "Sympathy in White Major" is another instance, and I have never been able to understand "Dry Point" in *The Less Deceived*.) My guess—and a guess is not as good as an intelligent deduction—is that the speaker is a lighthouse keeper. The way the snow ("O loose moth world") swerves against the black water and the line "Guarded by brilliance" seem somehow to suggest that: that, or something similar. Anyway, whoever he is, the narrator is right in among the elements, watching the exploding sea and the freezing slither from seventy feet up on a stormy night. But we see at the end that he, too, is safe indoors. On the radio he hears of elsewhere. He sets out his plate and spoon, cherishing his loneliness. In this central panel of his triptych, it seems to me, Larkin is saying that the civilizations described in the side-panels—one decaying, the other soon to lose its confidence—have an essence, and that this is it. The essence can be preserved in the soul of a man on his own. This is not to suggest that there is anything consolingly positive under Larkin's well-known negativism: the only consoling thing about Larkin is the quality of his art.

"High Windows," the next stand-out poem, shows an emotional progression Larkin had already made us used to.

> When I see a couple of kids
> And guess he's fucking her and she's
> Taking pills or wearing a diaphragm,
> I know this is paradise. . . .

Larkin is a master of language-levels and eminently qualified to use coarse language for shock effects. He never does, however. Strong language in Larkin is put in not to shock the reader but to define the narrator's personality. When Larkin's narrator in "A Study of Reading Habits" (in *The Whitsun Weddings*) said "Books are a load of crap," there were critics—some of them, incredibly, among his more appreciative—who allowed themselves to believe that Larkin was expressing his own opinion. (Kingsley Amis had the same kind of trouble, perhaps from the same kind of people, when he let Jim Dixon cast aspersions on Mozart.) It should be obvious at long last, however, that the diction describes the speaker. When the speaker is close to representing Larkin himself, the diction defines which Larkin it is—what mood he is in. Larkin is no hypocrite and has expressed envy of young lovers too often to go back on it here. The word "fucking" is a conscious brutalism, a protective way of not conjuring up what's meant. However inevitable it might be that Jake Balokowsky will identify this opening sentiment as a Muggeridgean gesture of contempt, it is incumbent on us to realize that something more interesting is going on.

Everyone young is going down "the long slide" to happiness. The narrator argues that his own elders must have thought the same about him, who was granted freedom from the fear of Hellfire in the same way that the kids are granted freedom from the fear of pregnancy.

But (and here comes the clincher) attaining either freedom means no more than being lifted up to a high window, through which you see

> . . . the deep blue air, that shows
> Nothing, and is nowhere, and is endless.

There is no doubt that the narrator is calling these callous sexual activities meaningless. What's open to doubt is whether the narrator believes what he is saying, or, given that he does, whether Larkin (wheels within wheels) believes the narrator. Later in the volume there is a poem called "Annus Mirabilis" which clearly contradicts the argument of "High Windows."

> Sexual intercourse began
> In nineteen sixty-three
> (Which was rather late for me)—
> Between the end of the Chatterley ban
> And the Beatles' first LP.

Evincing an unexpected sensitivity to tone, Jake could well detect an ironic detachment here. To help him out, there is a suggestion, in the third stanza, that the new liberty was merely licence.

> And every life became
> A brilliant breaking of the bank,
> A quite unlosable game.

It all links up with the bleak view of "High Windows." What Jake might not spot, however, is that it contrasts more than it compares. "Annus Mirabilis" *is* a jealous poem—the fake-naïve rhythms are there for self-protection as much as for ironic detachment. Larkin can't help believing that sex and love ought by rights to have been easier things for his generation, and far easier for him personally. The feeling of having missed out on something is one of his preoccupations. The thing Balokowsky needs to grasp is that Larkin is not criticizing modern society from a position of superiority. Over the range of his poetry, if not always in individual poems, he is very careful to allow that these pleasures might very well be thought meaningful. That he himself finds them meaningless might have something to do with himself as well as the state of the world. To the reader who has Larkin's poetry by heart, no poet seems more open. Small wonder that he finds it simply incomprehensible when critics discuss his lack of emotion. Apart from an outright yell for help, he has sent every distress signal a shy man can.

"The Old Fools"—even the ex-editor of the *Listener* blew his cool over that one, billing it as "marvellous" on the paper's mast-head. And marvellous it is, although very scary. There is a pronounced technical weakness in the first stanza. It is all right to rhyme "remember" with "September" if you make it quite clear why September can't be July. Does it mean that the Old Fools were in the Home Guard in September 1939? It's hard to know. Apart from that one point, though, the poem is utterly and distressingly explicit. Once again, the brutalism of the opening diction is a tip-off to the narrator's state of mind, which is, this time, fearful.

> What do they think has happened, the old fools,
> To make them like this? Do they somehow suppose
> It's more grown-up when your mouth hangs open and drools. . . .

Ill-suppressed anger. The crack about supposing "it's more grown-up" is a copy-book example of Larkin's ability to compact his intelligibility without becoming ambiguous. Supposing something to be "more grown-up" is something children do: ergo, the Old Fools are like children—one of the poem's leading themes stated in a single locution.

> Why aren't they screaming?

Leaving the reader to answer: because they don't know what's happening to them. The narrator's real fears—soon he switches to a personal "you" —are for himself. The second stanza opens with an exultant lyrical burst: stark terror never sounded lovelier.

> At death, you break up: the bits that were you
> Start speeding away from each other for ever
> With no one to see. It's only oblivion, true:
> We had it before, but then it was going to end,

And was all the time merging with a unique endeavour
To bring to bloom the million-petalled flower
Of being here.

The old, he goes on to suggest, probably live not in the here and now but "where all happened once." The idea takes some of its force from our awareness that that's largely where Larkin lives already—only his vision could lead to this death. The death is terrifying, but we would have to be like Larkin to share the terror completely. The reader tends to find himself shut out, glad that Larkin can speak so beautifully in his desperation but sorry that he should see the end in terms of his peculiar loneliness. There is always the edifying possibility, however, that Larkin is seeing the whole truth and the reader's defence mechanisms are working full blast.

If they are, "The Building" will quickly break them down. Here, I think, is the volume's masterpiece—an absolute chiller, which I find myself getting by heart despite a pronounced temperamental aversion. The Building is the house of death, a Dantesque hell-hole—one thinks particularly of *Inferno* V—where people "at that vague age that claims / The end of choice, the last of hope" are sent to "their appointed levels." The ambience is standard modernist humdrum: paperbacks, tea, rows of steel chairs like an airport lounge. You can look down into the yard and see red brick, lagged pipes, traffic. But the smell is frightening. In time everyone will find a nurse beckoning to him. The dead lie in white rows somewhere above. This, says Larkin with an undeflected power unique even for him, is what it all really adds up to. Life is a dream and we awake to this reality.

O world.
Your loves, your chances, are beyond the stretch
Of any hand from here! And so, unreal,
A touching dream to which we all are lulled
But wake from separately. In it, conceits
And self-protecting ignorance congeal
To carry life. . . .

There is no point in disagreeing with the man if that's the way he feels, and he wouldn't write a poem like "The Building" if he didn't feel that way to the point of daemonic possession. He himself is well aware that there are happier ways of viewing life. It's just that he is incapable of sharing them, except for fleeting moments—and the fleeting moments do not accumulate, whereas the times in between them do. The narrator says that "nothing contravenes / The coming dark." It's an inherently less interesting proposition than its opposite, and a poet forced to devote his creative effort to embodying it has only a small amount of space to work in. Nor, within the space, is he free from the paradox that his poems will become part of life, not death. From that paradox, we gain. The desperation of "The Building" is like the desperation of Leopardi, disconsolate yet doomed to being beautiful. The advantage which accrues is one of purity—a hopeless affirmation is the only kind we really want to hear when we feel, as sooner or later everybody must, that life is a trap.

There is no certain way of separating Larkin's attitude to society from his conception of himself, but to the extent that you can, he seems to be in two minds about what the world has come to. He thinks, on the one hand, that it's probably all up; and on the other hand that youth still has a chance. On the theme of modern life being an unmitigated and steadily intensifying catastrophe he reads like his admired Betjeman in a murderous mood—no banana blush or cheery telly teeth, just a tight-browed disdain and a toxic line of invective. "Going, Going" is particularly instructive here. In "How Distant" we hear about

> . . . the departure of young men
> Down valleys, or watching
> The green shore past the salt-white cordage
> Rising and falling

Between the "fraying cliffs of water" (always a good sign when there's a lot of water about) the young adventurers used to sail, in the time of what we might call *genuine newness*. Larkin's objections to modern innovation are centered on its lack of invention—it's all fatally predictable. Jimmy Porter was nostalgic for the future. Larkin is anticipatory about the past. He longs for the time when youth meant the possibility of a new start.

> This is being young,
> Assumption of the startled century
> Like new store clothes,

> The huge decisions printed out by feet
> Inventing where they tread,
> The random windows conjuring a street.

The implication being that the time of adventure is long over. But in "Sad Steps," as the poet addresses the Moon, youth is allowed some hope.

> One shivers slightly, looking up there.
> The hardness and the brightness and the plain
> Far-reaching singleness of that wide stare
>
> Is a reminder of the strength and pain
> Of being young; that it can't come again,
> But is for others undiminished somewhere.

An elegantly cadenced admission that his own view of life might be neurotic, and excellent fuel for Jake's chapter on the dialectical element in Larkin in which it is pointed out that his poems are judiciously disposed in order to illuminate one another, Yeats-style. The Sun and Moon, like Water, bring out Larkin's expansiveness, such as it is. It's there, but you couldn't call it a bear-hug. Time is running out, as we hear in the wonderfully funny *Vers de Société:*

> Only the young can be alone freely.
> The time is shorter now for company,
> And sitting by a lamp more often brings
> Not peace, but other things.

Visions of The Building, for example.

The book ends on an upbeat. Its next to last poem, "Show Saturday," is an extended, sumptuous evocation of country life ("Let it always be there") which has the effect of making the rural goings-on so enviably cosy that the reader feels almost as left out as the narrator. The final piece is an eery lyric called "The Explosion," featuring the ghosts of miners walking from the sun towards their waiting wives. It is a superb thought superbly expressed, and Larkin almost believes in it, just as in "An Arundel Tomb" (the closing poem of *The Whitsun Weddings*) he almost believed in the survival of love. Almost believing is all right, once you've got believing out of it. But faith itself is extinct. Larkin loves and inhabits tradition as much as Betjeman does, but artistically he had already let go of it when others were only just realizing it was time to cling on. Larkin is the poet of the void. The one affirmation his work offers is the possibility that when we have lost everything the problem of beauty will still remain. It's enough.

(*Encounter*, June 1974)

The Sherlockologists

Sir Arthur Conan Doyle wrote little about Sherlock Holmes compared with what has been written by other people since. Sherlock has always been popular, on a scale never less than world-wide, but the subsidiary literature which has steadily heaped up around him can't be accounted for merely by referring to his universal appeal. Sherlockology—the adepts call it that, with typical whimsy—is a sort of cult, which has lately become a craze. The temptation to speculate about why this should be is one I don't propose to resist, but first there is the task of sorting the weighty from the witless in the cairn of Sherlockiana—they say that, too—currently available. What follows is a preliminary classification, done with no claims to vocational, or even avocational, expertise. Most decidedly not: this is a field in which all credentials, and especially impeccable ones, are suspect. To give your life, or any significant part of it, to the study of Sherlock Holmes is to defy reason.

It is also to disparage Doyle, as John Fowles pointed out in his introduction to *The Hound of the Baskervilles,* one of the four Sherlock Holmes novels handsomely reissued in Britain early last year, each as a single volume. This is an expensive way of doing things, but the books are so good-looking it is hard to quarrel, although the childhood memory of reading all the Sherlock Holmes "long stories" in one volume (and all the short stories in another volume), well printed on thin but opaque paper, dies hard. Still, the new books look splendid all lined up, and the introductions are very interesting. Apart from Fowles, the men on the case are

Hugh Greene *(A Study in Scarlet),* his brother Graham Greene *(The Sign of Four)* and Len Deighton *(The Valley of Fear).* What each man has to say is well worth hearing, even if not always strictly relevant to the novel it introduces. When you add to this four-volume set of the novels the five-volume reissue of the short-story collections, it certainly provides a dazzling display.

To follow the order in which Doyle gave them to the world, the short-story collections are *The Adventures of Sherlock Holmes* (introduced by Eric Ambler), *The Memoirs of Sherlock Holmes* (Kingsley Amis), *The Return of Sherlock Holmes* (Angus Wilson), *His Last Bow* (Julian Symons) and *The Case-Book of Sherlock Holmes* (C. P. Snow). The dust-wrappers of all nine volumes are carried out in black and gold, a colour combination which in Britain is supposed to put you in mind of John Player Specials, a flash line in cigarettes. If you do it this way, it will set you back £21.20 in English money to read the saga through.

A less crippling alternative would be to purchase the Doubleday omnibus introduced by the old-time (in fact, late) Sherlockian Christopher Morley, which reproduces the whole corpus—four novels and fifty-six short stories—on goodish paper for slightly under nine bucks, the contents being as nourishing as in the nine-volume version. The question of just how nourishing that *is* is one that begs to be shirked, but honour demands I should stretch my neck across the block and confess that Holmes doesn't seem quite so fascinating to me now as he once did. Perhaps only an adolescent can get the full thrill, and the price of wanting to go on getting it is to remain an adolescent always. This would explain a lot about the Sherlockologists.

The best single book on Doyle is *Sir Arthur Conan Doyle, l'homme et l'œuvre,* a thoroughgoing monograph by Pierre Nordon which came out in its original language in 1964 and was translated into English as *Conan Doyle* a couple of years later. By no coincidence, it is also the best thing on Sherlock. In his chapter on "Sherlock Holmes and the Reading Public" Nordon says most of what requires to be said about the bases of Sherlock's contemporary appeal. On the sociological side our nine introducers can't do much more than amplify Nordon's points, but since all of them are working writers of fiction (with the exception of Hugh Greene, who has, however, a profound knowledge of the period's genre literature), they usually have something of technical moment to add—and disinterested technical analysis is exactly what the Sherlock saga has for so long lacked. The Sherlockologists can't supply it, partly because most of them are nuts, but mainly because the deficiencies of Doyle's stories are what they thrive on: lacunae are what they are in business to fill, and they see Doyle's every awkwardness as a fruitful ambiguity, an irrevocable licence for speculation. The professional scribes, even when they think highly of Doyle, aren't like that. They haven't the time.

Hugh Greene reminds us that the Sherlock stories were head and shoulders above the yellow-back norm. This is still an essential point to put: Doyle was the man who made cheap fiction a field for creative work. Greene also says that *A Study in Scarlet* is broken-backed, which it is. Graham Greene calls one of Doyle's (brief, as always) descriptive scenes "real writing from which we can all draw a lesson" but doesn't forget to insist that the sub-plot of *The Sign of Four* is far too like *The Moonstone* for comfort. (He also calls the meeting of Holmes and Watson in *A Study in Scarlet* unmemorable, an accurate perception denied to the Sherlockians who gravely installed a plaque in St. Bartholomew's hospital to commemorate it.)

Of *The Hound of the Baskervilles*, the only successful Sherlock novel, John Fowles gives an unsparing critical analysis, on the sound assumption that anything less would be patronizing. He sees that Doyle's great technical feat was to resolve "the natural incompatibility of dialogue and narration" but isn't afraid to call Doyle's inaccuracy inaccuracy. (He is surely wrong, however, to say that if Doyle had really wanted to kill Holmes he would have thrown *Watson* off the Reichenbach Falls. It is true that Sherlock couldn't exist without Watson, but there is no possible question that Doyle was keen to rub Holmes out.)

Len Deighton, a dedicated amateur of technology, assures us that Doyle really *did* forecast many of the police methods to come—the business with the typewriter in "A Case of Identity," for example, was years ahead of its time. Since Nordon, eager as always to demystify Sherlock, rather downrates him on this point, it is useful to have the balance redressed. Unfortunately Deighton says almost nothing pertaining to *The Valley of Fear*, the novel which he is introducing. It seems likely that there was no editor to ask him to.

. . .

So it goes with the introductions to the short-story collections. All of them are informative, but some of them tell you the same things, and only one or two illuminate the actual book. Kingsley Amis, as he did with Jane Austen and Thomas Love Peacock, gets down to fundamentals and admits that the Sherlock stories, for all their innovations in space and compression, are seldom "classical" in the sense of playing fair with the reader. Eric Ambler talks charmingly about Doyle's erudition; Angus Wilson pertinently about the plush nineties (1895–1898, the years of *The Return*, were Sherlock's times of triumph); Julian Symons penetratingly about how Doyle shared out his own personality between Holmes and Watson; and C. P. Snow—well, he, of all the nine, it seems to me, is the one who cracks the case.

His personality helps. Lord Snow not only sees but admits the attractions of the high position in society to which Sherlock's qualities eventually brought him, with Watson striding alongside. It might have been Sherlock's bohemianism that pulled in the crowds, but it was his conservatism that glued them to the bleachers. This was Pierre Nordon's salient observation on the sleuth's original appeal, but Lord Snow has outsoared Nordon by realizing that the same come-on is still operating with undiminished force. Sherlock was an eccentrically toothed but essential cog in a society which actually functioned.

The life led by Holmes and Watson in their rooms at 221B Baker Street is a dream of unconventionality, like Act I of *La Bohème*. (A Sherlockologist would step in here to point out that Henri Murger's *Scènes de la vie de bohème*, the book on which the opera was later based, is perused by Watson in *A Study in Scarlet*.) Although Len Deighton is quite right to say that the busy Sherlock is really running the kind of successful medical consultancy which Doyle never enjoyed, it is equally true to say that Holmes and Watson are living as a pair of Oxbridge undergraduates were popularly thought to—and indeed did—live. Holmes is a maverick scientist who treats science as an art, thereby combining the glamour of both fields while avoiding the drudgery of either. He is free of all ties; he does what he wants; he is afraid of nothing. He is above the law and dispenses his own justice. As with Baudelaire, boredom is his only enemy. If he can't escape it through an intellectual challenge, he takes refuge in drugs.

Sherlock in *The Sign of Four* was fixing cocaine three times a day for three months: if he'd tried to snort it in those quantities, his aquiline septum would have been in considerable danger of dropping off. Morphine gets a mention somewhere too—perhaps he was also shooting speedballs. Certainly he was a natural dope-fiend: witness how he makes a cocktail of yesterday's cigarette roaches in "The Speckled Band." In *The Valley of Fear* he is "callous from over-stimulation." All the signs of an oil-burning habit. Did he quit cold turkey, or did Watson ease him down? Rich pickings for the ex-Woodstock Sherlockologists of the future. All of this must have been heady wine for the contemporary reader endowed by the Education Act of 1870 with just enough literacy to read the *Strand* magazine, helped out by a Sidney Paget illustration on every page.

George Orwell thought Britain needed a boys' weekly which questioned society, but Sherlock, for all his nonconformity, set no precedent. He fitted in far more than he dropped out. Sherlock was the house hippie. His latter-day chummings-up with crowned heads (including the private sessions with Queen Victoria which drive card-carrying Sherlockologists to paroxysms of conjecture) were merely the confirmation of a love for royalty which was manifest as early as "A Scandal in Bohemia." "Your Majesty had not spoken," announces Holmes, "before I was aware that I was addressing Wilhelm Gottsreich Sigismond von Ormstein, Grand Duke of Cassel-Felstein, and Hereditary King of Bohemia." The language, as so often in the Holmes stories, is part-way a put-on, but the relationship is genuine: Sherlock is as eager to serve as any of his cultural descendants. From Sanders of the River and Bulldog Drummond down to Pimpernel Smith and James Bond, all those gifted amateur soldiers can trace their ancestry to Sherlock's bump of reverence. Physically a virgin, spiritually he spawned children numberless as the dust.

At least 30 per cent of London's population lived below the poverty line in Sherlock's heyday, but not very many of them found their way into the stories. Doyle's criminals come almost exclusively from the income-earning classes. They are clinically, not socially, motivated. There is seldom any suggestion that crime could be a symptom of anything more general than a personal disorder. Doyle's mind was original but politically blinkered, a condition which his hero reflects. When Watson says (in "A Scandal in Bohemia") that Holmes loathes "every form of society with his whole Bohemian soul," it turns out that Watson means socializing. Society itself Holmes never queries. Even when he acts above the law, it is in the law's spirit that he acts. Nordon is quite right to insist that Sherlock's London, for all its wide social panorama and multiplicity of nooks and crannies, shouldn't be allowed to get mixed up with the real London. (He is quite wrong, though, to suppose that Orwell—of all people—mixed them up. Orwell said that Doyle did, but Nordon has taken Orwell's paraphrase of Doyle's view for Orwell's own opinion. He was helped to the error by a misleading French translation. Pan-cultural-ism has its dangers.)

Holmes was a nonconformist in a conformist age, yet still won all the conformist rewards. It was a double whammy, and for many people probably works the same magic today. I suspect that such reassurance is at the centre of the cosy satisfaction still to be obtained from reading about Sherlock, but of course there are several things it doesn't explain. The first of these is the incessant activity of the hard-core Sherlockolo-gists, the freaks who are on the Baker Street beat pretty well full time. Most of them seem to be less interested in getting things out of the Sherlock canon than in putting things in. Archness is the keynote: coyly pedantic about imponderables, they write the frolicsome prose of the incorrigibly humourless. The opportunity for recondite tedium knows no limit. This playful racket has been going on without let-up since well before Doyle died. The output of just the last few months is depressing enough to glance through. Multiply it by decades and the mind quails.

Here is *Sherlock Holmes Detected*, by Ian McQueen. It is composed of hundreds of such pseudo-scholarly points as the contention that "A Case of Identity" might very well be set in September, even though Holmes and Watson are described as sitting on either side of the fire—because their landlady, Mrs. Hudson, is known to have been conscientious, and would have laid the fire ready for use even before winter. And anyway, Mr. McQueen postulates cunningly, Holmes and Watson would probably sit on either side of the fire *even if it were not lit.* Apparently this subtle argument puts paid to other Sherlockologists who hold the view that "A Case of Identity" can't possibly be set in September. Where that view originated is lost in the mists of fatuity: these drainingly inconse-quential debates were originally got up by Ronald Knox and Sydney Roberts and formalized as an Oxford *vs.* Cambridge contest in dead-pan whimsy, which has gradually come to include the less calculated ponderosity of interloping enthusiasts who don't even realize they are supposed to be joking. Mr. McQueen's book sounds to me exactly the same as Vincent Starrett's *The Private Life of Sherlock Holmes,* which came out in 1933 and seems to have set the pace in this particular branch of the industry.

Two other volumes in the same Snark-hunting vein are the *London of Sherlock Holmes* and *In the Footsteps of Sherlock Holmes,* both written by Michael Harrison, both published recently and both consisting of roughly the same information and photographs. Both bear the imprint of the same publishing house, which must have an editor whose blindness matches the blurb-writer's illiteracy. Mr. Harrison goes in for the same brand of bogus precision as Mr. McQueen. We hear a lot about what "must have" happened. We are shown a photograph of the steps which Sherlock's brother Mycroft "must have used" when going to his job at the Foreign Office. This music-hall "must have been visited" by Sherlock. There is the usual interminable speculation about the whereabouts of 221B, coupled with the usual reluctance to consider that Doyle himself obviously didn't give a damn for the plausibility of its location. The only authentic problem Mr. Harrison raises is the question of which of his two books is the sillier.

Messrs. McQueen and Harrison are toddling in the giant footsteps of W. S. Baring-Gould, who compiled *The Annotated Sherlock Holmes,* which went into such scholastic minutiae with the determination of mania. Baring-Gould was also the father of yet another branch of the business—fake biographies. In his *Sherlock Holmes: A Biography of the World's First Consulting Detective* (1962), Baring-Gould sent Sherlock to Oxford. In her contribution to H. W. Bell's *Baker Street Studies* thirty years earlier, Dorothy Sayers sent him to Cambridge. Doyle sent him to neither.

Current biographical efforts are in the same footling tradition. Here is an untiringly industrious novel by John Gardner called *The Return of Moriarty,* in which the Greatest Schemer of All Time returns alive from the Reichenbach. It doesn't daunt Mr. Gardner that he is transparently ten times more interested in Moriarty than Doyle ever was. In "The Final Problem," Sherlock tells Watson that the silent struggle to get the goods on Moriarty could be the greatest story of all, but Doyle never wrote it.

The reason, as Angus Wilson divines, is that Moriarty was a less employable villain than his sidekick, Moran. Moriarty was merely the Napoleon of Crime, whereas Moran was the "best heavy game shot that our Eastern Empire has ever produced"—which at least *sounded* less vague.

But the vagueness in Doyle is what the speculators like. And here is *The Seven-Per-Cent Solution,* pretending to be "a reprint from the reminiscences of John H. Watson, M.D., as edited by Nicholas Meyer." This time Sherlock and Mycroft turn out to be repressing a shameful, nameless secret. In books like this, speculation is supposed to be veering towards the humorous. The transgression would be funny, if only it made you laugh. Mr. Meyer's comic invention, however, is thin. But at least he is *trying* to be silly.

The most foolish book of the bunch, and quite frankly the loopiest stretch of exegesis since John Allegro dug up the sacred mushroom, is *Naked Is the Best Disguise,* by Samuel Rosenberg, which has been welcomed in the United States with reviews I find inexplicable. Mr. Rosenberg's thesis, briefly, is that Moriarty is Nietzsche and that Doyle is acting out a psycho-drama in which Sherlock is his super-ego suppressing his polymorphous perversity. Even if it had been reached by a convincing show of reasoning, this conclusion would still be far-fetched: fetched, in fact, from half-way across the galaxy. But it has been reached by no kind of reasoning except casuistry. Mr. Rosenberg argues in one place that if a Sherlock Holmes adventure is set in a house with two storeys, that means there are two *stories*—i.e., two levels of meaning. His arguing is of the same standard in every other place.

It seems that Mr. Rosenberg used to work as a legal eagle for a film studio, protecting it from plagiarism suits by finding a common literary ancestor who might have influenced both the plaintiff's script and the script the studio had in the works. He must have been well worth his salary, because he can see similarities in anything. (His standards of accuracy spring from the same gift: he spells A. J. Ayer's name wrongly on seven occasions.) It would be overpraising the book to call it negligible, yet both *Time* and *The New York Times,* among others, seem to have found it a meaty effort.

Though *Naked Is the Best Disguise* considers itself to be high scholarship, it reveals itself instantly as Sherlockology by worrying over the importance of minor detail in stories whose major action their author could scarcely be bothered to keep believable. The chronology of the Holmes saga is indefinitely debatable because Doyle didn't care about establishing it. Early on, Sherlock was ignorant of the arts and didn't know the earth went around the sun: later, he quoted poetry in several languages and had wide scientific knowledge. Sherlock was a minor occupation for Doyle and he was either content to leave such inconsistencies as they were or else he plain forgot about them. Mysteries arising from them are consequently unresolvable, which is doubtless their attraction. Programs for explicating Sherlock are like Casaubon's Key to All Mythologies, which George Eliot said was as endless as a scheme for joining the stars.

Uniquely among recent Sherlockiana, *The Sherlock Holmes Scrapbook*, edited by Peter Haining, is actually enjoyable. It reproduces playbills, cartoons, production stills and—most important—some of the magazine and newspaper articles which set Sherlockology rolling. (One of them is a piece of joky speculation by Doyle himself—a bad mistake. If he wanted to trivialize his incubus, he couldn't have chosen a worse tactic.) Basil Rathbone easily emerges as the most likely-looking movie incarnation of Holmes. Sidney Paget's drawings are better than anything else then or since. (What we need is a good two-volume complete *Sherlock Holmes* with all of Paget and none of Baring-Gould.) The whole scrapbook is a great help in seeing how the legend grew, not least because it shows us that legends are of circumscribed interest: too many supernumeraries— belletrist hacks and doodling amateurs with time to burn—contribute to them. As you leaf through these chronologically ordered pages, you can see the dingbats swarming aboard the bandwagon.

Doyle's brain-child could scarcely survive this kind of admiration if it did not possess archetypal attributes. Sherlockology is bastardized academicism, but academicism is one of the forces which Doyle instinctively set out to fight, and Sherlock, his Sunday punch, is not yet drained of strength. Sherlock was the first example of the art Dürrenmatt later dreamed of—the art which would weigh nothing in the scales of respectability. Doyle knew that Sherlock was cheap. What he didn't guess before it was too late to change his mind was that the cheapness would last. The only coherence in the Holmes saga is a coherence of intensity. The language is disproportionate and therefore vivid. "He was, I take it, the

most perfect reasoning and observing machine that the world has seen."
The images are unshaded and therefore flagrant. "I took a step forward:
in an instant his strange headgear began to move, and there reared itself
from among his hair the squat diamond-shaped head and puffed neck of
a loathsome serpent."

But Sherlock's world was all fragments, and no real world could or can
be inferred from it. In *The Valley of Fear* the Scowrers work mischief to
no conceivable political purpose. Moriarty machinates to no ascertainable
end. The Sherlockologists would like to believe that this abstract universe
is concrete, and that large questions of good and evil are being worked
out. But the concreteness is only in the detail; beyond the detail there is
nothing; and the large questions must always lack answers.

Doyle asked and tried to answer the large questions elsewhere, in the
spiritualist faith which occupied his full mental effort. Eventually his
seriousness went out of date, while his frivolity established itself as an
institution. But since his mind at play could scarcely have played so well
if it had not been so earnest a mind, there is no joke.

(*New York Review of Books*, 20 February 1975)

The Country Behind the Hill:
Raymond Chandler

"In the long run," Raymond Chandler writes in *Raymond Chandler Speaking*, "however little you talk or even think about it, the most durable thing in writing is style, and style is the most valuable investment a writer can make with his time." At a time when literary values inflate and dissipate almost as fast as the currency, it still looks as if Chandler invested wisely. His style has lasted. A case could be made for saying that nothing else about his books has, but even the most irascible critic or most disillusioned fan (they are often the same person) would have to admit that Chandler at his most characteristic is just that—characteristic and not just quirky. Auden was right in wanting him to be regarded as an artist. In fact Auden's tribute might well have been that of one poet to another. If style is the only thing about Chandler's novels that can't be forgotten, it could be because his style was poetic, rather than prosaic. Even at its most explicit, what he wrote was full of implication. He used to say that he wanted to give a feeling of the country behind the hill.

Since Chandler was already well into middle age when he began publishing, it isn't surprising that he found his style quickly. Most of the effects that were to mark *The Big Sleep* in 1939 were already present, if only fleetingly, in an early story like "Killer in the Rain," published in *Black Mask* magazine in 1935. In fact some of the very same sentences are already there. This from "Killer in the Rain":

> The rain splashed knee-high off the sidewalks, filled the gutters, and big cops in slickers that shone like gun barrels had a lot of fun carrying little girls in silk stockings and cute little rubber boots across the bad places, with a lot of squeezing.

Compare this from *The Big Sleep*:

> Rain filled the gutters and splashed knee-high off the pavement. Big cops in
> slickers that shone like gun barrels had a lot of fun carrying giggling girls across
> the bad places. The rain drummed hard on the roof of the car and the burbank
> top began to leak. A pool of water formed on the floorboards for me to keep
> my feet in.

So there is not much point in talking about how Chandler's style
developed. As soon as he was free of the short-paragraph restrictions
imposed by the cheaper pulps, his way of writing quickly found its outer
limits: all he needed to do was refine it. The main refining instrument was
Marlowe's personality. The difference between the two cited passages is
really the difference between John Dalmas and Philip Marlowe. Marlowe's name was not all that more convincing than Dalmas's, but he was
a more probable, or at any rate less improbable, visionary. In *The Big Sleep*
and all the novels that followed, the secret of plausibility lies in the style,
and the secret of the style lies in Marlowe's personality. Chandler once
said that he thought of Marlowe as the American mind. As revealed in
Chandler's *Notebooks* (edited by Frank McShane and published by the
Ecco Press, New York), one of Chandler's many projected titles was "The
Man Who Loved the Rain." Marlowe loved the rain.

Flaubert liked tinsel better than silver because tinsel possessed all silver's attributes plus one in addition—pathos. For whatever reason, Chandler was fascinated by the cheapness of L.A. When he said that it had
as much personality as a paper cup, he was saying what he liked about it.
When he said that he could leave it without a pang, he was saying why
he felt at home there. In a city where the rich were as vulgar as the poor,
all the streets were mean. In a democracy of trash, Marlowe was the only
aristocrat. Working for twenty-five dollars a day plus expenses (Jim Rockford in the TV series *The Rockford Files* now works for ten times that
and has to live in a trailer), Marlowe was as free from materialistic
constraint as any hermit. He saw essences. Chandler's particular triumph
was to find a style for matching Marlowe to the world. Vivid language was
the decisive element, which meant that how not to make Marlowe sound
like too good a *writer* was the continuing problem. The solution was a kind
of undercutting wit, a style in which Marlowe mocked his own fine
phrases. A comic style, always on the edge of self-parody—and, of course,

sometimes over the edge—but at its best combining the exultant and the sad in an inseparable mixture.

For a writer who is not trying all that hard to be funny, it is remarkable how often Chandler can make you smile. His conciseness can strike you as a kind of wit in itself. The scene with General Sternwood in the hot-house, the set piece forming Chapter Two of *The Big Sleep,* is done with more economy than you can remember: there are remarkably few words on the page to generate such a lasting impression of warm fog in the reader's brain. "The air was thick, wet, steamy and larded with the cloying smell of tropical orchids in bloom." It's the rogue verb "larded" which transmits most of the force. Elsewhere, a single simile gives you the idea of General Sternwood's aridity. "A few locks of dry white hair clung to his scalp, like wild flowers fighting for life on a bare rock." The fact that he stays dry in the wet air is the measure of General Sternwood's nearness to death. The bare rock is the measure of his dryness. At their best, Chandler's similes click into place with this perfect appositeness. He can make you laugh, he gets it so right—which perhaps means that he gets it *too* right. What we recognize as wit is always a self-conscious performance.

But since wit that works at all is rare enough, Chandler should be respected for it. And anyway, he didn't always fall into the trap of making his characters too eloquent. Most of Marlowe's best one-liners are internal. In the film of *The Big Sleep,* when Marlowe tells General Sternwood that he has already met Carmen in the hall, he says: "She tried to sit in my lap while I was standing up." Bogart gets a big laugh with that line, but only half of the line is Chandler's. All that Chandler's Marlowe says is "Then she tried to sit in my lap." The film version of Marlowe got the rest of the gag from somewhere else—either from William Faulkner, who wrote the movie, or from Howard Hawks, who directed it, or perhaps from both. On the page, Marlowe's gags are private and subdued. About Carmen, he concludes that "thinking was always going to be a bother to her." He notices—as no camera could notice, unless the casting director flung his net very wide—that her thumb is like a finger, with no curve in its first joint. He compares the shocking whiteness of her teeth to fresh orange pith. He gets you scared stiff of her in a few sentences.

Carmen is the first in a long line of little witches that runs right through the novels, just as her big sister, Vivian, is the first in a long line of rich bitches who find that Marlowe is the only thing money can't buy. The little witches are among the most haunting of Chandler's obsessions and the rich bitches are among the least. Whether little witch or rich bitch, both kinds of woman signal their availability to Marlowe by crossing their legs shortly after sitting down and regaling him with tongue-in-the-lung French kisses a few seconds after making physical contact.

All the standard Chandler character ingredients were there in the first novel, locked in a pattern of action so complicated that not even the author was subsequently able to puzzle it out. *The Big Sleep* was merely the first serving of the mixture as before. But the language was fresh and remains so. When Chandler wrote casually of "a service station glaring with wasted light," he was striking a note that Dashiell Hammett had never dreamed of. Even the book's title rang a bell. Chandler thought that there were only two types of slang which were any good: slang that had established itself in the language, and slang that you made up yourself. As a term for death, "the big sleep" was such a successful creation that Eugene O'Neill must have thought it had been around for years, since he used it in *The Iceman Cometh* (1946) as an established piece of low-life tough talk. But there is no reason for disbelieving Chandler's claim to have invented it.

Chandler's knack for slang would have been just as commendable even if he had never thought of a thing. As the *Notebooks* reveal, he made lists of slang terms that he had read or heard. The few he kept and used were distinguished from the many he threw away by their metaphorical exactness. He had an ear for depth—he could detect incipient permanence in what sounded superficially like ephemera. A term like "under glass," meaning to be in prison, attracted him by its semantic compression. In a letter collected in *Raymond Chandler Speaking,* he regards it as self-evident that an American term like "milk run" is superior to the equivalent British term "piece of cake." The superiority being in the range of evocation. As it happened, Chandler *was* inventive, not only in slang but in more ambitiously suggestive figures of speech. He was spontaneous as well as accurate. His second novel, *Farewell, My Lovely* (1940)—which he was always to regard as his finest—teems with show-stopping similes, many of them dedicated to conjuring up the gargantuan figure of Moose Malloy.

In fact some of them stop the show too thoroughly. When Chandler describes Malloy as standing out from his surroundings like "a tarantula on a slice of angel food" he is getting things backwards, since the surroundings have already been established as very sordid indeed. Malloy ought to be standing out from them like a slice of angel food on a tarantula. Chandler at one time confessed to Alfred A. Knopf that in *The Big Sleep* he had run his similes into the ground, the implication being that he cured himself of the habit later on. But the truth is that he was always prone to overcooking a simile. As Perelman demonstrated in "Farewell, My Lovely Appetizer" (a spoof which Chandler admired), this is one of the areas in which Chandler is most easily parodied, although it should be remembered that it takes a Perelman to do the parodying.

"It was a blonde," says Marlowe, looking at Helen Grayle's photograph, "a blonde to make a bishop kick a hole in a stained-glass window." I still laugh when I read that, but you can imagine Chandler jotting down such brainwaves *à propos* of nothing and storing them up against a rainy day. They leap off the page so high that they never again settle back into place, thereby adding to the permanent difficulty of remembering what happens to whom where in which novel. The true wit, in *Farewell, My Lovely* as in all the other books, lies in effects which marry themselves less obtrusively to character, action and setting. Jessie Florian's bathrobe, for example. "It was just something around her body." A sentence like that seems hardly to be trying, but it tells you all you need to know. Marlowe's realization that Jessie has been killed—"The corner post of the bed was smeared darkly with something the flies liked"—is trying harder for understatement, but in those circumstances Marlowe *would* understate the case, so the sentence fits. Poor Jessie Florian. "She was as cute as a washtub."

And some of the lines simply have the humour of information conveyed at a blow, like the one about the butler at the Grayle house. As always when Chandler is dealing with Millionaires' Row, the place is described with a cataloguing eye for ritzy detail, as if F. Scott Fitzgerald had written a contribution to *Architectural Digest*. (The Murdock house in *The High Window* bears a particularly close resemblance to Gatsby's mansion: *vide* the lawn flowing "like a cool green tide around a rock.") Chandler enjoyed conjuring up the grand houses into which Marlowe came as an interloper and out of which he always went with a sigh of relief, having hauled the family skeletons out of the walk-in cupboards and left the beautiful, wild elder daughter sick with longing for his incorruptible countenance. But in several telling pages about the Grayle residence, the sentence that really counts is the one about the butler. "A man in a striped vest and gilt buttons opened the door, bowed, took my hat and was through for the day."

In the early books and novels, before he moved to Laurel Canyon, when he still lived at 615 Cahuenga Building on Hollywood Boulevard, near Ivar, telephone Glenview 7537, Marlowe was fond of Los Angeles. All the bad things happened in Bay City. In Bay City there were crooked cops, prostitution, drugs, but after you came to (Marlowe was always coming to in Bay City, usually a long time after he had been sapped, because in Bay City they always hit him very hard), you could drive home. Later on the evil had spread everywhere and Marlowe learned to hate what L.A. had become. The set-piece descriptions of his stamping-ground got more and more sour. But the descriptions were always there—one of the strongest threads running through the novels from first to last. And even at their most acridly poisonous they still kept something of the wide-eyed lyricism of that beautiful line in *Farewell, My Lovely* about a dark night in the canyons—the night Marlowe drove Lindsay Marriott to meet his death. "A yellow window hung here and there by itself, like the last orange."

There is the usual ration of overcooked metaphors in *The High Window* (1942). Lois Morny gives forth with "a silvery ripple of laughter that held the unspoiled naturalness of a bubble dance." (By the time you have worked out that this means her silvery ripple of laughter held no unspoiled naturalness, the notion has gone dead.) We learn that Morny's club in Idle Valley looks like a high-budget musical. "A lot of light and glitter, a lot of scenery, a lot of clothes, a lot of sound, an all-star cast, and a plot with all the originality and drive of a split fingernail." Tracing the club through the musical down to the fingernail, your attention loses focus. It's a better sentence than any of Chandler's imitators ever managed, but it was the kind of sentence they felt able to imitate—lying loose and begging to be picked up.

As always, the quiet effects worked better. The backyard of the Morny house is an instant Hockney. "Beyond was a walled-in garden containing flower-beds crammed with showy annuals, a badminton court, a nice stretch of greensward, and a small tiled pool glittering angrily in the sun." The rogue adverb "angrily" is the word that registers the sun's brightness. It's a long step, taken in a few words, to night-time in Idle Valley. "The wind was quiet out here and the valley moonlight was so sharp that the black shadows looked as if they had been cut with an engraving tool." Saying how unreal the real looks make it realer.

"Bunker Hill is old town, lost town, shabby town, crook town." *The High Window* has many such examples of Chandler widening his rhythmic scope. Yet the best and the worst sentences are unusually far apart. On several occasions Chandler is extraordinarily clumsy. "He was a tall man with glasses and a high-domed bald head that made his ears look as if they had slipped down his head." This sentence is literally effortless: the clumsy repetition of "head" is made possible only because he isn't trying. Here is a useful reminder of the kind of concentration required to achieve a seeming ease. And here is another: "From the lay of the land a light in the living room . . ." Even a writer who doesn't, as Chandler usually did, clean as he goes, would normally liquidate so languorous an alliterative lullaby long before the final draft.

But in between the high points and the low, the general tone of *The High Window* had an assured touch. The narrator's interior monologue is full of the sort of poetry Laforgue liked—*comme ils sont beaux, les trains manqués.* Marlowe's office hasn't changed, nor will it ever. "The same stuff I had had last year, and the year before that. Not beautiful, not gay, but better than a tent on the beach." Marlowe accuses the two cops, Breeze and Spangler, of talking dialogue in which every line is a punch line. Criticism is not disarmed: in Chandler, everybody talks that kind of dialogue most of the time. But the talk that matters most is the talk going on inside Marlowe's head, and Chandler was making it more subtle with each book.

Chandler's descriptive powers are at their highest in *The Lady in the Lake* (1943). It takes Marlowe a page and a half of thoroughly catalogued natural detail to drive from San Bernardino to Little Fawn Lake, but when he gets there he sees the whole thing in a sentence. "Beyond the gate the road wound for a couple of hundred yards through trees and then suddenly below me was a small oval lake deep in trees and rocks and wild grass, like a drop of dew caught in a curled leaf." Hemingway could do bigger things, but small moments like those were Chandler's own. (Nevertheless Hemingway got on Chandler's nerves: Dolores Gonzales in *The Little Sister* is to be heard saying "I was pretty good in there, no?" and the nameless girl who vamps Marlowe at Roger Wade's party in *The Long Goodbye* spoofs the same line. It should be remembered, however, that Chandler admired Hemingway to the end, forbearing to pour scorn even on *Across the River and into the Trees*. The digs at Papa in Chandler's novels can mainly be put down to self-defence.)

The Little Sister (1949), Chandler's first post-war novel, opens with Marlowe stalking a bluebottle fly around his office. "He didn't want to sit down. He just wanted to do wing-overs and sing the Prologue to *Pagliacci.*" Ten years before, in "Trouble Is My Business," John Dalmas felt like singing the same thing after being sapped in Harriet Huntress's apartment. Chandler was always ready to bring an idea back for a second airing. A Ph.D. thesis could be written about the interest John Dalmas and Philip Marlowe take in bugs and flies. There is another thesis in the tendency of Chandler's classier dames to show a startling line of white scalp in the parting of their hair: Dolores Gonzales, who throughout *The Little Sister* propels herself at Marlowe like Lupe Velez seducing Errol Flynn, is only one of the several high-toned vamps possessing this tonsorial feature. "She made a couple of drinks in a couple of glasses you could almost have stood umbrellas in." A pity about that "almost"—it ruins a good hyperbole. Moss Spink's extravagance is better conveyed: "He waved a generous hand on which a canary-yellow diamond looked like an amber traffic light."

But as usual the would-be startling images are more often unsuccessful than successful. The better work is done lower down the scale of excitability. Joseph P. Toad, for example. "The neck of his canary-yellow shirt was open wide, which it had to be if his neck was going to get out." Wit like that lasts longer than hyped-up similes. And some of the dialogue, though as stylized as ever, would be a gift to actors: less supercharged than usual, it shows some of the natural balance which marked the lines Chandler has been writing for the movies. Here is Marlowe sparring with Sheridan Ballou.

"Did she suggest how to go about shutting my mouth?"
"I got the impression she was in favour of doing it with some kind of heavy blunt instrument."

Such an exchange is as playable as anything in *Double Indemnity* or *The Blue Dahlia.* And imagine what Laird Cregar would have done with Toad's line "You could call me a guy what wants to help out a guy that don't want to make trouble for a guy." Much as he would have hated the imputation, Chandler's toil in the salt-mines under the Paramount mountain had done things for him. On the other hand, the best material in *The Little Sister* is inextricably bound up with the style of Marlowe's perception, which in turn depends on Chandler's conception of himself. There could be no complete screen rendition of the scene with Jules Oppenheimer in the studio patio. With peeing dogs instead of hot-house steam, it's exactly the same layout as Marlowe's encounter with General Sternwood in *The Big Sleep*, but then there was no filming *that* either. The mood of neurotic intensity—Marlowe as the soldier-son, Sternwood/Oppenheimer as the father-figure at death's door—would be otiose in a film script, which requires that all action be relevant. In the novels, such passages are less about Marlowe than about Chandler working out his obsessions through Marlowe, and nobody ever wanted to make a film about Chandler.

In *The Long Goodbye* (1953), Marlowe moves to a house on Yucca Avenue in Laurel Canyon and witnesses the disintegration of Terry Lennox. Lennox can't control his drinking. Marlowe, master of his own thirst, looks sadly on. As we now know, Chandler in real life was more Lennox than Marlowe. In the long dialogues between these two characters he is really talking to himself. There is no need to be afraid of the biographical fallacy: even if we knew nothing about Chandler's life, it would still be evident that a fantasy is being worked out. Worked out but not admitted —as so often happens in good-bad books, the author's obsessions are being catered to, not examined. Chandler, who at least worked for a living, had reason for thinking himself more like Marlowe than like Lennox. (Roger Wade, the other of the book's big drinkers, is, being a writer, a bit closer to home.) Nevertheless Marlowe is a day-dream—more and more of a day-dream as Chandler gets better and better at making him believable. By this time it's Marlowe *vs.* the Rest of the World. Of all Chandler's nasty cops, Captain Gregorius is the nastiest. "His big nose was a network of burst capillaries." But even in the face of the ultimate nightmare Marlowe keeps his nerve. Nor is he taken in by Eileen Wade, superficially the dreamiest of all Chandler's dream girls.

It was a near-run thing, however. Chandler mocked romantic writers who always used three adjectives but Marlowe fell into the same habit when contemplating Eileen Wade. "She looked exhausted now, and frail, and very beautiful." Perhaps he was tipped off when Eileen suddenly caught the same disease and started referring to "the wild, mysterious, improbable kind of love that never comes but once." In the end she turns out to be a killer, a dream girl gone sour like Helen Grayle in *Farewell, My Lovely,* whose motherly clutch ("smooth and soft and warm and comforting") was that of a strangler. *The Long Goodbye* is the book of Marlowe's irretrievable disillusion.

> I was as hollow and empty as the spaces between the stars. When I got home I mixed a stiff one and stood by the open window in the living-room and sipped it and listened to the ground swell of the traffic on Laurel Canyon Boulevard and looked at the glare of the big, angry city hanging over the shoulder of the hills through which the boulevard had been cut. Far off the banshee wail of police or fire sirens rose and fell, never for very long completely silent. Twenty-four hours a day somebody is running, somebody else is trying to catch him.

Even Marlowe got caught. Linda Loring nailed him. "The tip of her tongue touched mine." His vestal virginity was at long last ravished away. But naturally there was no Love, at least not yet.

Having broken the ice, Marlowe was to be laid again, most notably by the chic, leg-crossing Miss Vermilyea in Chandler's next novel, *Playback* (1958). It is only towards the end of that novel that we realize how thoroughly Marlowe is being haunted by Linda Loring's memory. Presumably this is the reason why Marlowe's affair with Miss Vermilyea is allowed to last only one night. (" 'I hate you,' she said with her mouth against mine. 'Not for this, but because perfection never comes twice and with us it came too soon. And I'll never see you again and I don't want to. It would have to be for ever or not at all.' ") We presume that Miss Vermilyea wasn't just being tactful.

Anyway, Linda Loring takes the prize, but not before Marlowe has raced through all his usual situations, albeit in compressed form. Once again, for example, he gets hit on the head. "I went zooming out over a dark sea and exploded in a sheet of flame." For terseness this compares favourably with an equivalent moment in "Bay City Blues," written twenty years before.

> Then a naval gun went off in my ear and my head was a large pink firework exploding into the vault of the sky and scattering and falling slow and pale, and then dark, into the waves. Blackness ate me up.

Chandler's prose had attained respectability, but by now he had less to say with it—perhaps because time had exposed his day-dreams to the extent that even he could see them for what they were. The belief was gone. In *The Poodle Springs Story*, his last, unfinished novel, Marlowe has only one fight left to fight, the war against the rich. Married now to Linda, he slugs it out with her toe to toe. It is hard to see why he bothers to keep up the struggle. Even heroes get tired and not even the immortal stay young for ever. Defeat was bound to come some time, and although it is undoubtedly true that the rich are corrupt at least Linda knows how corruption ought to be done: the classiest of Chandler's classy dames, the richest bitch of all, she will bring Marlowe to a noble downfall. There is nothing vulgar about Linda. (If that Hammond organ-*cum*-cocktail bar in their honeymoon house disturbs you, don't forget that the place is only rented.)

So Marlowe comes to an absurd end, and indeed it could be said that he was always absurd. Chandler was always dreaming. He dreamed of being more attractive than he was, taller than he was, less trammelled than he was, braver than he was. But so do most men. We dream about our ideal selves, and it is at least arguable that we would be even less ideal if we didn't. Marlowe's standards of conduct would be our standards if we had his courage. We can rationalize the discrepancy by convincing ourselves that if we haven't got his courage he hasn't got our mortgage, but the fact remains that his principles are real.

Marlowe can be hired, but he can't be bought. As a consequence, he is alone. Hence his lasting appeal. Not that he is without his repellent aspects. His race prejudice would amount to outright Fascism if it were not so evident that he would never be able to bring himself to join a movement. His sexual imagination is deeply suspect and he gets hit on the skull far too often for someone who works largely with his head. His taste in socks is oddly vile for one who quotes so easily from Browning ("the poet, not the automatic"). But finally you recognize his tone of voice.

It is your own, day-dreaming of being tough, of giving the rich bitch the kiss-off, of saying smart things, of defending the innocent, of being the hero. It is a silly day-dream because anyone who could really do such splendid things would probably not share it, but without it the rest of us would be even more lost than we are. Chandler incarnated this necessary fantasy by finding a style for it. His novels are exactly as good as they should be. In worse books, the heroes are too little like us: in better books, too much.

(1977)

Bitter Seeds: Solzhenitsyn

I wonder if, despite the critical success of *The Gulag Archipelago*, Solzhenitsyn's reputation is quite as high as it was when *August 1914* had not yet seen the light, when its author was still in Russia and when the K.G.B. were obviously looking for some plausible means of stopping his mouth. Even at that arcadian stage, however, I can well remember arousing the scorn of some of my brighter contemporaries by calling Solzhenitsyn a great imaginative writer. This was put down to my customary hyperbole, to my romanticism, to my bad taste or to all three. Yet it seemed to me a sober judgement, and still seems so. I think Solzhenitsyn is a creative artist of the very first order.

What tends to disguise this is an historical accident—the accident that most of his imaginative energy has had to be expended on the business of reconstructing reality. He has been trying to remember what a whole country has been conspiring, for various reasons, to forget. In such a case it is a creative act simply to find a way of telling some of the truth, as many people realized instinctively when they greeted Nadezhda Mandelstam's first volume of memoirs as the poetic work it is. But to tell as much of the truth as Solzhenitsyn has already told—and all of this truth must be *recovered,* from sources whose interests commonly lie in yielding none of it up—is a creative act of such magnitude that it is hard to recognize as a work of the imagination at all. On the whole, it seems, we would rather think of Solzhenitsyn as an impersonal instrument, a camera photographing the surface of another, airless planet. Hence the common complaint that he is a bit short on human warmth, the general agreement that there is something eerily mechanical about him. Even before *August 1914* (whose characters tended to be described by reviewers as having keys sticking out of their backs) there was talk of how *Cancer Ward* and *The First Circle* proved that Solzhenitsyn was not Tolstoy.

I can recall this last point being made in an argument I had with one of the more gifted members of what I must, I suppose, with chagrin, get used to thinking of as the next generation. He hadn't yet got round to reading *War and Peace* or *Anna Karenina* or *Resurrection,* but in the intervals of urging upon me the merits of Northrop Frye he nevertheless conveyed that he thought he had a pretty fair idea of what Tolstoy had been all about, and that Solzhenitsyn's novels weren't in the same league.

Not only did I concede the truth of such a judgement, I insisted on it. Solzhenitsyn's novels are not Tolstoy's, and never could have been. Tolstoy's novels are about the planet Earth and Solzhenitsyn's are about Pluto. Tolstoy is writing about a society and Solzhenitsyn is writing about the lack of one. My argument might have a touch of sophistry (perhaps one is merely rationalizing Solzhenitsyn's limitations), but surely there is something wilfully unhistorical about being disappointed that Pierre Bezukhov or Andrey Bolkonsky or Natasha Rostov find no equivalents in *Cancer Ward.* Characterization in such wealthy detail has become, in Solzhenitsyn's Russia, a thing of the past, and to expect it is like expecting the fur-lined brocades and gold-threaded silks of the Florentine Renaissance to crop up in Goya's visions of the horrors of war. Solzhenitsyn's contemporary novels—I mean the novels set in the Soviet Union—are not really concerned with society. They are concerned with what happens after society has been destroyed. And *August 1914,* an historical novel in the usual sense, looks to be the beginning of a long work which will show the transition from one state to the other. It is already fairly clear that Solzhenitsyn plans to carry the novel forward until he ends up telling the story of the 1917 Revolution itself, as well as, if he is granted time enough, of the Civil War afterwards. Here one should remember his talks with Susi in the "eagle's perch" of the Lubyanka, in *Gulag Archipelago,* Part I, Chapter 5. While recollecting them he writes: "From childhood on, I had somehow known that my objective was the history of the Russian Revolution and that nothing else concerned me."

Solzhenitsyn is explicit about his belief that he is linked to Tolstoy in some sort of historical mission. His detractors have made much of the meeting between Tanya and Tolstoy in Chapter 2 of *August 1914.* But Solzhenitsyn, even though he is a proud man (and it is a wonder that his pride isn't positively messianic, considering what he has been through and the size of the task which circumstances have posed him), isn't, it seems to me, an especially conceited one. He doesn't see his connection with Tolstoy as one of rivalry. What he sees is an apostolic succession. He knows all about Tolstoy's superiority. But when Tanya fails to get Tolstoy to admit that love might not be the cure for everything, Solzhenitsyn is showing us (by a trick of retroactive prophecy, or clairvoyance through hindsight) that Tolstoy's superiority will be a limitation in the age to come. What will count above everything else for the writer in the Russian future is *memory*. In the prison state, you should own only what you can carry with you and let your memory be your travel bag. "It is those bitter seeds alone which might sprout and grow someday." (*Gulag Archipelago*, Part II, Chapter 1.) The lesson is Tolstoyan, but the context is not. Solzhenitsyn's argument has nothing to do with the perfecting of one's soul. All he is saying—in a tone unifying realism and irony—is that if you try to keep anything tangible the prison-camp thieves will break what is left of your heart when they take it. (An instructive exercise here is to read some of, say, *Resurrection* just after having absorbed a chapter or two of *Gulag Archipelago*. The unthinkable has occurred: Tolstoy seems to have become irrelevant to Russia.)

There can't be much doubt that *August 1914* did damage to Solzhenitsyn's stature in the short run. But in the long run it will probably be the better for him to be liberated from the burden of fashionable approval, and anyway it is far too early to judge *August 1914* as a novel. Most of the reviewers who found it wanting in comparison with *War and Peace* had probably not read *War and Peace* recently or at all; certainly those who talked of its shape or construction had never read it, since *War and Peace* is a deliberately sprawling affair which takes ages to get started. *August 1914* reads like a piece of scene-setting, a slow introduction to something prodigious. I would like to see a lot more of the project before deciding that Solzhenitsyn has failed as a novelist. But it is possible to concede already that he might have failed as a nineteenth-century novelist.

It can be argued that because the setting of *August 1914* is pre-Revolutionary the characters and situations ought therefore to be more earthily lifelike than they are—more Tolstoyan, in a word. I suppose there is something to this. Tolstoy was a transfigurative genius and probably Solzhenitsyn is not; probably he just doesn't possess Tolstoy's charm of evocative utterance. But the loss in afflatus is surely a small thing compared to what we gain from Solzhenitsyn's panoramic realism. In clarifying the history of the Soviet Union (and Solzhenitsyn is already, by force of circumstance, the pre-eminent modern Russian historian), he is making a large stretch of recent time his personal province. He has been writing a bible, and consequently must find it hard to avoid the occasional God-like attribute accruing to him: omniscience, for example. It must be a constant temptation to suggest more than he knows. Yet when dealing with events taking place in the course of his own lifetime he never seems to, and I would be surprised if he ever did much to break that rule when writing about the pre-Revolutionary period. The use of documents in *August 1914* has been called a weakness. The inspiration for this technique is supposed to come from John Dos Passos, and the purported result is that *August 1914* is as flawed as *U.S.A.* Well, for any novel to rank with *U.S.A.* would not be all that bad a fate, and anyway critics who take this line are underestimating the importance to Solzhenitsyn of documentation of all kinds. He goes in for this sort of thing not because he lacks imagination but because that *is* imagination—to suppose that the facts of the Russian past can be recovered, to suppose that evidence can still *matter,* is an imaginative act. But to assess the boldness of that act, we must first begin to understand what has happened to the truth in the Soviet Union. And it's Solzhenitsyn who more than anyone else has been helping us to understand.

In writing about World War I, Solzhenitsyn can't help having the benefit of his peculiar hindsight. Everything in *August 1914* and its succeeding volumes is bound to be illuminated by what we know of his writings about the Soviet Union. There is no way he can escape this condition and it is childish, I think, to wish that he could. It could well be that the war novel will be artistically less than fully successful because we will have to keep thinking of its author as the author of *Gulag Archipelago* or else miss out on its full force. But we had better accept such a possibility and learn to be grateful that at least the novel is being written. Because nobody else—certainly not Sholokhov—could have written it: Solzhenitsyn's war novel is based on the idea that the truth is indivisible.

At a guess, I would say that Solzhenitsyn's lack of the Tolstoyan virtues will turn out to be an artistic strength as well as a philosophical one. Until recently the key Russian novel about World War I, the Revolution and the Civil War was *Dr. Zhivago.* The book was overrated on publication and is underrated now, but it will always be an instructive text for the attentive reader. One defends Pasternak's right, argued through the leading character, to live and create without taking sides. One can see the importance of the principle which Pasternak is eager to incarnate in Zhivago and Lara. Lara is, if you like, the Natasha that Solzhenitsyn seems doomed never to create. Lara and Yuri are Natasha and Andrey, lovers surrounded by chaos, a private love in the middle of public breakdown. But Pasternak can't seem to avoid an effect of Tolstoy-and-water. Really the time for all this is past, and the rest of his book helps to tell us so. The point about the Civil War lies with the millions who are *not* surviving it—Pasternak, in focussing on these blessed two, is luxuriating despite himself.

However reluctantly and fragmentarily, *Dr. Zhivago* affirms that Life Goes On: Pasternak is old-world. Solzhenitsyn, one of the "twins of October" (his term for Russians who were born in the first years of the Revolution and came of age just in time to witness the 1937–1938 purges, fight in World War II and be imprisoned by Stalin), doesn't believe that life went on at all. He thinks that it stopped, and that death started. In his World War I novel we can expect to hear portents of the future strangeness. But the predominant tone—and this we can already hear—will almost certainly be one of scrupulous political realism. Not *realpolitik*, but the truth about politics. This is what Pasternak was in no position to treat and what the great common ancestor Tolstoy simply got wrong. Tolstoy's early appearance in *August 1914* is undoubtedly strategic: he is the innocent, dreaming genius who just has no idea whatsoever of the new world to come.

Two representative moments serve to show how the force of *August 1914* is potentiated by acquaintance with Solzhenitsyn's later work, especially with *Gulag Archipelago*. In Chapter 6 we are told that Roman thinks of himself as superior and imagines that his superiority lies in his brutal frankness. But the truly illustrative detail, presented without comment, is Roman's admiration for Maxim Gorky. (Solzhenitsyn's contempt for Gorky is touched on in *The First Circle* and expressed at length in *Gulag Archipelago*.) And in Chapter 61, when the two engineers Obodovsky and Arkhangorodsky meet in amity, their friendly optimism is a mere hint of the intense, regretful passage in *Gulag Archipelago* I, 5, where Solzhenitsyn laments the destruction of the engineers in the 1920s as the blasting of Russia's best hope. In the *August 1914* passage we read:

Although there was no similarity or even contact between the lives, experience and specialised interest of the two men, they shared a common engineering spirit which like some powerful, invisible wing lifted them, bore them onwards and made them kin.

In the *Gulag Archipelago* passage the same emotion is multiplied, in the kind of paragraph which led several critics to comment (approvingly, let it be admitted) on the book's supposed lack of sobriety:

> An engineer? I had grown up among engineers, and I could remember the engineers of the twenties very well indeed: their open, shining intellects, their free and gentle humour, their agility and breadth of thought, the ease with which they shifted from one engineering field to another, and, for that matter, from technology to social concerns and art. Then, too, they personified good manners and delicacy of taste; well-bred speech that flowed evenly and was free of uncultured words; one of them might play a musical instrument, another dabble in painting; and their faces always bore a spiritual imprint.

It is evident that the optimism of the two friends about the new Russia to come is being treated ironically, but unless we know about Solzhenitsyn's feelings concerning what happened subsequently to the engineers (whose show trials in 1928 are treated at length in Robert Conquest's *The Great Terror*, but without, of course, the epigrammatic power Solzhenitsyn unleashes on the subject in *Gulag Archipelago*), we are unlikely to realize just how bitterly ironical he is being. Whether this is a weakness of the novel isn't easily decided. My own view is that Solzhenitsyn has done the right thing in neutralizing his viewpoint. We have to provide a context from our own knowledge—knowledge which Solzhenitsyn is busy supplying us with in other books. The most pressing reason he writes history is to make the truth public. But a subsidiary reason, and one that will perhaps become increasingly important, is to make his own fiction intelligible. He writes history in order that his historical novel might be understood.

Because Solzhenitsyn deals with modern events over which there is not merely dispute as to their interpretation, but doubt as to whether they even happened, he is obliged to expend a great deal of effort in saying what things were like. The task is compounded in difficulty by the consideration that what they were like is almost unimaginable. To recover the feeling of such things is an immense creative achievement. In Coleridge's sense, it takes imagination to see things as they are, and Solzhenitsyn possesses that imagination to such a degree that one can be excused for thinking of him as a freak. He is a witness for the population of twentieth-century shadows, the anonymous dead: all the riders on what Mandelstam in his poem called the Lilac Sleigh. Solzhenitsyn can imagine what pain is like when it happens to strangers. Even more remarkably, he is not disabled by imagining what pain is like when it happens to a *million* strangers—he can think about individuals even when the subject is the obliteration of masses, which makes his the exact reverse of the ideological mentality, which can think only about masses even when the subject is the obliteration of individuals. Camus said it was a peculiarity of our age that the innocent are called upon to justify themselves. Nowhere has this been more true than in Soviet Russia, where the best the condemned innocent have been able to hope for is rehabilitation. But Solzhenitsyn has already managed, at least in part, to bring them back in their rightful role—as prosecutors.

Of the ideological mentality Solzhenitsyn is the complete enemy, dedicated and implacable. Here, perhaps, lies the chief reason for the growing uneasiness about the general drift of his work. Nobody in the Left intelligentsia, not even the Marxists, much minds him suggesting that in the Soviet Union the Revolution went sour. But almost everybody, and not always covertly, seems to mind his insistence that the Revolution should never have happened, and that Russia was better off under the Romanovs. In *Dr. Zhivago* Pasternak showed himself awed by the magnitude of historical forces: reviewers sympathized, since being awed by historical forces is a way of saying that what happened should have happened, even though the cost was frightful. Nobody wants to think of horror as sheer waste. Solzhenitsyn says that the Soviet horror was, from the very beginning, sheer waste. Politically this attitude is something of a gift to the Right, since it practically aligns Solzhenitsyn with Winston Churchill. It is no great surprise, then, that on the liberal Left admiration is gradually becoming tinctured with the suspicion that so absolute a fellow might be a bit of a crank.

In *The Great Terror* Robert Conquest valuably widened the field of attention from the purges of 1937–1938 to include the trials of the late twenties—a reorientation which meant that the age of destruction overlapped the golden era of the Soviet Union instead of merely succeeding it, and also meant that while Stalin still got the blame for the Terror, Lenin got the blame for Stalin. But in *Gulag Archipelago* Solzhenitsyn does a more thorough job even than Conquest of tracing the Terror back to the Revolution itself: he says that the whole court procedure of the typical Soviet show trial was already in existence in 1922, and that the activities of the Cheka from the very beginning provided a comprehensive model for everything the "organs," under their various acronyms, were to perpetrate in the decades to come. He has no respect for the Revolution even in its most pristine state—in fact he says it never *was* in a pristine state, since pre-Revolutionary Russia was totally unsuited for any form of Socialism whatsoever and no organization which attempted to impose it could escape pollution. It is the overwhelming tendency of Solzhenitsyn's work to suggest that the Russian Revolution should never have happened. He can summon respect for ordinary people who were swept up by their belief in it, but for the Revolutionary intelligentsia in all its departments his contempt is absolute. The hopeful young artists of the golden era (see the paragraph beginning "Oh ye bards of the twenties," *Gulag Archipelago* I, 9) were, in his view, as culpable as the detested Gorky. Solzhenitsyn's critique of the Soviet Union is a radical critique, not a revisionist one. In condemning him as a class enemy, the regime is scarcely obliged to lie.

(Nevertheless it lies anyway—or perhaps the citizens invent the lies all by themselves. Not much is known of these matters inside the Soviet Union and Solzhenitsyn is generally just a name. One sometimes forgets that *One Day in the Life of Ivan Denisovich* is the only book of his which has ever been published there. A friend of mine just back from Russia tells me that he got into an argument with the director of a metalworkers' sanatorium on the Black Sea. This man was in his early fifties and had fought in World War II. He declared that Solzhenitsyn not only *is* a traitor, but *was* a traitor during the war—that he had been a Vlasov man. Now Solzhenitsyn's understanding of Vlasov is an important element of *Gulag Archipelago*. But Solzhenitsyn was a Red Army artillery officer who fought *against* Germany, not with it. In view of how this elementary truth can be turned on its head, it's probably wise of Solzhenitsyn to harbour as he does the doubt that the facts, once rediscovered, will spread, like certain brands of margarine, straight from the fridge. There is nothing automatic about the propagation of the truth. As he often points out, not even experience can teach it. The prison-camps and execution cells were full of people who were convinced that their own innocence didn't stop all these others being guilty.)

Solzhenitsyn finds it no mystery that the Old Bolsheviks condemned themselves. He resolves the apparent conflict between Koestler's famous thesis in *Darkness at Noon* (Koestler said 'they co-operated because the Party required their deaths and they had no spiritual resources for disobeying the Party) and Khrushchev's much later but equally famous insistence that they were tortured until they gave up ("Beat, beat, beat . . ."). According to Solzhenitsyn, the Old Bolsheviks were devoid of individuality in the first place, and simply had no private convictions to cling to: certainly they weren't made of the same moral stuff as the engineers they had connived at destroying ten years before, many of whom had preferred to be tortured to death rather than implicate the innocent. In the second place, the Old Bolsheviks had never been as marinated in suffering as they liked to pretend. Koestler was wrong in supposing that torture alone could not have cracked them, and Khrushchev was apparently also wrong in supposing that they needed to be tortured all that hard. Czarist imprisonment was the only kind the Old Bolsheviks had ever known and it was a picnic compared to the kind they themselves had become accustomed to dishing out. Solzhenitsyn sees no tragedy in the Old Bolsheviks. He doesn't talk of them with the unbridled hatred he reserves for the prosecutors Krylenko and Vyshinsky, but there is still no trace of sympathy in his regard. Here again is an example of his disturbing absolutism. He shows inexhaustible understanding of how ordinary people could be terrified into compliance. But for the ideologues trapped in their own system his standards are unwavering—they ought to have chosen death rather than dishonour themselves and their country further. He pays tribute to the Old Bolsheviks who suicided before they could be arrested (Skrypnik, Tomsky, Gamarnik) and to the half dozen who died ("silently but at least not shamefully"—*Gulag Archipelago* I, 10) under interrogation. He condemns the rest for having wanted to live. They should have been beyond that.

Solzhenitsyn takes a lot upon himself when he says that it was shameful for men not to die. Yet one doesn't feel that his confidence is presumptuous—although if one could, he would be less frightening. I remember that when I first read *The First Circle* the portrait of Stalin seemed inadequate, a caricature. My dissatisfaction, I have since decided—and Solzhenitsyn's writings have helped me decide—was a hangover from the romantic conviction that large events have large men at the centre of them. Tolstoy really did sell Napoleon short in *War and Peace*: Napoleon was a lot more interesting than that. But Stalin in *The First Circle* must surely be close to the reality. The only thing about Stalin on the grand scale was his pettiness—his mediocrity was infinite. Solzhenitsyn convinces us of the truth of this picture by reporting his own travels through Stalin's mind: the Archipelago is the expression of Stalin's personality, endlessly vindictive, murderously boring. Time and again in his major books, Solzhenitsyn makes a sudden investigative jab at Stalin, seemingly still hopeful of finding a flicker of nobility in that homicidal dullard. It never happens. That it could produce Stalin is apparently sufficient reason in itself for condemning the Revolution.

With Solzhenitsyn judgement is not in abeyance. He doesn't say that all of this happened in aid of some inscrutable purpose. He says it happened to no purpose. There is little solace to be taken and not much uplift to be had in the occasional story of noble defiance. First of all, the defiant usually died in darkness, in the way that Philip II denied Holland its martyrs by drowning them in secret. And when Solzhenitsyn somehow manages to find out who they were, he doesn't expect their example to light any torches. There are no eternal acts of faith or undying loves. (The typical love in Solzhenitsyn is between the Love Girl and the Innocent, or that unsatisfactory non-affair at the end of *Cancer Ward*—just a brushing of dazed minds, two strangers sliding past each other. No parts there for Omar Sharif and Julie Christie.) Everything is changed: there is no connection with the way things were.

It should be an elementary point that Solzhenitsyn is a critic of the Soviet Union, not of Russia. Yet even intelligent people seemed to think that there may have been "something in" his expulsion—that he had it coming. (It was edifying to notice how the construction "kicked out" came to be used even by those nominally on his side.) This sentiment has, I think, been intensified by Solzhenitsyn's argument with Sakharov. It has become increasingly common to hint that Solzhenitsyn has perhaps got above himself, that in telling the world's largest country what it ought to do next he is suffering from delusions of grandeur. Yet it seems to me perfectly in order for Solzhenitsyn to feel morally superior to the whole of the Soviet political machine. Its human integrity is not just compromised but fantastic, and he has lived the proof. He has good cause to believe himself Russia personified, and I am more surprised by his humility in this role than by his pride. To the suggestion that he is a mediocre artist with great subject-matter, the answer should be: to see that such stuff *is* your subject-matter, and then to go on and prove yourself adequate to its treatment—these are in themselves sufficient qualifications for greatness. Solzhenitsyn's forthcoming books (apparently there are to be at least two more volumes of *Gulag Archipelago*) will, I am convinced, eventually put the matter beyond doubt. But for the present we should be careful not to understand the man too quickly. Above all we need to guard against that belittling tone which wants to call him a reactionary because he has lost faith in dreams.

(*The New Review*, October 1974)

It Is of a Windiness:
Lillian Hellman

Much praised in the United States, *Pentimento* deals mainly with people
other than its author, but there is still a good deal of Lillian Hellman in
it—possibly more than she intended—and it's hard not to think of the
book as finishing off *An Unfinished Woman,* a memoir which was inun-
dated with laurels but left at least one reader doubting its widely proclaimed first-rateness. Meaty details about Dorothy Parker, Hemingway,
Scott Fitzgerald and Dashiell Hammett were not quite compensation
enough for a garrulous pseudo-taciturnity—distinction of style, it seemed
to me, was precisely the quality *An Unfinished Woman* had not a particle
of. The very first time Hammett's drinking was referred to as "the drinking," you knew you were in for a solid course of bastardized Heming-
wayese. The drinking got at least a score more mentions. There were also
pronounced tendencies towards that brand of aggressive humility, or
claimed innocence, which finds itself helpless to explain the world at the
very moment when the reader is well justified in requiring that a writer
should give an apprehensible outline of what he deems to be going on.
Miss Hellman was with the Russian forces when Majdanek was liberated.
It struck me, as I read, that her account of her feelings, though graphic,
was oddly circumscribed. She had vomited, but in recounting the fact had
apparently failed to realize that no physical reaction, however violent, is
quite adequate to such a stimulus. What we needed to hear about was
what she *thought,* and it appeared that what she thought was, as usual,
a sophisticated version, decked out with Hem-Dash dialogue, of "I don't
understand these things."

On a larger scale, the same applied—and I think still applies—to her reasoning on the subject of Soviet Russia. She comes over in these two books—implicitly, since her political views have mainly to be pieced together from more or less revealing hints—as an unreconstructed and unrepentant Stalinist. There is no gainsaying her consistency and strength in such matters, even if those qualities are founded in some primal injury to the imaginative faculty. She was brave during the McCarthy era and has a right to be proud of never having turned her coat. Nevertheless it is impossible to grant much more than a token admiration to a professional clerical who can go on being "realistic" about Russia in the sense (by now, surely, utterly discredited) of believing that the Terror was simply an aberration disturbing an otherwise constructive historical movement. The "I don't understand these things" syndrome came in depressingly handy whenever she wandered onto the scene of an event about which she might have been obliged to say something analytical if she *had* understood. She was well-regarded in Russia, was even there during the war and met a lot of people. Her reporting of character and incident couldn't help but be interesting. Nevertheless, one felt, she missed out on the fundamentals. On the day she was due to meet Stalin, she was told he was busy. Shortly after which, she recorded, Warsaw fell. The implication being that Warsaw was what he was busy with. But for some reason it just doesn't cross her mind to give an opinion on the fundamental question—which remains a contentious issue to this day—of whether Stalin was busy liberating it or *not* liberating it: whether, that is, his first aim was to liberate the city or else to delay liberation until the insurrectionists of the ideologically unacceptable Uprising had been wiped out by the Germans.

Lillian Hellman was an early and impressive example of the independent woman, but she never completely forsakes feather-headed femininity as a ploy, and her continuing ability not to comprehend what was going on in Russia is a glaring demonstration. In a section of *An Unfinished Woman* dealing with a later trip to Russia, she finds herself tongue-tied in the presence of a Russian friend. We are asked to believe that her own feelings about the McCarthy period were welling up to block her speech, just as the Russian friend's experience of the recent past had blocked hers. The two communed in silence. That this equation was presented as a profundity seemed to me at the time to prove that Lillian Hellman, whatever her stature in the theatre, possessed, as an essayist, an attitudinizing mind of which her mannered prose was the logically consequent expression. One doesn't underrate the virulence of McCarthyism for a minute, and it may well be that such goonery is as fundamental to America's history as terror is to Russia's. But the two things are so different in nature, and so disparate in scale, that a mind which equates them loses the ability to describe either. For all its Proustian pernicketiness of recollected detail, *An Unfinished Woman* was a very vague book.

Still, it shimmered with stars. Parker and Hammett, especially, shone brightly in its pages. There are some additional facts about them scattered through *Pentimento* (Hammett's name is omnipresent, as you might expect), and in a section on the theatre and related performing arts we hear about Edmund Wilson, Theodore Roethke, Tyrone Guthrie, Samuel Goldwyn and Tallulah Bankhead. Just as she was good on Parker's decline, she is good on Bankhead's: Hellman's *grandes dames* go down to defeat in a flurry of misapplied talcum. Roethke features as the falling-down drunk he undoubtedly was most of the time. Lowell gets a mention. It's all good gossip, and all helps.

The bulk of the volume, however, is devoted to memoirs of non-famous characters from Miss Hellman's past. The transatlantic reviewers seem to have convinced themselves that this material is pretty quintessential stuff. We learn from Richard Poirier, quoted on the blurb, that it "provides one of those rare instances when the moral value of a book is wholly inextricable from its immense literary worth, where the excitations, the pacing, and the intensifications offered by the style manage to create in us perceptions about human character that have all but disappeared from contemporary writing." I certainly agree that the perceptiveness, such as it is, is closely linked to the style. What I can't see for a moment is how trained literati can imagine that the style is anything less than frantically mannered and anything more than painfully derivative.

"The drinking" has not reappeared, but "the joking" is there to make up for it. We hear of an historical period called "the time of Hitler." "It is of a windiness," says someone in a German train, and although this might just conjecturably sound like half-translated German, what it can't *help* sounding like is Hemingway's half-translated Spanish. Out-takes from *The Old Man and the Sea* abound:

> You are good in boats not alone from knowledge, but because water is a part of you, you are easy on it, fear it and like it in such equal parts that you work well in a boat without thinking about it and may be even safer because you

don't need to think too much. That is what we mean by instinct and there is no way to explain an instinct for the theatre, although those who have it recognize each other and a bond is formed between them.

Such passages read like E. B. White's classic parody "Across the Street and into the Grill," in which White established once and for all that Hemingway's diction could not be copied, not even by Hemingway. Nor are these echoes mere lapses: her whole approach to moral-drawing is Hemingway's—the excitations, the pacing and the intensifications, if I may borrow Richard Poirier's terminology.

That is what I thought about Aunt Lily until I made the turn and the turn was as sharp as only the young can make when they realize their values have been shoddy.

Or try this:

There are many ways of falling in love and one seldom is more interesting or valid than another unless, of course, one of them lasts so long that it becomes something else, like your arm or leg about which you neither judge nor protest.

Her approach to anecdote is Hemingway's as well. Not just in the dialogue, which is American Vernacular to the last degree ("You are fine ladies," I said after a while, "the best"), but in the withholding of information—the tip-of-the-iceberg effect. On occasions this works. She is good at showing how children get hold of the wrong end of the stick, giving their loyalties passionately to the wrong people. The first chapter, set in her childhood New Orleans and dealing with a girl called Bethe, shows us the young Lillian failing to understand that Bethe is a hoodlum's girl-friend. We are supplied with this information so grudgingly ourselves that it is easy to identify with the young Lillian's confusion. In other chapters, dealing with characters who entered her life much later on, we are already equipped with knowledge of our own about the relevant period and tend to find the by now less young Lillian's slowness to comprehend a bit of a strain, especially when the period in question is the Time of Hitler.

For action, the chapter about a girl called Julia is the best thing in the book. A childhood friend who went back to Europe, Julia was in the Karl

Marx Hof in Vienna when the Austrian Government troops (abetted by the local Nazis) bombarded it. She lost a leg, but kept on with the fight against Fascism. Apparently Miss Hellman, passing through Germany on her way to Russia, smuggled fifty thousand dollars to Julia in her hat. The money was used to spring five hundred prisoners. Miss Hellman was in no small danger when engaged on this enterprise and the results unquestionably constituted a more impressive political effectiveness than most of us ever accomplish. She still revels in the nitty-grittiness of it all: she liked thirties radicalism a lot better than twenties "rebellion"—the twenties were all style and she is properly contemptuous of style in that vitiated sense.

But with all that said, we are still left with key questions unanswered. Miss Hellman says that she has changed Julia's name because she is "not sure that even now the Germans like their premature anti-Nazis." Since they like them well enough to have made one of them Chancellor of West Germany, it's permissible to assume that Miss Hellman means something more interesting, and that Julia was a member of the Communist Party. If she was, it's difficult to see why Miss Hellman can't come straight out and say so. If she fears that we might think the less of the young Julia for it, she surely overestimates the long-term impact of McCarthyism on her readership. Or is she just *compelled* to be vague?

For the truth is that the Julia chapter, like all the others, happens in a dream. Despite the meticulously recollected minutiae, the story reads like a spy-sketch by Nichols and May, even down to the bewilderingly complicated instructions ("You have two hours, but we haven't that long together because you have to be followed to the station and the ones who follow you must have time to find the man who will be with you on the train until Warsaw in the morning") Julia breathes to Lillian under the noses of the lurking Gestapo.

To have been there, to have seen it, and yet still be able to write it down so that it rings false—it takes a special kind of talent. But there are stretches of her writing which somehow manage to sound true, even through the blanket of her supposedly transparent prose. She liked Samuel Goldwyn and has the guts to say so. Whether or not it took bravery to like him, it still takes bravery to admit it. She is, of course, perfectly right to admire Goldwyn above Irving Thalberg. Here again her suspicion of Style led her to the truth. Scott Fitzgerald, infinitely more sensitive but over-endowed with reverence, fell for Thalberg full length.

Less prominent this time but still compulsively invoked, the true hero of *Pentimento* is Dashiell Hammett. Theirs, I think, will be remembered as a great love. The only thing that could possibly delay the legend would be Miss Hellman's indefatigable determination to feed its flames. In this volume the Nick and Nora Charles dialogue reads as much like a screenplay as it did in the previous one.

> I phoned the Beverly Hills house from the restaurant. I said to Hammett, "I'm in New Orleans. I'm not coming back to Hollywood for a while and I didn't want you to worry."
> "How are you?" he said.
> "O.K. and you?"
> "I'm O.K. I miss you."
> "I miss you, too. Is there a lady in my bedroom?"
> He laughed. "I don't think so, but they come and go. Except you. You just go."
> "I had good reason," I said.
> "Yes," he said, "you did."

I like it now and my mother liked it then, when William Powell and Myrna Loy rattled it off to each other in the thirties. The *Thin Man* movies, with their unquestioned assumption that man and wife were equal partners, played a vital part in raising the expectations of women everywhere. Such are the unappraised impulses of modern history—when the fuss dies down it turns out that turns of speech and tones of voice mattered just as much as battles.

On Broadway Lillian Hellman took her chances among the men, a pioneer women's liberationist. Her plays were bold efforts, indicative social documents which are unlikely to be neglected by students, although as pieces for the theatre they will probably date: they are problem plays whose problems are no longer secrets, for which in some measure we have her to thank. She is a tough woman who has almost certainly not been relishing the patronizing critical practice—more common in America than here, and let's keep it that way—of belatedly indicating gratitude for strong early work by shouting unbridled hosannas for pale, late stuff that has a certain documentary value but not much more. She says at one point in *Pentimento* that in her time on Broadway she was always denied the benefits of the kind of criticism which would take her properly to task.

(The New Review, May 1974)

Mailer's *Marilyn*

"She was a fruit-cake," Tony Curtis once told an interviewer on BBC television, and there can't be much doubt that she was. Apart from conceding that the camera was desperately in love with her, professional judgements of Marilyn Monroe's attributes rarely go much further. It would be strange if they did: there's work to be done, and a girl blessed with equivalent magic might happen along any time—might even not be a fruit-cake. Amateur judgements, on the other hand, are free to flourish. Norman Mailer's new book, *Marilyn,* is just such a one.

Even if its narrative were not so blatantly, and self-admittedly, cobbled together from facts already available in other biographies, the Mailer *Marilyn* would still be an amateur piece of work. Its considerable strength lies in that limitation. As far as talent goes, Marilyn Monroe was so minimally gifted as to be almost unemployable, and anyone who holds to the opinion that she was a great natural comic identifies himself immediately as a dunce. For purposes best known to his creative demon, Mailer planes forward on the myth of her enormous talent like a drunken surfer. Not for the first time, he gets further by going with the flow than he ever could have done by cavilling. Thinking of her as a genius, he can call her drawbacks virtues, and so deal—unimpeded by scepticism—with the vital mystery of her presence.

Mailer's adoration is as amateurish as an autograph hunter's. But because of it we are once again, and this time ideally, reminded of his extraordinary receptivity. That the book should be an embarrassing and embarrassed rush job is somehow suitable. The author being who he is, the book might as well be conceived in the most chaotic possible circumstances. The subject is, after all, one of the best possible focal points for his chaotic view of life. There is nothing detached or calculating about that view. It is hot-eyed, errant, unhinged. Writhing along past a gallery of yummy photographs, the text reads as the loopiest message yet from the Mailer who scared Sonny Liston with thought-waves, made the medical breakthrough which identified cancer as the thwarted psyche's revenge and first rumbled birth control as the hidden cause of pregnancy. And yet *Marilyn* is one of Mailer's most interesting things. Easy to punish, it is hard to admire—like its subject. But admire it we must—like its subject. The childishness of the whole project succeeds in emitting a power that temporarily calls adulthood into question: The Big Book of the Mad Girl. Consuming it at a long gulp, the reader ponders over and over again Mailer's copiously fruitful aptitude for submission. Mailer is right to trust his own foolishness, wherever it leads—even if the resulting analysis of contemporary America impresses us as less diagnostic than symptomatic.

Not solely for the purpose of disarming criticism, Mailer calls his *Marilyn* a biography in novel form. The parent novel, we quickly guess, is *The Deer Park,* and we aren't seventy-five pages into this new book before we find Charles Francis Eitel and Elena Esposito being referred to as if they were people living in our minds—which, of course, they are. The permanent party of *The Deer Park* ("if desires were deeds, the history of the night would end in history") is still running, and the atom bomb that lit the desert's rim for Sergius O'Shaugnessy and Lulu Meyers flames just as bright. But by now Sergius is out from under cover: he's Norman Mailer. And his beloved film star has been given a real name too: Marilyn Monroe. Which doesn't necessarily make her any the less fictional. By claiming the right to launch vigorous imaginative patrols from a factual base, Mailer gives himself an easy out from the strictures of verisimilitude, especially when the facts are discovered to be contradictory. But Mailer's fantasizing goes beyond expediency. Maurice Zolotow, poor pained scrivener, can sue Mailer all he likes, but neither he nor the quiescent Fred Lawrence Guiles will ever get his Marilyn back. Mailer's Marilyn soars above the known data, an apocalyptic love object no mundane pen-pusher could dream of reaching. Dante and Petrarch barely knew Beatrice and Laura. It didn't slow them down. Mailer never met Marilyn at all. It gives him the inside track.

Critical fashion would have it that since *The Deer Park* reality has been busy turning itself into a novel. As Philip Roth said it must, the extremism of real events has ended up by leaving the creative imagination looking like an also-ran. A heroine in a fifties novel, Lulu was really a girl of the forties—she had some measure of control over her life. Mailer now sees that the young Marilyn was the true fifties heroine—she had no control over her life whatsoever. In the declension from Lulu as Mailer then saw her to Marilyn as he sees her now, we can clearly observe what is involved in dispensing with the classical, shaping imagination and submitting one's talent (well, Mailer's talent) to the erratic forces of events. Marilyn, says Mailer, was every man's love affair with America. He chooses to forget now that Sergius was in love with something altogether sharper, just as he chooses to forget that for many men Marilyn in fact represented most of the things that were to be feared about America. Worshipping a doll was an activity that often came into question at the time. Later on, it became a clever critical point to insist that the doll was gifted: she walks, she talks, she plays Anna Christie at the Actors Studio. Later still, the doll was canonized. By the time we get to this book, it is as though there had never been any doubt: the sickness of the fifties lay not in over-valuing Marilyn Monroe but in under-valuing her.

Marilyn, says Mailer, suggested sex might be as easy as ice cream. He chooses to forget that for many men at the time she suggested sex might have about the same nutritional value. The early photographs by André De Dienes—taken before her teeth were fixed but compensating by showing an invigorating flash of pantie above the waistline of her denims —enshrine the essence of her snuggle-pie sexuality, which in the ensuing years was regularized, but never intensified, by successive applications of oomph and class. Adorable, dumb tomato, she was the best of the worst. As the imitators, and imitators of the imitators, were put into the field behind her, she attained the uniqueness of the paradigm, but that was the sum total of her originality as a sex-bomb. Any man in his right mind would have loved to have her. Mailer spends a good deal of the book trying to drum up what mystical significance he can out of that fact, without even once facing the possibility of that fact representing the *limitation* of her sexuality—the criticism of it, and the true centre of her tragedy. Her screen presence, the Factor X she possessed in the same quantity as Garbo, served mainly to potentiate the sweetness. The sweetness of the girl bride, the unwomanly woman, the *femme* absolutely not *fatale*.

In her ambition, so Faustian, and in her ignorance of culture's dimensions, in her liberation and her tyrannical desires, her noble democratic longings intimately contradicted by the widening pool of her narcissism (where every friend and slave must bathe), we can see the magnified mirror of ourselves, our exaggerated and now all but defeated generation, yes, she ran a reconnaissance through the 50's. . . .

Apart from increasing one's suspicions that the English sentence is being executed in America, such a passage of rhetorical foolery raises the question of whether the person Mailer is trying to fool with it might not conceivably be himself. If "magnified mirror of ourselves" means anything, it must include Mailer. Is Mailer ignorant of culture's dimensions? The answer, one fears, being not that he is, but that he would like to be —so that he could write more books like *Marilyn*. As Mailer nuzzles up beside the shade of this poor kitten to whom so much happened but who could cause so little to happen, you can hear the purr of sheer abandon. He himself would like very much to be the man without values, expending his interpretative powers on whatever the world declared to be important. Exceptional people, Mailer says (these words are almost exactly his, only the grammar having been altered, to unveil the epigram), have a way of living with opposites in themselves that can be called schizophrenia only when it fails. The opposite in Mailer is the hick who actually falls for all that guff about screen queens, voodoo prize-fighters and wonder-boy Presidents. But his way of living with it hasn't yet quite failed. And somehow, it must be admitted, he seems to get further, see deeper, than those writers who haven't got it to live with.

In tracing Marilyn's narcissism back to her fatherless childhood, our author is at his strongest. His propensity for scaling the mystical ramparts notwithstanding, Mailer in his Aquarius/Prisoner role is a lay psychologist of formidable prowess. The self-love and the unassuageable need to have it confirmed—any fatherless child is bound to recognize the pattern, and be astonished at how the writing generates the authentic air of continuous panic. But good as this analysis is, it still doesn't make Marilyn's narcissism ours. There is narcissism and there is narcissism, and to a depressing degree Marilyn's was the sadly recognizable version of the actress who could read a part but could never be bothered reading a complete script. Mailer knows what it took Marilyn to get to the top: everything from betraying friends to lying down under geriatric strangers. Given the system, Marilyn was the kind of monster equipped to climb through it. What's debilitating is that Mailer seems to have given up imagining other systems. He is right to involve himself in the dynamics of Hollywood; he does better by enthusiastically replaying its vanished games than by standing aloof; but for a man of his brains he doesn't *despise* the place enough. His early gift for submitting himself to the grotesqueness of reality is softening with the years into a disinclination to argue with it. In politics he still fights on, although with what effect on his allies one hesitates to think. But in questions of culture—including, damagingly, the cultural aspects of politics—he has by now come within an ace of accepting whatever is as right. His determination to place on Marilyn the same valuation conferred by any sentimentalist is a sure token.

On the point of Marilyn's putative talents, Mailer wants it both ways. He wants her to be an important natural screen presence, which she certainly was; and he wants her to be an important natural actress, which she certainly wasn't. So long as he wants it the first way, he gets it: *Marilyn* is an outstandingly sympathetic analysis of what makes somebody look special on screen, and reads all the better for its periodic eruptions into incoherent lyricism. But so long as he wants it the second way, he gets nowhere. He is quite right to talk of *Some Like It Hot* as her best film, but drastically overestimates her strength in it. Mailer knows all about the hundreds of takes and the thousands of fluffs, and faithfully records the paroxysms of anguish she caused Billy Wilder and Tony Curtis. But he seems to assume that once a given scene was in the can it became established as a miracle of assurance. And the plain fact is that her salient weakness—the inability to read a line—was ineradicable. Every phrase came out as if it had just been memorized. *Just* been memorized. And that film was the high point of the short-winded, monotonous attack she had developed for getting lines across. In earlier films, all the way back to the beginning, we are assailed with varying degrees of the irrepressible panic which infected a voice that couldn't tell where to place emphasis. As a natural silent comedienne Marilyn might possibly have qualified, with the proviso that she was not to be depended upon to invent anything. But as a natural comedienne in sound she had the conclusive disadvantage of not being able to speak. She was limited ineluctably to characters who rented language but could never possess it, and all her best roles fell into that category. She was good at being inarticulately abstracted for the same reason that midgets are good at being short.

To hear Mailer overpraising Marilyn's performance in *Gentlemen Prefer Blondes* is to wonder if he has any sense of humour at all. Leaving out of account an aberration like *Man's Favourite Sport?* (in which Paula Prentiss, a comedienne who actually knows something about being funny, was entirely wasted), *Gentlemen Prefer Blondes* is the least entertaining comedy Howard Hawks ever made. With its manic exaggeration of Hawks's already heavy emphasis on male aggressiveness transplanted to the female, the film later became a touchstone for the Hawksian cinéastes (who also lacked a sense of humour, and tended to talk ponderously about the role reversals in *Bringing Up Baby* before passing with relief to the supposed wonders of *Hatari!*), but the awkward truth is that with this project Hawks landed himself with the kind of challenge he was least likely to find liberating—dealing with dumb sex instead of the bright kind. Hawks supplied a robust professional framework for Marilyn's accomplishments, such as they were. Where I lived, at any rate, her performance in the film was generally regarded as mildly winning in spite of her obvious, fundamental inadequacies—the *in spite of* being regarded as the secret of any uniqueness her appeal might have. Mailer tells it differently:

> In the best years with DiMaggio, her physical coordination is never more vigorous and athletically quick; she dances with all the grace she is ever going to need when doing *Gentlemen Prefer Blondes,* all the grace and all the bazazz —she is a musical comedy star with panache! Diamonds Are a Girl's Best Friend! What a surprise! And sings so well Zanuck will first believe her voice was dubbed. . . .

This is the language of critical self-deception, fine judgement suppressed in the name of a broader cause. What does it mean to dance with all the grace you are ever going to need? It doesn't sound the same as being good at dancing. The fact was that she could handle a number like the "Running Wild" routine in the train corridor in *Some Like It Hot* (Wilder covered it with the marvellous cutaways of Lemmon slapping the back of the bull-fiddle and Curtis making Ping-Pong-ball eyes while blowing sax), but anything harder than that was pure pack-drill. And if Zanuck really believed that her voice was dubbed, then for once in his life he must have made an intuitive leap, because to say that her singing voice didn't sound as if it belonged to her was to characterize it with perfect accuracy. Like her speaking voice, it was full of panic.

It took more than sympathy for her horrible death and nostalgia for her atavistic cuddlesomeness to blur these judgements, which at one time all intelligent people shared. The thing that tipped the balance towards adulation was Camp—Camp's yen for the vulnerable in women, which is just as inexorable as its hunger for the strident. When Mailer talks about Marilyn's vulnerability, he means the inadequacy of her sense of self. Camp, however, knew that the vulnerability which mattered was centred in the inadequacy of her talent. She just wasn't very good, and was thus eligible for membership in the ever-increasing squad of Camp heroines who make their gender seem less threatening by being so patently unaware of how they're going over. On the strident wing of the team, Judy Garland is a perennial favourite for the same reason. If common sense weren't enough to do it, the Camp enthusiasm for Monroe should have told Mailer—Mailer of all people—that the sexuality he was getting set to rave about was the kind that leaves the viewer uncommitted.

Mailer longs to talk of Monroe as a symbolic figure, node of a death-wish and foretaste of the fog. Embroiled in such higher criticism, he doesn't much concern himself with the twin questions of what shape Hollywood took in the fifties and of how resonantly apposite a representative Marilyn turned out to be of the old studio system's last gasp. As the third-string blonde at Fox (behind Betty Grable and June Haver), Marilyn was not—as Mailer would have it—in all that unpromising a spot. She was in luck, like Kim Novak at Columbia, who was groomed by Harry Cohn to follow Rita Hayworth in the characteristic fifties transposition which substituted apprehensiveness for ability. For girls like them, the roles would eventually be there—mainly crummy roles in mainly crummy movies, but they were the movies the studios were banking on. For the real actresses, times were tougher, and didn't ease for more than a decade. Anne Bancroft, for example, also started out at Fox, but couldn't get the ghost of a break. Mailer isn't careful enough about pointing out that Fox's record as a star-maker was hopeless in all departments: Marilyn was by no means a unique case of neglect, and in comparison with Bancroft got a smooth ride. Marilyn was just another item in the endless catalogue of Zanuck's imperviousness to box-office potential. James Robert Parish, in his useful history, *The Fox Girls,* sums up the vicissitudes of Marilyn's career at Fox with admirable brevity and good sense, and if the reader would like to make up his own mind about the facts, it's to that book he should turn.

Right across Hollywood, as the films got worse, the dummies and the sex-bombs came into their own, while the actresses dropped deeper into limbo. Considering the magnitude of the luminary he is celebrating, it might seem funny to Mailer if one were to mention the names of people like, say, Patricia Neal, or (even more obscure) Lola Albright. Soon only the most fanatic of students will be aware that such actresses were available but could not be used. It's not that history has been rewritten. Just that the studio-handout version of history has been unexpectedly confirmed—by Norman Mailer, the very stamp of writer who ought to know better. The studios created a climate for new talent that went on stifling the best of it until recent times. How, for example, does Mailer think Marilyn stacks up against an artist like Tuesday Weld? By the criteria of approval manifested in *Marilyn,* it would be impossible for Mailer to find Weld even mildly interesting. To that extent, the senescent dream-factories succeeded in imposing their view: first of all on the masses, which was no surprise, but now on the élite, which is.

Mailer is ready to detect all manner of bad vibes in the fifties, but unaccountably fails to include in his read-out of portents the one omen pertinent to his immediate subject. The way that Hollywood divested itself of *intelligence* in that decade frightened the civilized world. And far into the sixties this potato-blight of the intellect went on. The screen was crawling with cosmeticized androids. Not content with gnawing her knuckles through the long days of being married to a test pilot or the long nights of being married to a band leader, June Allyson sang and danced. Betty Hutton, the ultimate in projected insecurity, handed over to Doris Day, a yelping freckle. The last Tracy-Hepburn comedies gurgled nostalgically in the straw like the lees of a soda. The new Hepburn, Audrey, was a Givenchy clothes-horse who piped her lines in a style composed entirely of mannerisms. And *she* was supposed to be class. Comedy of the thirties and forties, the chief glory of the American sound cinema, was gone as if it had never been. For those who had seen and heard the great Hollywood high-speed talkers (Carole Lombard, Irene Dunne, Rosalind Russell, Katharine Hepburn, Jean Arthur) strut their brainy stuff, the let-down was unbelievable. Comic writing was pretty nearly wiped out, and indeed has never fully recovered as a genre. In a context of unprecedented mindlessness, Marilyn Monroe rose indefatigably to success. She just wasn't clever enough to fail.

Marilyn came in on the fifties tide of vulgarity, and stayed to take an exemplary part in the Kennedy era's uproar of cultural pretension. Mailer follows her commitment to the Actors Studio with a credulousness that is pure New Frontier. The cruelty with which he satirizes Arthur Miller's ponderous aspirations to greatness is transmuted instantly to mush when he deals with Mrs. Miller's efforts to explore the possibilities hitherto dormant within her gift. That such possibilities existed was by no means taken as gospel at the time of her first forays into New York, but with the advent of the Kennedy era the quality of scepticism seemed to drain out of American cultural life. *Marilyn* is a latter-day Kennedy-era text, whose prose, acrid with the tang of free-floating charisma, could have been written a few weeks after Robert Kennedy's death rounded out the period of the family's power. Mailer's facility for confusing the intention with the deed fits that epoch's trust in façades to perfection. He is delicately tender when evoking the pathos of Marilyn's anxious quest for self-fulfilment, but never doubts that the treasure of buried ability was there to be uncovered, if only she could have found the way. The true pathos—that she was simply not fitted for the kind of art she had been led to admire —eludes him. Just as he gets over the problem of Marilyn's intellectual limitations by suggesting that a mind can be occupied with more interesting things than thoughts, so he gets over the problem of her circumscribed accomplishments by suggesting that true talent is founded not on ability but on a state of being. Nobody denies that the snorts of derision which first greeted the glamour queen's strivings towards seriousness were inhuman, visionless. In rebuttal, it was correctly insisted that her self-exploration was the exercise of an undeniable right. But the next, fatal step was to assume that her self-exploration was an artistic activity in itself, and had a right to results.

Scattered throughout the book are hints that Mailer is aware that his loved one had limited abilities. But he doesn't let it matter, preferring to insist that her talent—a different thing—was boundless. Having overcome so much deprivation in order to see that certain kinds of achievement were desirable, she had an automatic entitlement to them. That, at any rate, seems to be his line of reasoning. A line of reasoning which is really an act of faith. The profundity of his belief in the significance of what went on during those secret sessions at the Actors Studio is unplumbable. She possessed, he vows, the talent to play Cordelia. One examines this statement from front-on, from both sides, through a mirror and with rubber gloves. Is there a hint of a put-on? There is not. Doesn't he really mean something like: she possessed enough nerve and critical awareness to see the point of trying to extend her range by playing a few fragments of a Shakespearian role out of the public eye? He does not. He means what he says, that Marilyn Monroe possessed the talent to play Cordelia. Who, let it be remembered, is required, in the first scene of the play, to deliver a speech like this:

> Good my lord,
> You have begot me, bred me, lov'd me: I
> Return those duties back as are right fit,
> Obey you, love you, and most honour you.
> Why have my sisters husbands, if they say
> They love you all? Haply, when I shall wed,
> That lord whose hand must take my plight shall carry
> Half my love with him, half my care and duty:
> Sure I shall never marry like my sisters,
> To love my father all.

Leave aside the matter of how she would have managed such stuff on stage; it is doubtful she could have handled a single minute of it even on film: not with all the dialogue coaches in the world, not even if they had shot and edited in the way Joshua Logan is reputed to have put together her performance in some of the key scenes of *Bus Stop*—word by word, frame by frame. The capacity to apprehend and reproduce the rhythm of written language just wasn't there. And even if we were to suppose that such an indispensable capacity could be dispensed with, there would still be the further question of whether the much-touted complexity of her character actually contained a material resembling Cordelia's moral steel: it is not just sweetness that raises Cordelia above her sisters. We are bound to conclude (if only to preserve from reactionary scorn the qualities Marilyn really *did* have) that she was debarred from the wider range of classical acting not only by a paucity of ability but by a narrowness of those emotional resources Mailer would have us believe were somehow a substitute for it. Devoid of invention, she could only draw on her stock of feeling. The stock was thin. Claiming for her a fruitful complexity, Mailer has trouble conjuring it up: punctuated by occasional outbreaks of adoration for animals and men, her usual state of mind seems to have been an acute but generalized fear, unreliably counterbalanced by sedation.

Mailer finds it temptingly easy to insinuate that Marilyn's madness knew things sanity wots not of, and he tries to make capital out of the tussle she had with Olivier in *The Prince and the Showgirl.* Olivier, we are asked to believe, was the icy technician working from the outside in, who through lack of sympathy muffed the chance to elicit from his leading lady miracles of warm intuition. It's a virtuoso passage from Mailer, almost convincing us that an actor like Olivier is a prisoner of rationality forever excluded from the inner mysteries of his profession. You have to be nuts, whispers Mailer from the depths of his sub-text, to be a *real* actor. The derivation from Laing's psychology is obvious.

The author does a noble, loyal, zealous job of tracing his heroine's career as an artist, but we end by suspecting that he is less interested in her professional achievement than in her fame. The story of Norma Jean becoming Somebody is the true spine of the book, and the book is Mailer's most concise statement to date of what he thinks being Somebody has come to mean in present-day America. On this theme, *Marilyn* goes beyond being merely wrong-headed and becomes quite frightening.

As evidence of the leverage Marilyn's fame could exert, Mailer recounts a story of her impressing some friends by taking them without a reservation to the Copacabana, where Sinatra was packing the joint to the rafters every night. Marilyn being Monroe, Sinatra ordered a special table put in at his feet, and while lesser mortals were presumably being asphyxiated at the back, he sang for his unexpected guest and her friends, personally. Only for the lonely. Mailer tells such stories without adornment, but his excitement in them is ungovernable: it infects the style, giving it the tone we have come to recognize from all his previous excursions into status, charisma, psychic victory and the whole witchcraft of personal ascendancy. *Marilyn* seems to bring this theme in his work to a crisis.

In many ways *The Naked and the Dead* was the last classic novel to be written in America. The separately treated levels of the military hierarchy mirrored the American class structure, such as it was, and paralleled the class structure of the classic European novel, such as it had always

been. With *The Deer Park* the American classes were already in a state
of flux, but the society of Hollywood maintained cohesion by being aware
of what conditions dictated the mutability of its hierarchy: Sergius the
warrior slept with Lulu the love queen, both of them qualifying, while
fortune allowed, as members of the only class, below which was the ruck
—the unlovely, the unknown, the out. *The Deer Park* was Mailer's last
attempt to embody American society in fictional form: *An American
Dream* could find room only for its hero. Increasingly with the years, the
broad sweep of Mailer's creativity has gone into the interpretation of
reality as it stands, or rather flows, and he has by now become adept at
raising fact to the level of fiction. Meanwhile society has become even
more fluid, to the extent that the upper class—the class of celebrities—
has become as unstable in its composition as the hubbub below. Transfor-
mation and displacement now operate endlessly, and the observer (heady
prospect) changes the thing observed. Mailer's tendency to enrol himself
in even the most exalted action is based on the perception, not entirely
crazed, that the relative positions in the star-cluster of status are his to
define: reality is a novel that he is writing.

On her way to being divorced from Arthur Miller, Marilyn stopped off
in Dallas. In Dallas! Mailer can hardly contain himself. "The most electric
of the nations," he writes, "must naturally provide the boldest circuits of
coincidence." Full play is made with the rumours that Marilyn might have
had affairs with either or both of the two doomed Kennedy brothers, and
there is beetle-browed speculation about the possibility of her death having placed a curse on the family—and hence, of course, on the whole era.
Mailer himself calls this last brainwave "endlessly facile," thereby once
again demonstrating his unfaltering dexterity at having his cake and
eating it. But this wearying attempt to establish Marilyn as the muse of
the artist-politicians is at one with the book's whole tendency to weight
her down with a load of meaning she is too frail to bear. Pepys could be
floored by Lady Castlemaine's beauty without ascribing to her qualities
she did not possess. The Paris intellectuals quickly learned that Pompa-
dour's passion for china flowers and polite theatre was no indication that
artistic genius was in favour at Versailles—quite the reverse. Where
hierarchies were unquestioned, realism meant the ability to see what was
really what. Where the hierarchy is created from day to day in the mind
of one man interpreting it, realism is likely to be found a hindrance.

Mailer doesn't want famous people to mean as little as the sceptical tongue says they do. To some extent he is right. There *is* an excitement in someone like Marilyn Monroe coming out of nowhere to find herself conquering America, and there *is* a benediction in the happiness she could sometimes project from the middle of her anguish. Without Mailer's receptivity we would not have been given the full impact of these things; just as if he had listened to the liberal line on the space programme we would not have been given those enthralling moments in *Of a Fire on the Moon* when the launch vehicle pulls free of its bolts, or when the mission passes from the grip of the earth into the embrace of its target —moments as absorbing as our first toys. Mailer's shamelessness says that there are people and events which mean more than we in our dignity are ready to allow. He has nearly always been right. But when he starts saying that in that case they might as well mean what he wants them to mean, the fictionalist has overstepped the mark, since the patterning that strengthens fiction weakens fact.

Mailer's Marilyn is a usurper, a democratic monarch reigning by dint of the allegiance of an intellectual aristocrat, the power of whose regency has gone to his head. Mailer has forgotten that Marilyn was the people's choice before she was his, and that in echoing the people he is sacrificing his individuality on the altar of perversity. Sergius already had the sickness:

> Then I could feel her as something I had conquered, could listen to her wounded breathing, and believe that no matter how she acted other times, these moments were Lulu, as if her flesh murmured words more real than her lips. To the pride of having so beautiful a girl was added the bigger pride of knowing that I took her with the cheers of millions behind me. Poor millions with their low roar!

At the end of *The Deer Park* the dying Eitel tells Sergius by telepathy that the world we may create is more real to us than the mummery of what happens, passes, and is gone. Whichever way Sergius decided, Mailer seems finally to have concluded that the two are the same thing. More than any of his essays so far, *Marilyn* tries to give the mummery of what happens the majestic gravity of a created world. And as he has so often done before, he makes even the most self-assured of us wonder if we have felt deeply enough, looked long enough, lived hard enough. He comes close to making us doubt our conviction that in a morass of pettiness no great issues are being decided. We benefit from the doubt. But the price he pays for being able to induce it is savage, and Nietzsche's admonition is beginning to apply. He has gazed too long into the abyss, and now the abyss is gazing into him. Bereft of judgement, detachment, or even a tinge of irony, *Marilyn* is an opulent but slavish expression of an empty consensus. The low roar of the poor millions is in every page.

(*Commentary*, October 1973)

A NOTE ON THE TYPE

The text of this book was set via computer-driven cathode-ray tube in Avanta, a film version of Electra, a typeface designed by W(illiam) A(ddison) Dwiggins for the Mergenthaler Linotype Company and first made available in 1935. Electra cannot be classified as either "modern" or "old-style." It is not based on any historical model, and hence does not echo any particular period or style of type design. It avoids the extreme contrast between thick and thin elements that marks most modern faces, and is without eccentricities that catch the eye and interfere with reading. In general, Electra is a simple, readable typeface that attempts to give a feeling of fluidity, power and speed.

Composed by The Haddon Craftsmen, Inc.,
ComCom Division, Allentown, Pennsylvania
Printed and bound by The Haddon Craftsmen, Inc.
Scranton, Pennsylvania
Designed by Judith Henry